Praise for
The Double Bottom Line

"It's time for all corporations to be truly committed to meeting the needs of all stakeholders and to playing an essential role in improving our society. Tramuto's new book, *The Double Bottom Line*, is the essential playbook for compassionate, forward-looking leaders."

—**Alex Gorsky,** chairman and CEO, Johnson & Johnson

"Compassion is an action that shows in the way you move throughout the world. Let *The Double Bottom Line* be your roadmap to compassionate action that will strengthen your business and better the world."

—**Thasunda Brown Duckett,** president and CEO at TIAA

"Can you have unfettered capitalism and compassionate leadership? Donato Tramuto shows you how they can be perfectly compatible."

—**Katie Couric,** award-winning journalist, co-founder, Katie Couric Media, co-founder, Stand Up to Cancer, author of the new memoir, *Going There*

"Maximizing only financial interest is not sustainable. Leaders who drive the highest levels of long-term success know how to maximize the interests of all. Compassion is an essential element in that. *The Double Bottom Line* gives actionable examples of how compassionate leaders do this with terrific results. The time is right for this book."

—**Bruce Broussard,** CEO at Humana

"*The Double Bottom Line* is required reading for the next generation."

—**Governor John Baldacci**

"We have the choice to be the difference in our own lives. When we connect with compassion it drives passion and purpose within ourselves. We can then elevate others as individuals, companies can elevate their employees and members, and together, I think we can change the world. Donato Tramuto's book, *The Double Bottom Line*, gives us examples and inspiration to help us do just that."

—**Janine Broussard,** founder, H.U.G. Reading Program

"We all have the power to make a difference, whether through instituting large-scale changes or by helping others in the course of our daily lives—in our community, workplace, or home. Compassion is the heart of what drives our ability to make this impact. Donato Tramuto's book illustrates the power we all have to help make the world a better place."

—**Senator William Frist,** MD, acclaimed heart-lung transplant surgeon, humanitarian, former US Senate majority leader, and founding partner, Frist Cressey Ventures

"Having compassion doesn't mean that you can't be tough, that you can't be results oriented. This book shows that compassionate leadership is, in fact, strong leadership that leads to higher-performing teams, greater innovation, and better results overall."

—**Jeff Arnold,** co-founder, chairman, and CEO of Sharecare; Founder, WebMD

"I see the mission of leadership as the unrelenting effort to improve the conditions of people within an organization, a community, or a society. It's not always the easy thing to do. This book will provide leaders with valuable insights and actionable examples that will help them in their pursuit of a more compassionate world."

—**Dr. Sandro Galea,** dean, Boston University School of Public Health

"Donato Tramuto leads with compassion in addition to writing about it. We can trust his voice and heart to guide us toward becoming more compassionate leaders. The advice and inspiration he shares, along with the wisdom of the leaders he interviewed, creates a beautiful map for anyone seeking places and spaces to help others, and themselves."

—**Reverend Becca Stevens,** founder and president, Thistle Farms, speaker, Episcopal priest, and author of the new book, *Practically Divine*

The Double Bottom Line

HOW COMPASSIONATE LEADERS CAPTIVATE HEARTS AND DELIVER RESULTS

Donato Tramuto
with Tami Booth Corwin

FAST COMPANY *Press*

Fast Company Press
New York, New York
www.fastcompanypress.com

Distributed by Greenleaf Book Group

For ordering information or special discounts for bulk purchases, please contact Greenleaf Book Group at PO Box 91869, Austin, TX 78709, 512.891.6100.

Design and composition by Greenleaf Book Group and Lindsay Starr
Cover design by Greenleaf Book Group and Lindsay Starr
Tami Booth Corwin author photo by Marco Calderon

Publisher's Cataloging-in-Publication data is available.

Print ISBN: 978-1-63908-004-5

eBook ISBN: 978-1-63908-005-2

Part of the Tree Neutral® program, which offsets the number of trees consumed in the production and printing of this book by taking proactive steps, such as planting trees in direct proportion to the number of trees used: www.treeneutral.com

TreeNeutral

Printed in the United States of America on acid-free paper

21 22 23 24 25 26   10 9 8 7 6 5 4 3 2 1

First Edition

THIS BOOK IS DEDICATED TO the memory of Maeve Kennedy McKean and Gideon McKean, who lost their lives in a canoe accident during the COVID-19 lockdown, and to their quest for a more compassionate world.

I first met Maeve right after the launch of my first book in 2016. She was moved by my willingness to share my struggle with a severe hearing loss and resulting loneliness. I remember our first telephone conversation, in which she shared her work in addressing social isolation, especially with the hearing impaired. Her words were eloquent and pointed, yet it was her passion, courage, wit, and unwavering commitment to do her part in the world to ensure that no one—no matter their race, their disability, their sexual orientation, or whatever the difference might be—was left out. She lived compassion to the fullest and clearly understood the connection between empathy and taking action.

It was a year later when I met her five-year-old son Gideon. To say Gideon was far beyond his years would be an understatement. He certainly lit up a room, as he did that evening with his infectious smile, yet what I remember most was how this young boy was so full of love, kindness, and curiosity. Perhaps the lesson we can take from the tragic loss of these two extraordinary individuals is that you do not have to wait a hundred years to show compassion and love for others.

The new currency for this generation of leaders is compassion. This is what I have learned from writing this book. It was amplified for me when Maeve and Gideon left this world to make heaven brighter. The best way we can honor them is to unite and embrace compassion, not only for those we know very well, but also, in equal amount, for the stranger on the street or in the restaurant.

Contents

Foreword

by Kathleen Kennedy Townsend

CONGRATULATIONS TO DONATO TRAMUTO for challenging us to think about what compassionate leadership means. In this book, he convinces us of its effectiveness and shows us how to put it into practice. His stories bring these insights to life, as do the reflections and examples of dozens of powerful leaders woven throughout this book. It was inspiring and instructive to see how they exhibit compassionate leadership in the realms of business, politics, education, and beyond, and how they learned to be compassionate—some from their parents, others as a result of the pain they have suffered, the breadth of their readings, their acquaintances, or their circumstances. Donato not only shares his personal experiences and those of other proven leaders—with many practical pieces of advice included—but also shares compelling research that reinforces each aspect of strong, compassionate leadership.

One common denominator among these leaders is their ability to reflect, to think about their perception and the world around them. They could engage in a conversation about how they chose their goals, how they would respect their followers, and how they would treat those with whom they disagree. Reading about their practices and the compelling results they deliver is proof of the power of applied compassion!

Donato Tramuto is a great source of knowledge on compassion and a wonderful conduit through which we learn the stories of others. He has practiced compassionate leadership in different ways for essentially his whole, from his early days studying in a Catholic seminary—literally a student of compassion!—to his long career as a CEO in the health-care industry.

I came to know Donato when he joined the board at the Robert F. Kennedy Human Rights Foundation, an organization that was created in my father's honor and fights for human rights for all. Donato's leadership and advocacy for justice and human dignity show his strong commitment to compassion and his skilled application of it in a leadership role.

Compassionate leadership is not a one-and-done event. What I have observed about Donato is his extraordinary capacity to connect to a situation and then do something about it. When he observed in his company in 2018 that bullying in the workplace was as prevalent as bullying in schools, his foundation committed the dollars that launched the RFK Workplace Dignity Program. I know how important this is, having been the executive director of Operation Respect, the national anti-bullying effort led by Peter Yarrow, of Peter, Paul and Mary. In 2015, Donato was one of the first health-care leaders to point out that loneliness and social isolation is the new chronic condition of the 21st century, and he launched the first rural aging summit to address this situation. My daughter Maeve was working with him to host a conference at Georgetown University, before she died.

In 2014, the Robert F. Kennedy Human Rights Foundation honored Donato with the RFK Ripple of Hope Award, alongside Robert De Niro, Hillary Clinton, and Tony Bennett. In Donato's acceptance speech, in front of nearly 2,000 people, he openly shared his years of isolation, loneliness, and being bullied as a result of his severe hearing loss. He shared the pain he endured from the 9/11 loss of his dear friends and their three-year-old son aboard United flight 175, a flight on which he was originally scheduled to be. He shared his story to help others understand that their story matters and that only through compassion can we achieve the highest level of *connectiveness.*

I have long been a believer in the power of this form of leadership. In fact, I wrote a paper on it when I was at Yale Law School. When I served as lieutenant governor of Maryland from 1995 to 2003, I made sure we had character education in public schools. Of course, we taught reading, writing, and arithmetic. We also taught courage, compassion, bravery, and respect. Too often, the message to students was negative. *Just say NO. DON'T get pregnant. DON'T lie, cheat, or steal.* I wanted a positive message. *Serve your community, solve problems, advocate for a cause you care about. You can be a HERO.* Our slogan was: "The Courage to Care, the Strength to Serve."

I've learned that another important element of this type of leadership is strength. When Donato lost his friends on September 11, after having spent the weekend with them, he did not retreat to bitterness or to anger, although one would have understood had he gone down that path. Rather, he launched two not-for-profit foundations as a means to channel tragedy into doing good. He felt the pain of children like the one he once was, living with disabilities, wanting to pursue their dream of a college education yet needing help both monetarily and spiritually. He visited villages in Kenya and Haiti and saw the injustice of women delivering babies in a crowded room and on dirt floors. Over the last two decades, the Tramuto Foundation has helped thousands of young adults pursue their dreams, and Health eVillages has helped nearly a dozen countries increase access to health care, reducing maternal, infant, and pediatric mortality. He did more than show empathy. He also took action!

Compassionate leadership takes steely courage. Think of Abraham Lincoln visiting his troops, who he knew had been injured due to his decisions. He felt their pain and knew that some would die. Yet he persisted as he signed the Emancipation Proclamation and fought to keep the Union together.

Think of John Lewis in his nonviolent march from Selma to Montgomery, during which he was beaten, along with his fellow marchers—including children. Again, he persisted. The photos of the police beating the unarmed marchers moved the nation and helped enact the 1964 Civil Rights Bill.

One of my compassionate leadership heroes is Eleanor Roosevelt. There are many stories I could tell that demonstrate her strength and compassion. My favorite is how she helped the soldiers at St. Elizabeth's Hospital after World War I. These men were manacled to their beds in the same hospital as the criminally insane, attended to by Washington, DC, prisoners who had been recruited for the job. It was a horror show and a total abandonment of those who had fought for our country. It was extremely difficult for Eleanor to even go there; she shrank from anything having to do with mental illness because her own father had committed suicide.

But she went. Her mantra was, "You must do the thing you think you cannot do."

While there, she did three things. She was kind and gentle with each of the men, giving them hope. She used her position as the wife of the assistant secretary of the navy to get many more resources to St. Elizabeth's. She got the secretary of the interior to launch an investigation into St. Elizabeth's. As he said, "The most unforgivable sin in governing was a lack of generosity."

I love this story, for it shows how personal commitment—to helping on a one-on-one basis, and also to advocacy—can change the system.

Donato Tramuto provides countless examples of this type of help and advocacy in his experience as a leader in the business world and in his work as a philanthropist, human rights advocate, and non-profit leader.

I think compassionate leadership should combine those two aspects. One-on-one help is important, but it doesn't go far enough because the system doesn't change. On the other hand, people who just deal with systems often don't know what really goes on at the ground level. It is just ideas for them, not the blood, sweat, and tears of real people with names and fathers, mothers, friends, and children.

The goals and the ways these compassionate leaders reach their goals provide us with examples for our own time. Abraham Lincoln, John Lewis, and Eleanor Roosevelt knew that government had to change. Slavery had to be outlawed, discrimination eliminated, and horrendous hospital conditions alleviated.

Each felt enormous pain. None turned away from it or became hardened in the face of suffering.

I would say the same thing about my family.

When my uncle, President Kennedy, died, my father wrote me from the White House:

Dear Kathleen,

You seem to understand that Jack died and was buried today. As the oldest of the Kennedy grandchildren you have a special responsibility to Joe and Jack. Be kind to others. And work for your country.

Love,
Daddy

He did not have to take the time to write. And he could just as easily have expressed bitterness, anger, or sadness. Why not? But if he had, the consequences would have been very different for him, for his family. If he had, we—his family—could have spent the next generation tracking down rumors, living in the past, angry about what could have been. Instead, he set himself and our family in a different direction, one of service to our country and kindness. One of big goals and treating others with kindness, compassion, mercy, and love. Not that we always succeeded, but we knew that this was the path that we should follow.

Where did he learn this? His father and mother had already lost two children: my uncle Joe in World War II and my aunt Kathleen in a plane crash. While both of their parents were devasted, particularly my grandfather, neither withdrew from public life. They continued to make an impact with grace. After my uncle Jack died in office, my father stayed in government, focusing on poverty, the Civil Rights Act, voting rights, the Immigration Bill, hunger, and the rights of working people. He wanted to make the government work for people.

When Martin Luther King Jr. died, my father could walk into the inner city of Indianapolis, where the police chief would *not* go because he said it was not safe.

He calmed the crowd. He quoted Aeschylus:

> *"In our sleep, pain which cannot forget falls drop by drop upon the heart until in our despair, against our will, comes wisdom through the awful grace of God." What we need in the United States is not hatred, what we need is not violence and lawlessness, but rather love and wisdom and compassion toward one another and a feeling of justice toward those who still suffer in this country whether they be white or they be black.*

He asked the crowd to go home and asked for "compassion for all those, whether they be white or they be black." He then asked for a "prayer of love and that compassion of which I spoke."

More than 100 cities burned that night, but not Indianapolis. My father's compassionate leadership made the difference.

It is not easy to replicate the leadership of Lincoln, Lewis, Roosevelt, or my father. They had unique positions at a special moment in history. Each came to their positions with enormous pain, suffering, and deep reading and study in scripture, literature, and history. They had built their bona fides through years of work. Their examples can inspire and enlarge our own efforts.

This book is filled with stories of people who have built up their bona fides in their own communities, who have learned how to combine compassion with competence, strength, and commitment to produce meaningful results—whether in their neighborhoods or schools or to their bottom line. Donato's hope is that they will send ripples of hope throughout many communities and workplaces. I share that hope.

Different people would choose different starting points, some in the for-profit sector, others in the nonprofit area. In this book are stories of leaders who have used their talents in many different ways to open up opportunities for others by wealth creation, access to health, and better legislation.

I came from a family in which I knew that I had a responsibility to make a difference, and that I could. When I ran for Congress in 1986, I recruited many students to help. After the election, they told me that it was the most exciting thing they had ever done and that they would love to keep working with me. Since the voters had not been as excited as they, I wasn't quite sure exactly what to do at first. But then I got it.

I started the Maryland Student Service Alliance and made Maryland the first and only state to make service a graduation requirement. I visited hundreds of high schools. Students would tell me, "We have been taught to be seen and not heard," or they'd ask, "Why should I care what happens ten miles down the road?"

I made sure that the service was accompanied by preparation and reflection so the young people would understand why they were tutoring, picking up trash, or visiting the elderly.

For visits to the elderly, we would sometimes get the students to wear blurry glasses or put cotton in their ears or tie up one leg so they could feel how it is to be less mobile or lose your hearing or eyesight. And we made sure that they would reflect on their experiences. Compassion does not grow from just doing but also from thinking, understanding, asking questions, and discussing.

When I was elected lieutenant governor working with the Department of Education, I included character education in the curriculum so that students would learn respect, responsibility, and forgiveness as well as reading, writing, and mathematics. We had teachers, staff, and parent education on this! Turns out the staff were particularly important to include because students can be very rude to kitchen staff and janitors.

I find that if you teach certain values in school, it can also help at home. I grew up in a time when people did not use car seat belts. My children were much more adamant than I about seat belts. And, if at times I was not as kind as I should be, they were very happy to point that out!

Students are happy to be leaders. I visited a school in a rough part of town. I asked the eighth graders if they were bothered being in a character education school. "No, we like it," they said. "We have the responsibility to be leaders. And we have the courage and compassion to do what is right."

Who knows what will happen when they reach high school. The pressures are enormous. But as they grow older, they will remember the wonderful idealistic young person they were in eighth grade. They will have the language to guide them. They will have stories to remember.

That is the purpose of this book. Each of us needs guides, needs language, needs hope. And each of us can be a leader, whether we're high school students or CEOs. This book shows that there are numerous ways to be a compassionate leader. One size doesn't fit all. And if you don't find it here, you can create your own.

Good luck.

Acknowledgments

M Y FATHER ONCE SAID, "Be happy if you have as many friends as the number of fingers on your two hands." For whatever reason, God has given me multiple hands. In the pre-work for the writing of this book, I reached out to more than 40 colleagues, friends, and other individuals whom I knew over the many decades of my career and lifetime to ascertain their appetite to be interviewed for the book. Only two were unable to participate. I thank all of the amazing people who accepted our request to share their insights, experiences, and passion for a more compassionate world. I was simply taken aback by the unequivocal commitment of their time and energy to launching this movement to help current and future leaders understand how compassionate leadership can lead to more sustainable results. Each and every one of these contributors has had an indelible impact on my life, and their guidance has helped foster growth in my personal, professional, and spiritual journey.

As for my writing partner, Tami Corwin, compared to the feelings near and dear to my heart, words are simply insignificant in expressing my deep appreciation for her unwavering support. From the first moment I shared with her the idea of a book on compassion, she took a personal and deep interest in the topic, and for more than a year, she devoted countless hours to listening, interviewing, and researching to assemble the words that would ultimately explain the notion of tough compassion.

Many thanks also to Dr. Adam Leach, who brought the research skills as well as the wisdom and knowledge that ultimately created the rich and insightful original research data highlighted throughout this book. His own sense of compassion has helped thousands of young individuals find their way to fulfilling their dreams. Thank you to Steve Woods and TideSmart Health for providing their database and research capabilities to conduct the qualitative survey for the book.

I'd also like to acknowledge my parents, who taught me and my siblings that life is not about what you get but rather about what you give. We did not grow up with privilege, yet they taught us how to be tough with love and kindness, to always be kind to people, and to never take for granted the moments you spend with one another. While they left this world all too soon, there is not a single day that goes by that I do not think about them and the fact that I would not be where I am today if they had not pushed me to believe that the sky is the limit in one's journey to becoming a better person.

In addition, I'd like to thank Abby Snyder, Catherine Marcoullier, Jane Lane, Ethan Wright-Magoon, my brothers and sisters who never wavered in their belief in me, and all those who have impacted my life in a way that has contributed to my own sense of compassion.

And last but not least, I'd like to thank my partner of 30 years, Jeff. I first met Jeff in 1992, at the height of the AIDS epidemic and just two months following the sudden death of my beloved father. We met on the first anniversary of the loss of his dear partner, Bobby. What struck me about Jeff was the fact that he had entered into a committed relationship with Bobby knowing that he had AIDS and that his time on this earth was limited. Jeff was just 24 when they met. He could have simply said "nice to meet you" and moved in a different direction, given the reality in 1992 that anyone living with AIDS was, unfortunately, living on borrowed time. But instead, Jeff devoted more than four years to creating wonderful memories with

Bobby and using whatever time had been gifted to their relationship as an opportunity to grow and love deeply. I never knew Bobby, and yet I am certain he must have felt a wonderful sense of commitment, compassion, and unconditional love coming from Jeff. Without question, I have been the beneficiary of that same sense of commitment, compassion, and love for the last three decades. This book would not have been possible without Jeff's devotion and gentle spirit, his reminders about my shortcomings and areas in need of improvement, his support of my dreams, and his encouragement to always explore the unknown.

Introduction

W E'VE BEEN LIVING IN UNPRECEDENTED TIMES. Never before in my lifetime has there been as much widespread disruption in our daily lives and as many seismic shifts in how people work and live as those I've witnessed during the COVID-19 pandemic. As a result of the pandemic and the civil, political, and social upheaval we've been living through, important trends that were emerging prior to these events quickly accelerated: remote work and flexible hours, flexibility and adaptability that allow businesses to pivot quickly, and the need for a more modern approach to leadership that's better suited to today's workforce and marketplace all increased.

Now more than ever, leaders need to upgrade skills such as communication, transparency, adaptability, and understanding and support of employees' needs. They need to embrace diversity and inclusion, create stronger teams, and take responsibility for the impact they have on the communities in which they work and on the world. And, most importantly—as we are seeing how these shifts affect our neighbors, families, employees, and coworkers—we need to raise empathy and compassion to the top of the list.

During the pandemic, many companies struggled to stay open or simply had to shut their doors. Still others rose to the challenge, not only weathering the storm but also finding breakthrough ideas and moving from strength to strength to drive their businesses. They've seen that this test has solidified their organizations and unified their teams. There are many variables that separate those who have survived and thrived from those who have suffered, but it's clear that the most effective leaders are putting *people* at the top of their priority list and embracing compassion and humanity to a greater degree than ever before in their workplace. They are finding that putting people first and delivering results are not two separate goals. Rather, a strong focus on people *drives* strong results. That what I call *The Double Bottom Line*.

Forces of Change

It's not only the pandemic that makes compassion-driven skills and a more "fully human" approach so important. Rapidly accelerating technological advances have had a counterintuitive impact on the needs of the workforce. Workers do not necessarily need highly technical skills as automation and artificial intelligence become pervasive. Instead, workers need to develop more human dimensions, like creativity and compassion.

Another fundamental shift that is just as profound is the generational shift in the workplace. The percentage of younger generation—millennial and Gen Z—workers is growing, and the workforce has more diversity in general. Five generations make up the workforce as the youngest generation enters it and older workers delay retirement. Workers come from different backgrounds, experiences, and perspectives. Every demographic has changed. For example, since I started my career in 1980, the proportion of the workforce that was white has dropped from eighty-three percent to sixty-three percent today.[1] Only around half of millennials in the workforce are white today. Along with the shifting demographics come shifting economic and work trends.[2] The bottom line: things have changed!

Are leaders and managers ready for the future workforce? I believe, in many cases, the answer is no. Most senior leaders in CEO or C-suite jobs are in their late fifties. That means they started out working in businesses led by executives who began working in the 1950s, when businesses were more manufacturing-based. The technological boom had not yet happened. The workforce was not diverse. They learned skills and a work style from more traditional, top-down leaders focused on efficiency and productivity. Those things don't work anymore. Conversely, younger, up-and-coming leaders will be managing workers older than themselves. A new approach to leadership is needed to create understanding across generations.

Leadership Needs an Upgrade

If you look at the engagement of the workforce now, and at how satisfied people are in their jobs, things haven't changed much over the past several decades. There is a big gap between the current level of engagement (only about one-third of workers are engaged) and what companies should be striving for, both for their bottom lines and for the well-being of their workers.

The new order requires a new approach to leading, managing, and participating at work and in the world. At every company or organization that I have recently been engaged in or led, and in every conversation that I've had with workers, whether they are CEOs or recent college grads, a new set of vital leadership skills and traits are being identified. The new workforce needs leaders they trust who empower them, understand differences among people in diverse workplaces, and act to build bridges. It's now vital for leaders to communicate that what workers do has purpose and meaning and to demonstrate how each individual's work connects with a larger mission.

I believe without a doubt that there is one dimension that both underlies and drives all others. That common denominator is compassion.

The Study of Compassion

I have long been a student of compassion. I had a series of tragedies as a child, including an illness that resulted in nearly complete hearing loss for many years. I faked my way by letting others believe I could understand what they were saying when I could not, succumbing to the peer pressure that perfection is synonymous with youth. I watched as my parents struggled with loss, illness, and economic hardship while still putting other people's needs before their own. I studied for six years in a Catholic seminary, where I completed my undergraduate education, worked as a hospital chaplain, and studied to be a priest.

Though I ultimately decided to not become a priest and instead became an entrepreneur and a public company CEO, I took with me the calling to serve, the values that were cemented there, and a deep understanding of the practice of compassion. After my time in the seminary, I pursued an MBA part time for two years and enjoyed a long career in health care, starting as a sales rep and eventually becoming a CEO, a position I held at multiple companies over a span of twenty-five years. Spending decades in health care, where there is vast and deep human suffering and need, kept me deeply immersed in the understanding and practice of compassion.

All of these experiences shaped me and cultivated in me a deeper practice of compassion. But one event changed everything and took my commitment to compassion to a new level, where it remains today. On September 11, 2001, I lost two dear friends and their three-year-old son in one of the planes that hit the south tower of the World Trade Center. They were on that plane returning to Los Angeles after visiting me. In fact, I was supposed to be on that plane with them, but a toothache and a last-minute change in plans to get to the dentist prevented me from getting on that plane and dying on that day. That deeply painful experience brought me to a crossroads. I could be bitter, or I could channel that pain into something productive and hopeful to honor the memory of my friends. I chose the latter and have dedicated myself and the foundation I launched in their memory to the pursuit and application of compassion-driven work. This also deepened my belief in applying compassion in my career and in the organizations that I worked with and led.

A New Leadership Model

During my career, I've seen many approaches to leadership and management. My early bosses were old-school, dictatorial managers who drove their teams to win at all costs. On the other side of the coin, I've had bosses and colleagues who led by empowering employees and consistently showed great compassion. Both types of leaders are around today. But, perhaps because of all the forces at work over recent years, I'm seeing an acceleration in the rise of the latter. Leading with compassion is taking hold. It brings success in the short term as well as in the long term to a business and to people. It's more imperative than ever.

Leaders of some of the most successful companies in the world, like Apple, PayPal, and Microsoft, have long utilized compassion as a core leadership principle. It obviously works for the strongest of leaders. Yet, many still view compassion as a weak approach, an unnecessary "soft skill," or a low priority in contrast to the pressing need to drive performance and profits. Leaders who prioritize it, though, know that compassion is a powerful driver of success. It correlates to greater creativity and innovation, higher employee engagement, better morale, increased loyalty, consistently better performance, and higher profits. When leaders take an opposite approach, they actually create headwinds for themselves that could be avoided with more consciousness and compassion.

I've watched some leaders struggle to grasp the importance of this fundamental. And worse, I've met others who truly believe that winning at all costs, that leading through force of will, is what it means to be a strong leader. This could not be further from the truth.

For some, compassion is an off-putting word in the competitive world of dog-eat-dog business, and it's looked down upon by many.

Some think being compassionate is weak, that it means copping out of doing the really hard thing. Or, they regard it as "nice to do" but not by any means a must. Or, they believe that people are either born compassionate or they're not. In all those estimates, they couldn't be more wrong. Men and women around the world have used the model with outstanding success on both the human and profit-making fronts.

I've championed compassion as a leadership practice for a long time, in many ways. I've instituted antidiscrimination and anti-bullying initiatives in the workplace. I founded the Robert F. Kennedy (RFK) Human Rights Workplace Dignity Program. I've committed to a years-long study of the topic of loneliness and how compassion in policy and leadership can address it. Then in 2020, after a year in the making, I stepped away from a full-time CEO role and started work on what I think of as a compassion campaign to take the next step to help cultivate more compassion within organizations and in the world at large. My foundation, the Tramuto Foundation, is now committed to compassion as its core mission.

I believe my background uniquely positions me to further this mission: I was steeped in compassion from birth, even studying it in my undergraduate work as a would-be priest. Knowing that I might have had circumstances different from others that allowed me to focus on and practice compassion from an early age and in depth, I wanted to understand how other people become compassionate. Did they have compassionate parents? Is it developed through experience with deep suffering? Is it possible to learn compassion as you would learn a new language?

I also wanted to know how the best leaders practice this type of leadership in a way that brings out the best in their workers and their bottom-line results. How do they combine compassion with the tough aspects of the job? How do they combine purpose with performance? I knew how I did it, but I wanted to learn from other strong leaders who had been doing it with great success.

I decided to study compassion with more depth and focus. I assembled a small team of committed and compassionate collaborators to dive in fully to this work. We talked with hundreds of people over the course of a year, many of whom were CEOs or executives, others who were college students or recent college graduates, and many in between. We conducted a formal survey among 1,500 workers in the United States to study the dimensions of compassion in the workplace. We then did in-depth interviews with forty successful compassionate leaders and asked them key questions. These handpicked proven leaders also completed the compassionate leadership survey so that I could compare the similarities and differences between them and a general population of senior leaders.

The Compassionate Leadership Gap

The results of the formal survey research were both validating and concerning. Mostly, they underscored the need for this book. For example:

Most workers believe a compassionate workplace leads to cooperation, which leads to greater productivity and profitability. Yet most workers believe the workplace is more competitive than cooperative.

- Eighty-four percent of respondents believe that a compassionate workplace encourages cooperation, which in turn leads to greater productivity and profitability.

- Sixty-eight percent believe the workplace is more competitive than cooperative.

Most leaders and workers believe that compassion can be part of a double bottom line that favors both profitability and care for workers and communities. Yet, at the same time, most workers see their leaders as rejecting this notion.

- Eighty-four-and-a-half percent of our leadership group and seventy-seven percent of our survey group believe that compassionate leadership can be part of a double bottom line.

- Sixty-and-a-half percent of all workers believe that leaders in general reject compassion because they see it as contradictory to productivity or profit.

- Sixty percent of workers said that the beliefs and attitudes held by leaders are insufficient in the promotion of compassion.

Most workers see compassionate acts by their leaders as good examples, yet a majority also view compassionate leadership as weak or distracted.

- Eighty percent of workers believe that leaders who demonstrate compassionate acts set a good example for others to follow.

- Fifty-seven percent of respondents strongly or somewhat strongly agree that leaders who emphasize compassion are seen as weak or distracted from normal priorities.

Part of the research focused on the comparison between the responses, views, and beliefs of the most senior leaders and the lowest-level employees. One statement read:

Leaders in my current organization inspire others to be compassionate in their work and personal lives.

- Eighty-six percent of the most senior leaders (e.g., CEOs, C-suite executives) said they agreed with this statement.

- Sixty-five percent of the lowest-level employees agree with this statement.

Leaders in my organization seek input and support from employees and other stakeholders to promote a compassionate workplace.

- Eighty-five percent of the most senior leaders agreed with this statement.

- Fifty-nine percent of the lowest-level employees agreed with this statement.

These gaps between belief and practice, between the ideal and current states, are exactly why this book is needed. Most of us, if asked, would say of course we believe in compassion. Most of us believe compassion-driven leadership can improve workers' engagement and well-being as well as a business's financial results. In fact, study after study shows this is true. So, the core issue is that we believe in it—*but we're not doing it*. Either our leaders think they're doing it but the effect isn't being felt, or they say they're doing it but they're not.

In this book, I have found compelling evidence, both quantitative and anecdotal, that proves that compassion makes stronger leadership across all meaningful measures. And, perhaps most importantly, I want to show people what this really means, and how to apply it. Time after time, I've observed that if a leader with skill, knowledge, and vision combines these fundamentals with a compassion-driven approach, results soar even higher.

What Compassionate Leadership Is *Not*

I've been looking at the world and at business through the lens of compassion throughout my life. I've observed many other compassionate leaders empower people while accomplishing their goals and delivering amazing financial results. There are countless examples of compassionate leadership throughout history, courageous acts of leadership that have even *changed* history. In reviewing existing research and the results of original research done for this book, I see that most agree that compassionate leadership is a good thing. The majority of people believe it drives performance, and plenty of studies and analyses show that *it does drive performance* across many measures, including the bottom line.

In light of all this, I've asked myself many times, *Why isn't everyone doing it?*

I've come to some broad conclusions. There are certainly long-established societal and systemic influences, such as financial markets and corporate boards that tell leaders there is only one set of results that matter—financial results. These are deeply entrenched and will take time to change. I also believe there is a fear of being compassionate in the workplace, and a resistance or reluctance to spend time trying, that is driven by a lack of real understanding of what compassionate leadership is, how it's executed, and what its impact is. Which brings me to a key point: There are powerful myths and misconceptions about compassion in leadership that prevent broad acceptance of this approach. These misconceptions are standing in the way of important change.

So, before I get into what compassionate leadership really means and how successful leaders are practicing it, I want to wipe the slate clean and correct some old ideas and misconceptions that hold people back from embracing compassion—and from being more successful. I'll address those myths head-on by explaining what compassionate leadership *is not*.

I'll show some of the most surprising insights from our original survey research that reveal the prevalence of these myths and the negative effect of executing on compassionate values or policies either partially or incorrectly. Insights from our research show a few things, but one of the most interesting is the gap between what senior leaders think they're doing and how their lower-level employees are experiencing it.

Let's Clear Up the Myths

Myth 1: Being compassionate is the same as being nice.

Myth 2: Compassionate leadership is a "soft skill," not a driver of real results.

Myth 3: Compassionate leadership is weak leadership. If you're compassionate, you'll be walked all over by your employees and colleagues.

I've observed that most people have an incomplete understanding of what compassion-driven leadership really is in practice. In this book, I will take a deep dive into what compassionate leadership really means and what it looks like from the perspectives of compassionate leaders and from the perspective of those led. While many view compassion in the same vein as empathy and kindness, I will show the dimensions of compassion that set it apart. I'll show both anecdotal and measurable benefits of compassionate leadership in a company or organization and in society as a whole. I will show how compassionate organizations are doing it well and how anyone can borrow from their playbooks.

Compassion Is a Strength

I will challenge leaders to see compassion in a different light, as a strength, a critical skill, and as an imperative. I will explain how leaders can be strong, firm, and tough while sticking to their values and principles. I will make the case that compassion is power. Adding this component to one's overall leadership approach boosts its effectiveness. I will demonstrate that adopting these attributes is not just nice to do but also a "must-do" by providing compelling examples of the people I interviewed, reporting the survey results of our original research study, and sharing what I've learned in my lifetime.

I will share evidence-based findings that demonstrate how compassion is as good for those practicing it as it is for those receiving it. Could it be that the key to compassionate leadership is also the key to happiness? I believe I'll help convince you of this.

Importantly, I will show how compassion can be taught and how it's learned. In our own research, we saw that ninety-four-and-a-half percent of senior leaders believe that compassionate leadership can be taught, and eighty percent across the whole population believed so as well. A recent study featured in the *Harvard Business Review* found that **eighty percent of managers want to be more compassionate but they do not know how**.[3] This book and the great leaders represented in it will show you how.

My firm belief is that compassionate leadership should be taught in some way, in every school, at every level, especially in college and MBA programs. Robert F. Kennedy would often use this quote from French philosopher Albert Camus: "We live in a world where children go hungry. Our job is to lessen the number of children who are hungry." Perhaps we live in a world where many individuals are incompassionate, and perhaps this project can lessen the number of those incompassionate individuals. That is our goal.

I wrote this book because I've seen firsthand that it is possible to be compassionate, to empower people and help them grow while also delivering strong results, not just on a parallel track but also because compassionate leadership makes results stronger. I believe its messages are imperative for our current and future workforce and world. I know it's possible to implement *The Double Bottom Line* in any organization that does indeed captivate and light up hearts and minds while delivering stronger results. It is a uniquely opportune time to help spread the word, to grow the movement, to be part of what we see as a coming leadership revolution.

Part 1

Defining a New Model of Leadership

Chapter 1

It's Time to Flip Traditional
Leadership on Its Head

I f I asked you what training to be a priest has in common with training to sell drugs, I'm pretty certain you'd say, "Nothing!" But, in 1980, I was doing both.

After years of training to be a priest, I was wavering on whether the priesthood was right for me. I decided to take a sabbatical from the seminary until I had more certainty. During that time, I worked as a hospital chaplain, taught a course in philosophy, and generally contemplated my future. One day, when I was reading the newspaper, I saw an ad for a pharmaceutical sales position with Marion Labs. On a whim, I decided to apply. That became my first job in the business world.

After years of preparing for a life of ministry, I wanted to find some kind of purpose or deeper meaning in this new job, something more than reaching sales goals. Years before, my sister-in-law Rosemary had died tragically during childbirth because of a simple and preventable medication error. I adored Rosemary and had trouble making sense of her loss. I tried to see this job as an opportunity to educate doctors, in the hope that I might help prevent future senseless deaths like Rosemary's.

I started work at the beginning of what many have since referred to as the "decade of greed." My boss Hank seemed to fit right in. A former college hockey player, he was still very competitive and wanted to win above all else. He made sure that his employees knew that his only focus was to make *a lot* of money. He was tough and far from compassionate. Hank was an example of the type of old-school manager who set aggressive goals and used toughness to push his employees to achieve those goals.

I was miserable. I lasted less than a year in that job and left it disillusioned about the workplace and still confused about my future. Hank showed me a business world with no heart. I wasn't sure that world was right for someone who was more influenced by the seminary than by sales. The competitive life in a high-pressure sales job was a jarring change from the contemplative life of the seminary.

Despite this experience, I ultimately concluded that Hank's way was not the only way. I also came to see that working for a for-profit company still allowed me to have an opportunity to help other people. I decided not to finish my seminary studies and to commit to a career in business instead. But the experience with Hank cemented a belief that still drives me: Leaders can be successful without sacrificing their values.

I entered an MBA program at the University of Buffalo. While pursuing an MBA, I went back to work again as a sales rep for a pharmaceutical company, this time for Boehringer Ingelheim. Fortunately, there I worked for a manager named Markus whose team leadership and goal achievement style was quite different from Hank's. I thrived under this positive leadership; so did the whole team. We consistently exceeded our sales goals, and I quietly noticed that we all did it together and without misery!

My first two managers were a study in leadership contrasts. Hank, an aggressive, old-school, win-at-all-costs manager, and Markus, a positive, empowering, team-oriented leader. There were two lessons in this:

1. You can learn just as much from negative leadership examples as you can from positive ones. Hank proved that to me.

2. A positive manager can produce better results than a negative one. In fact, more often than not, positive leaders with skill and knowledge excel at producing positive results.

The Evolution of Leadership

In the 1980s, there was a tension between the human-centered and money/power-centered forces that are still competing in our workplaces and society today. On the human- or team-centered side, surely one of the most notable business leaders of the time was Lee Iacocca, the CEO of Chrysler. He got a lot of press; he was frequently interviewed, observed, and—though often critiqued—emulated.

Lee Iacocca was famous for saving Chrysler. In manufacturing, Chrysler was a monolithic, union worker–driven business. Charged with leading it, Iacocca took it from the brink of bankruptcy and transformed it into a successful and innovative company.

He was a transformational leader who focused on the concept of teamwork. Unlike many dictatorial, "the-CEO-knows-best" leaders before him, he believed that a CEO didn't have to have all the answers. He described his leadership approach in this quote: "I hire people who are brighter than me, and then I get out of the way."

Around that time, a more rank-and-file-empowering and less top-down-controlling management style started to take hold and unfold in business, and Lee Iacocca no doubt fit that mold. Certainly, the older, more traditional, top-down-controlling type of leadership persisted. In fact, we still see it today in all sorts and sizes of businesses.

The 1980s also produced plenty of win-at-all-costs leaders. In fact, that was probably still the dominant style. There were plenty of infamous examples on Wall Street who took the model to an extreme and ended in disaster, like Ken Lay, the founder of Enron; Dick Fuld, whose hubris was reportedly responsible for the collapse of one of the most prestigious banks at the time, Lehman Brothers; and Jordan Belfort, the real-life inspiration for the movie *The Wolf of Wall Street*.

I believe that the difference today—four decades later—is that the human-centered leadership approach is finally pulling ahead and taking hold as the better fit for the challenges and opportunities that lie before leaders. Its influence is strengthening, and its adoption is spreading in organizations big and small. I believe its momentum will allow it to become the standard.

As Victor Hugo said, "No army can withstand the strength of an idea whose time has come." I'm certain that compassionate leadership's time has come.

Defining Compassionate Leadership

I see compassionate leadership as listening to others' challenges, needs, or problems; having empathy for them; and then actually doing something about it. To me, empathy—the ability to think about and feel for another person's problems, suffering, or experience—is a critical component. Compassion, on the other hand, usually starts with or coexists with empathy, but it adds the desire and action to relieve that person's suffering, help them overcome a challenge, or otherwise better their situation.

Compassion shows that you have committed to the person. You've embraced the dignity of that individual. I've always loved the line from *Man of La Mancha*, "Be willing to march into hell for a heavenly cause," and I think that's also what compassion is sometimes: being willing to take that road less traveled and set yourself apart from what others might be afraid to do. In an organization, because it is only people who get results, I think it means that you invest your time in individuals, and that is how the organization prospers. In other words, people are your true focus.

As I mentioned in the introduction, I reached out to more than forty of the most compassionate leaders I knew to interview them in depth for this book. I chose leaders who had demonstrated success in their own arenas as well as exhibited a compassionate leadership style. These are leaders who have practiced and refined this approach and can speak to it from a place of wisdom and experience. The first question I asked every leader we interviewed for this book was how they defined compassionate leadership. Their words were different, but they all conveyed the same essence.

Jeff Arnold, founder and CEO of Sharecare, defined compassionate leadership in terms of how it can be practiced in an organization. I've known Jeff since he founded WebMD, and I've long admired his leadership. When asked about how he sees compassion in practice, he explained: "I'm very mission driven. I've been around digital health for a long time trying to solve the complicated problems of the health-care system and how to improve well-being. I think of compassion as how we put ourselves in the shoes of another person. Sometimes that person is a consumer; sometimes they are a patient, an employee, a health-plan member, or a friend. It's trying to put myself in their shoes and know what they're dealing with. It's feeling that shared compassion and then trying to take action to work through solutions together."

As a pioneer in digital health, Jeff is, among other things, data driven. He spoke about the importance of pairing empathy with action in that context: "Data is only as good as the insight, and the insight is only as good as the action. That's our approach. Can I understand the situation? What insights can I get from that? Then what do I do about it?" In short, yes, Jeff is a data-*driven* leader. At the same time, he is a people-*focused* one. He sees getting outstanding bottom-line results not as separate from his leadership style but rather as a *result* of it.

Jeff Arnold is a great example of how compassionate leaders can be tough *and* compassionate, people-focused *and* very successful. He has been an ambitious entrepreneur, and anyone who has negotiated a deal with him knows he is a tough negotiator. After founding WebMD in the nineties, Jeff became a billionaire before the age of thirty and has gone on to continue his focus on how to help people by improving health care.

Top Down Is Out

The great leaders we interviewed for this book described this shift to compassionate leadership as a movement from head to heart. They described the place from which a leader leads as no longer from the top of an organization, dictating down. Instead, they lead from the center or bottom up. The focus moves from leader-centric to team- and customer-centric. The drive moves from profit-first to people-first and from shareholder value to stakeholder value. Practicing this form of leadership focuses on the actions a leader can take to operationalize empathy in a sincere and effective way to help the organization or the community reach goals and become better along the way.

Traditional leadership models have been hierarchical and top-down. This type of leadership is often about senior leaders thinking they need to have or do have all the answers, that they need to give all the direction and must supply the big ideas. The leader assumes the role of sole strategist. This often comes with dictatorial communication from the top down and, at its extreme, can be management by force, even bullying, which still happens in too many organizations.

This model is top heavy in terms of who is expected to contribute and who has power or a voice in an organization. If the ideas are coming from the top down, companies and organizations are missing ideas from the ranks. Given that the average CEO in America is fifty-nine years old, male, and white,[1] and the total workforce is younger and more diverse, it also suggests that companies with an old-school style are going to be missing ideas, innovations, and a deep understanding of their customer base that their more diverse, recently schooled, and digitally and globally savvy workforces can offer. In addition, if there isn't a regular and true many-way communication that reaches all those within the organization, leaders will miss issues and, as a result, live with the consequences of not resolving them.

The new compassion-driven model is much more flexible, as the stories throughout this book demonstrate. The top-down model is literally being flipped on its head by unquestionably great leaders who practice a more modern leadership style. It's more about bottom-up or center-out structures, in which the leader is the central facilitator of innovation and problem-solving, using the great ideas that come from all members of the team, regardless of where in the business they work, to serve the customers. Meanwhile, everyone participates in the innovations, changes, and successes, and thrives.

Great leaders who use this approach understand that people and profits are concerns that are not mutually exclusive but actually dovetail naturally. They see that infusing their leadership with a deep commitment to compassion is the accelerant that gives it added power.

Leading from the Center

I see the role of a leader as a facilitator of ideas, communication, and culture among employees, team members, and constituents. The leader is like an orchestra conductor who knows how to get the best from the unique contribution of each instrument while never playing the instrument in the musician's place. The leader is an influencer who knows how to get the best work from staff and how to support them as they work together to create a beautiful and powerful result.

Stefano Lucchini, a great friend of mine from my second home in Italy, described the disparity between the old and new models of leadership well. I work with Stefano on initiatives with the RFK Foundation, where he is chairman of the RFK Human Rights Foundation of Italy and where I serve on the board and support him as cochairman. Stefano said: "Leadership could be narrowly constructed, focused on how to manage teams, stay on the top, plan, and direct for the next issue. I take a broader view of leadership and subscribe to the eastern philosophy of leaders not at the top of a hierarchy but at the center of a network of talents, connections, and issues. Leadership in this sense is about understanding the different positions and points of view at stake, acting as a servant leader with compassion and understanding for the people I work with, our clients, our competitors, and the many other important stakeholders with whom we interact while fulfilling our range of societal responsibilities."

The culture has to be one in which the leader recognizes that their role is not to have all the answers. On the contrary, their role is to have all the questions, and then to listen to the individuals around them in a way that creates a sense of unity and a respect for dignity. As a leader, when you listen to the stories of others as they open up for perhaps the first time in a work environment, you become more vulnerable. Which, as you'll learn, is a good thing.

You're not cultivating a culture of similarities. Your business's culture and how you harmoniously thrive and prosper together is the result of having built upon differences. And I think that's what I have fostered the most: inclusion. The reality of culture is that nobody can get anything done in any role without other people.

In 2020, I had the honor of joining St. Joseph's College in Maine as their first-ever Honorary Scholar-in-Residence. One of the great benefits of this role is spending time with their president, Jim Dlugos, a true compassionate leader. When he was appointed president, he was described as a collaborator who can forge a common vision among people. I asked him about this, since it is an important part of compassionate leadership.

He told me that he was asked by someone at Maine Public Radio about his vision before he started in the role. He recalled that when asked, he was down in New Jersey and said he didn't have a vision for St. Joseph's, as "he wasn't anywhere near the place." He said: "I have to go there first and get to know those folks before I can begin to talk about not what *my* vision is but what *our* vision is. One of the roles I have as president is to be the chief storyteller, the gatherer of people's memories and hopes and frustrations, in some cases, and then to tie those together in a more coherent narrative. If we're going to move forward together effectively, each of us has to have enough buy-in for the thing that we end up sharing. In the middle of that Venn diagram, that's the space where we overlap." In Jim's role, he works from the center of that Venn diagram, bringing together those diverse voices and facilitating a way forward while making sure each one is heard and represented.

This type of leadership strives to accomplish a couple of things. The first goal is to get the best from each contributor, allowing individuals to work to their best potential. The second goal is to create the conditions that allow all people to collaborate and work in harmony with each other, cultivating the greatest potential from the entire organization.

As part of this, I see the leader as a chief obstruction remover. As CEO, I used to ask the question all the time, "What obstacles can I help you remove to get your job done?" Believe me, most people had an answer to that question! I took that role seriously. It not only helped us all get more done and materialize a better result, but also it let my people know I cared about them.

Laying the foundation for this model of compassionate leadership starts with how you define your values. By that, I don't mean it's about what the leader says are the values, and it's not the leader dictating those values. I mean, it starts with how you define them, the process by which you define them. I believe that leaders need to empower teams to collectively develop a company's culture and values. Some company CEOs force values on the organization, but there is a richer opportunity to empower the organization to participate. Remember, the focus is center out or bottom up, allowing people from all levels in an organization to participate and have a voice in the creation of this compassionate culture.

I've been fortunate to know many leaders who practice compassionate leadership. Most of the leaders interviewed for this book described their practice in one of three ways: team-centric, community-centric, or people-centric. In the end, all three are really just about the people.

Team-Centric Leadership

Dr. Craig Samitt is a good friend and health-care industry colleague of mine. He was recently president and CEO of Blue Cross and Blue Shield of Minnesota and its parent company, Stella, and is a nationally recognized expert and thought leader on health-care delivery and policy. He was named one of 50 Most Influential Physician Executives and Leaders by *Modern Healthcare*.[2]

Craig is someone who has lived, worked, and succeeded for decades as a strong and compassionate leader. He delineated a style of leadership in which "the leaders' focus is not about themselves." For him, embracing a compassionate leadership style is not just good but also *essential* to hitting your goals and, in his case, to transforming the health-care industry. Craig told us: "We live in a world that is very leader-centric and physician-centric, not teammate-centric and patient-centric. As I work to reinvent health care, it's very much through this philosophy, that to lead compassionately it's about the team, it's about the patient. It's not about the leader." For him, it's very simple. "We put people before profits," he said. "We put kindness before fear. It creates a followership when folks lead this way."

Like all of the leaders interviewed in this book, Craig had to respond to the coronavirus pandemic and help his team navigate it. The way he did so is a case study in compassion, and it paid off. "It was very clear to me that our team was our number one priority," said Craig. "So, the very first thing we were going to do, without thinking twice, was to send people home. We would get them all that they needed, and more than anything else, we wanted to keep every one of our teammates safe, out of the hospital, and healthy."

I asked Craig how his role changed during the pandemic. "No one really teaches how to lead in the midst of double or triple crises," he said, "and so I felt like I was no longer a chief executive officer. I immediately became a chief communications officer and a chief vulnerability officer, because our team wanted to know that I was struggling with the same things they were. I was. Compassionate leadership is removing a mask, removing a shield, or removing a protective coating. It's being as raw and vulnerable, as emotional and challenged as one's teammates. It opened us up to have more candid and transparent discussions about what people needed so that we could listen and then act.

"One of the early things we found was that the physical safety of our teammates was not enough," Craig continued. "We were worried about people's well-being, about their at-home workplace comfort. Some of our teammates were not just full-time employees, they were also full-time teachers and full-time parents. So, we asked, 'What can we do in this unprecedented time to help you cope?' We did a round of surveys. The first was an introductory 'How is it going at home?' I think at the beginning folks found it sort of unique and a bit fun to be at home. That quickly evolved. Folks were uncomfortable working at home; they didn't have separate workspaces that were conducive for them to work. So, we offered resources to make the home more comfortable. We added several resources that focused on people's well-being, their mental state. We also wanted to be sure they were staying connected. We started contests; some departments had virtual Olympics as a way to make sure that people were staying engaged. If we were just a run-of-the-mill employer, we might have made sure folks had the technical tools and left it at that. But in addition to an employer, we wanted to be colleagues, we wanted to be friends, we wanted to be caregivers in many respects."

Craig and his team also noticed that they were seeing a decline in demand for services and were worried that people would feel underutilized and be fearful for their jobs. They offered an opportunity for their teammates to give back to the state and to the community by volunteering to be contact tracers to help prevent the further spread of COVID-19. So, if they felt that they weren't busy enough doing their day jobs, they had the chance to find great fulfillment by helping their community stay well.

Craig Samitt's leadership through crises has paid off for the organization and made his connection to his team stronger. He did ongoing work to improve company culture and measures this work with noted consulting firm Heidrick & Struggles's culture-shaping division, Senn Delaney. Measured after months of the pandemic, the most recent employee engagement results skyrocketed. The jump in scores across the whole company was the biggest they've ever recorded. This was due to very intentional actions at every level. A big component was Craig's leadership and his authentic engagement with employees through the crisis. One employee noted: "Now, more than ever, it's comforting to me to know that my CEO is not some *Wizard of Oz*–type figure up at the top, but is instead someone who truly cares about and appreciates the rest of us."

Community-Centric Leadership

In addition to the Tramuto Foundation, I founded a second non-profit organization called Health eVillages with the specific mission of helping to bring modern health care to underserved areas around the world. In reviewing the name via a closer lens, you will see it really stands for "Heal the Villages." Our first project was helping to support services at a health clinic in the small Kenyan village of Lwala that is now called the Lwala Community Alliance. This is an amazing story of life-changing community-centric leadership started by two brothers from the village of Lwala.

When founders Milton and Fred Ochieng were boys, their village was poor and lacked access to health care. When women had babies, they had no care during their pregnancies, and children were delivered by unskilled village midwives. According to Lwala's annual reports, in the entire county, only twenty-six percent of births had a skilled health-care provider in attendance, which meant that if there were complications, there was no one to help, resulting in high infant and maternal mortality rates. There was no hospital, no doctor, and no cell service. But they did have a strong community, and Milton and Fred's father had a dream of bringing a health clinic to their village.

As the boys grew older, it was apparent that they had great academic promise. They got scholarships from Dartmouth College. Their village sold chickens, goats, and cows to pay for airfare to the United States with only one request: "Do not forget us." The brothers went on to Vanderbilt University Medical School and became doctors.

While away, their mother and father died tragically of AIDS. Milton and Fred returned to Lwala to follow through on their father's dream of building a health clinic, which they opened in 2007. The clinic has since expanded to become the Lwala Community Alliance. The first project Health eVillages supported there was the building of a maternity ward.

I'll never forget my first visit to Lwala. It was a long and arduous journey from the United States, first to Nairobi, and then from there to Lwala via a small plane that looked too old to fly. Doctors Without Borders escorted our team by car from the plane's landing site to our destination to make sure we were safe. Minutes into my drive, I looked out the window and saw a young boy dead on the road, struck by a car and left there. I learned that it happened all the time—poor children with no place to go in dangerous surroundings.

But when I got to Lwala, I felt safe and at home. I was overwhelmed by the love in this village. I was greeted with a huge hug by Lillian, a mother of twins. She told me that she had been rushed to the hospital after a complication during her pregnancy. If it weren't for the medical app we provided to the clinic, she and her babies would have died. To this day, I think of those boys as part of my extended family.

Help Communities Solve Their Own Problems

The Lwala Community Alliance is led by co-CEOs Julius Mbeya and Ash Rogers. They have shown how compassionate leadership can foster innovative solutions to very big problems, and how compassionate communities can be empowered to solve their own problems. Their approach highlights how compassionate leadership is not about a leader stepping in to single-handedly deliver the solution to a problem; it's about knowing that the best and most lasting outcomes for a community come when the leader supports or facilitates the community in solving the problem themselves. This is especially important in a community like many in Kenya that have a history of oppression by external forces, which results in a lack of trust toward actions that are offered to or imposed on them by outsiders.

The co-CEOs use the term "community-led" to describe this approach. Ash Rogers explained that one way they understand the level of community-driven development is by charting progress along a continuum of participation. On the left end of the continuum, the community is not participating in solving the problem, and the solution is being given to them or even forced on them. On the other end of the continuum, communities design and deliver their own solutions. The goal is always to move further to the right on this spectrum, to the full participation end of the continuum.

Julius Mbeya grew up in a neighboring village that was very poor. His father only had a third-grade education. His mother never went to school at all, though he calls her the most influential person he knows. Because he comes from the area he now serves, he told us that he felt humbled by the chance to help. Based on where he came from, the suffering he has seen—brothers and sisters who died of AIDS—he knew that could have easily been him. While he does have a unique understanding of the needs of the community, even more important is that he knows that the people who are experiencing the problems or suffering now are the ones who understand the problem best.

Julius described it like this: "Most of the time, solutions are implemented without communities. What has been a blessing for us is this idea of 'working from below,' so that we have knowledge and research and the ability to have the best solutions that can be implemented. Compassion is about accepting that the people who are experiencing the problem understand the problem better, and they have valid solutions. Compassion is the driver of innovation, of creating room for people to be able to think.

"Compassion is about responding to the community in a way that answers their deep questions and deep fears," he continued. "And, bringing back hope—I think that is what the organization has been able to do. Despite the challenges, the people of Lwala can still hope for a better future for themselves and their children." The results back this up. What was a twenty-six percent skilled health provider–performed infant-delivery rate before the Lwala Community Alliance is now up to 100 percent.[3]

People-Centric Leadership

For me, one of the most exciting developments in the movement toward more compassion in leadership was the campaign of President Joe Biden, a campaign that had compassion at its core. President Biden embodies the nature of compassionate leadership. At his inauguration, he addressed a deeply divided nation still hurting from all that led up to that day. His words were compassionate, and they exemplify this new type of leader. He said, "We celebrate the triumph not of a candidate, but of a cause, the cause of democracy. . . . The American story depends not on any one of us, not on some of us, but on all of us." He suggested that empathy might bridge our division, that "if we show a little tolerance and humility, and if we are willing to stand in the other people's shoes—as my mom would say—just for a moment, stand in their shoes."

Regardless of party affiliation, I think Biden's focus on human values will inspire the new generation of leaders. I've been fortunate to meet Joe Biden on several occasions, and the empathy born of his lifetime of losses emanates. Around the time of his election, headline after headline focused on his compassionate and empathetic style: From *The Atlantic*, "Biden's Empathy Is What Matches Him to This Moment"; from CNBC, "Biden Is Leading by Example When He Cries in Public. Emotional Honesty Makes Men Strong"; and from *The American Prospect*, "Biden's Secret Weapon—Compassion." Leading up to the election, Dr. Jill Biden tweeted, "Compassion is on the ballot." In this case, compassion won.

In many of our interviews, compassionate leadership was described as not just being about employees, customers, or community members, but also about people. I interviewed former governor of Maine, John Baldacci, because he really lives this philosophy. I've known John for years after meeting him through his sister Rosemary. He described his philosophy of compassionate leadership being about the people.

We're All In It Together

Governor John Baldacci had a long career in public service, starting at age twenty-three, when he was the youngest member of the Bangor City Council. He went on to serve in the Maine State Senate, in the US House of Representatives, and then as the first Democrat to be elected governor of Maine in twenty years. His leadership was clearly embraced. In his career, he never lost an election.

During his service, Governor Baldacci focused on efforts to improve lives through economic development, health-care initiatives, and equal rights. He passed legislation in Maine that prohibited discrimination based on sexual orientation, and, after quite a fight, legalized gay marriage. He also focused on education and worked to improve Maine's public schools.

His view on leadership can be distilled down to some very simple yet powerful philosophies, which he described to me in our conversation. "I think when you think of compassion or empathy, some people think it's a weakness," he said. "I think compassion is when you can relate to people and understand where they're coming from. Then you're able to put that into your decision-making. You may come up with a difficult decision that needs to be made for the best interests of the country, but at the same time you've taken into consideration a compassion, a new empathy about their struggles. To me, it's hard to be a leader and be compassionate, but at the same time I think it's required reading for this next generation."

John Baldacci comes from a large and close-knit family, so it didn't surprise me to hear that he thinks about those who he serves in the same way he thinks about family. He said: "We're all part of a large family. We're all in the same boat. Sometimes my friends would say they came over on the *Mayflower*, and I'd say, well we came over on the *Niña*, the *Pinta*, and the *Santa Maria*, but we're all in the same boat now. So, I think that we're all in it together.

"That we are all in it together is what I think this coronavirus pandemic has been showing us. I think it's showed all of us that the homeless person on the street in front of Starbucks or the person struggling on the park bench in New York should have health care. They all should have access to vaccinations. They all should have opportunities. To think, 'Oh, this is not going to happen to me,' is being shortsighted, seeing things with rose-colored glasses on."

Baldacci's family kept him humble. That humility is a common trait among compassionate leaders. "People in my campaign felt like I wasn't talking enough about what I was doing," Baldacci said, "that I had to promote myself more. I told them, in a family of eight, seven brothers and sisters, you can't be thinking you're the big shot in the family. You have to be able to realize that you have to keep yourself and your ego in check."

Baldacci's father had a big impact on his focus on people. "My father used to wash dishes at our family's restaurant," Baldacci recalls, "so I could go to a desk and be in the State Senate. I used to come back from the Senate to work with my father on Thursday, Friday, and Saturday. I'd be rushing to get the bar set up and get everything done, and my father would tell me to stop. I'd say, 'Dad, you've got a lot of work to do.' He'd say, 'I didn't wash dishes to send you to school and have you not tell me what you did for the people today. Instead, tell me what you've done for the people today.' So, he would stand there, and he would give me a test: What did I do for the people today? I had a sign made up with that question on it to hang in the governor's office to remind everybody that we were to always ask ourselves what we did for the people today. I think that was what he instilled in me from the beginning. I didn't think of it at the time, but I was lucky to have that. It gave me the opportunity to be governor of the state and to be able to set the agenda and to work and get things done." And he did get things done! Motivating and optimizing your biggest asset—your people—is the most effective way to get things done, and that's at the core of compassionate leadership.

In the next chapters I'll be highlighting some key concepts that are vital for the deeper understanding of this leadership style, including the essential ingredients of action, toughness, and heart—and how this style gets more from people, solves problems better, and creates more productivity.

END-OF-CHAPTER EXERCISES

WHAT KIND OF LEADER ARE YOU?

Take this self-assessment to gauge where you fall on the continuum between very traditional and modern leadership.

1. In a meeting with people who report to you or are junior to you in role or experience, you tend to:

   a. Talk most of the time

   b. Talk a lot but make time for others who want to speak

   c. Talk less and later in the meeting, allowing others to be heard or give input before you

2. When making important decisions, you:

   a. Make them on your own and direct your team accordingly

   b. Sometimes ask for input, more so from others who are expert or experienced

   c. Seek input from all levels and from many perspectives (when appropriate)

3. You ask those who report to you about how you can help them remove obstacles in their way:

   a. Never

   b. Occasionally

   c. Regularly

4. Your team is:

   a. Not very diverse in terms of race, ethnicity, background, age, or expertise

   b. Somewhat diverse but could be more diverse

   c. Very diverse

5. You put the following person's needs first:

   a. Yours

   b. Shareholders/investors

   c. Employees/customers

6. You ask your direct reports/employees about their well-being:

   a. Never

   b. Sometimes

   c. Often

7. You explain how your employees' jobs relate to a broader purpose and mission:

   a. Not at all

   b. Sometimes, but I don't reinforce it

   c. Often, and I reinforce it regularly

Self-Assessment: If you selected mostly *A* answers, you are likely a traditional, possibly old-school type of leader. If you chose more *B*s or a mix of *A*s, *B*s, and *C*s, your leadership style is a mixture of traditional and modern. If you picked more *C*s, you are a more modern leader.

Chapter 2

Empathy Isn't Enough

E MPATHY IS TODAY'S LEADERSHIP BUZZWORD, and it's often confused with compassion. In this chapter I'm going to show you that empathy isn't enough, and that it can even backfire if leaders' actions don't back up their words.

Empathy can be a confusing concept because it suggests more feeling than doing. The key to having compassionate leadership—which includes empathy—is making empathy actionable. I'll show what empathy is, its critical place in a workplace or organization, and how today we're seeing a gap between stated importance of empathy and the feeling employees have about how empathetic their leaders are. I'll also caution you on the pitfalls of too much empathy paired with too little action.

One of my most impactful lessons in compassionate leadership came when I was a general manager at what was known at the time as Caremark Home Health in Long Island, New York, which delivered home health care and nutrition to populations that included Crohn's patients and people with HIV.

Keith Grenz was an assistant on my team at the time. He was in his midtwenties, very intelligent, and handsome, with an infectious personality and a zest for life. Even when he revealed his stubborn side, his smile and gentle spirit always pulled you back in. It was 1990 when Keith was diagnosed with AIDS.

Keith was an amazing person and accepted his fate with courage. Imagining what this illness would ultimately do to Keith and the discrimination that was coming his way, I felt deep empathy for him. Not all of his colleagues felt the same. Fearful of his disease, they wanted to stay away from him, and I simply could not understand how we could be working in an industry whose medical providers were supposed to be aligned with the Hippocratic Oath yet were unwilling to embrace a population whose own families and communities were shunning them. And it was just wrong that we were making money delivering home health care to AIDS patients in our business yet were ready to turn our back on Keith, who was part of our work family.

There was one colleague of his who came to me and said, "If you don't get rid of him, I'm going to quit." I said, "Well, I'm not going to get rid of Keith, so I think you have your answer. You will need to quit because we're not going to discriminate in this organization."

This was perhaps the first time I had an opportunity as an operational leader to demonstrate what compassion is—it's about empathy *and* action. Yes, I clearly understood the person's viewpoint and was willing to educate her about how one can contract AIDS; however, I was unwilling to let one person educate an entire office on how to *not* be compassionate.

From there, I started to educate the entire branch about how you can remain safe when working with someone who has HIV. Not everyone got on board. There was a group of people who actually hated me for that and for other standard operating procedures we would employ to ensure that we had a culture of compassion and empowerment. This small group did everything imaginable to get rid of me. It started first with their efforts to build a coalition of associates who wrote a letter to the corporate office sharing with high-level executives that my leadership approach was wrong for the Long Island branch. Then, it escalated to the point where they managed to enter my office and place cannoli on my desk—a reference to a scene in *The Godfather*. I was shaken. They even went to the level of hiding my airline tickets when I was supposed to travel to meet with my boss, hoping that I would miss the meeting and get fired.

It got to the point that I considered resigning. News of the situation got around to the entire branch. The next day, ninety-eight percent of the branch wore green, my favorite color, to support me. They said, "We are with you. You are doing the right thing." I summoned all the courage and fortitude that I could, and I stuck it out.

There were leaders above me in the company who shared my ideals. As a result, I was promoted eight months later and went on to become executive vice president overseeing sixteen other facilities. We were awarded Branch of the Year. I would later launch the Arthur Ashe workplace AIDS program to help educate more people about how to handle AIDS in the workplace. I was fortunate to be introduced to Arthur Ashe, and he shared my ideals about the need to educate employers around how to create a compassionate workplace culture. We were scheduled to launch the program in February of 1993; however, the day we were going to kick it off, Arthur Ashe, my friend and supporter, was rushed to the hospital, and he died the next day. His associates tasked me and my chief of staff at the time, John Doherty, with communicating the news to the many hundreds of people who had gathered for this educational program, without informing anyone of the gravity of his illness. I decided at that moment to carry the torch to help educate others that AIDS needed to "come out of the workplace closet."

Keith Grenz died on November 3, 1992. He was just twenty-five. I remember to this day receiving the news at six a.m., and the impact this had on me at that moment still stays with me as I now approach my seventh decade. His family asked me to eulogize him at his funeral service. Keith would humor my tendency to always dress in a suit and wing tips. He would joke with me about it and say, "Donato, someday I would love to see you in sneakers." I eulogized him with sneakers on. The entire church broke into laughter, a moment Keith would have loved.

Empathy with Action

The experience I had supporting Keith and educating my team (and deciding to not resign) was one of the earliest moments in my career that demanded not just sympathy or empathy but real action—and commitment to my values. I've long believed that action is a must-have component to empathy. I think it comes from the many years when I couldn't hear. The way I perceived the world and other people was by observing their actions first. This became the critical link. The compassionate leaders I had in-depth interviews with agreed. Across all of the interviews I conducted, when asked, "What is compassionate leadership?" their answers were consistent: *The most defining feature of compassionate leadership is that it combines empathy with action.*

Empathy involves not only the art of listening but also understanding what someone else is feeling or experiencing. It's often cited as "walking a mile in their shoes." It's the exercise of actively imagining what it might feel like to experience what they're going through. Or, as Atticus Finch said in *To Kill a Mockingbird*, "You never really understand a person until you consider things from his point of view, until you climb inside of his skin and walk around in it."

Empathy on its own has important applications in business, education, politics, and relationships. Anyone developing products, services, or solutions needs to understand the experience of the customer or constituency they serve. To deliver a solution to a problem, you have to understand what it feels like to face that problem. Cultivating empathy is essential. Many business leaders know this, and it leads to their success. Satya Nadella of Microsoft, one of the business world's most passionate proponents of compassionate leadership, said, "Our core business is connected with the customers' needs, and we will not be able to satisfy them if we don't have a deep sense of empathy."

Empathy is also an essential skill when it comes to managing employees. But does everyone apply it in the workplace? The 2020 State of Workplace Empathy study published by benefit company Businessolver found that more than ninety percent of employees,

HR professionals, and CEOs believe that empathy is important.[1] Yet this survey also showed a gap in how—or if—empathy is made actionable. For example, ninety-one percent of CEOs said their own company is empathetic, but only sixty-eight percent of employees agreed. Conversely, seventy-six percent of employees believed that an empathetic organization inspires more motivated employees. Yet only about fifty percent of CEOs agreed. A 2020 Gallup poll on the state of the workplace found that only twenty-one percent of employees strongly agree that they're being managed in a way that motivates them to do outstanding work.[2]

Action is the fuel that brings empathy to life. I believe to bridge this gap between how CEOs see the role of empathy and how employees expect to see empathy show up in their organizations, we must first effectively listen and communicate, then combine empathy with actions that address employees' specific challenges, hardships, and needs.

Imagine the untapped potential, the enormous upside, if more managers and leaders practiced compassionate leadership! It's one of the most effective yet underutilized leadership skills that can bridge the gap between leaders and those they lead.

The Pitfalls of Empathy

A few words of caution before diving deeper into what compassionate leadership looks like. In some ways, using empathy without compassion leaves a gap in expectations. It could lead to a situation in which the leaders' "talk" doesn't match their "walk," which in turn leads to disappointment, frustration, or lack of trust. But there are other pitfalls to empathy on its own.

There is a danger of having too much empathy, as it can lead to too much emotional involvement, which can then lead to frustration, sadness, and emotional burnout. Some call it "empathy distress." This happens when you experience someone else's pain, really feeling it as if it were your own. This can have an incapacitating impact. A piece from the BBC quoted philosopher Susanne Langer, who called empathy an "involuntary breach of individual separateness."[3] The piece went on to describe brain scan studies that have shown that when people watched others in pain, their brain activity in the regions associated with pain partially mirrored that of those experiencing the pain. At its worst, people feel "empathic distress," which can become a barrier to action. Such distress leads to apathy, withdrawal, and feelings of helplessness, and can even be bad for your health.

It's helpful to draw a distinction between taking on someone else's pain and experiencing it yourself, between bringing suffering to yourself and putting yourself in someone else's shoes to understand their pain, and then acting to try to help alleviate it (this is compassion). Keeping a bit of distance between yourself and someone else's pain can help you be of more help to them. You can sometimes tap into your own pain or suffering in order to understand others' pain and empathize with them.

Turn Pain into Action

My friend Janine Broussard described how pain she experienced as a teen changed her life and gave her the impetus to help others. She explained, "When I was young, I lost a lot of loved ones, one loved one per year for four years in a row. I lost my brother, my dad, my grandma, and my other grandma. That was a lot of deaths to process when I was sixteen. Then I saw my mom go downhill because of all the despair in her life. But counterintuitively, that inspired me to be more positive, saying, 'Thank God that I was able to share their lives for that small amount of time I had with them.' I decided that every single happy moment should be celebrated and not forgotten. Since then, I celebrate everything, like a good phone call, friendships, and moments of kindness. So that was the route from all of those deaths to celebrating life and creating purposeful moments. Then I lived through my mom's isolation and sadness. She was very depressed, so we had to take care of her. The empathy I felt for my mom led me to care for the elderly. I asked myself, 'How do we bring the elder along with the younger population and make something significant?' I founded HUGS, a nonprofit organization that pairs senior volunteers with children who need help reading. The volunteers really enhanced the children's lives. We've run this program for six years. We touched 300 kids and had around 700 volunteer tutors."

The result of Janine's empathy-turned-into-action? She described the impact the program has had on the kids: "The parents and teachers tell us the kids are a lot more confident, that they're raising their hands more, that they're actually a changed student, many of them. One particular boy, who was in the office in third grade almost every day, was so touched by his tutor, he changed. Everyone just needs a little bit of kindness, a little bit of support, and that's all he needed. He became an A-plus student, he was actually helping other kids read in school. He went from being in the principal's office all the time to being a role model for other kids. And the senior volunteers enjoy the program so much, they have formed a community of their own. Some of them even started dating each other!"

Empathy + Action = Impact

In 2020 and 2021, the pandemic and the social and political upheaval that we experienced globally accelerated the shift toward more compassionate leadership and provided us with many examples of those leaders. My good friend Bruce Broussard is a standout among them. Bruce is president and CEO of Humana, one of the largest health-care companies in the United States. At the time of this writing, it's number fifty-two in the Fortune 500, with $64.8 billion in revenue, 20 million members, and 46,000 employees. In 2020, the company's growth, revenues, and profits outperformed its industry by a significant margin.

What I find most impressive is that Bruce accomplished this growth while putting stakeholders, members, and employees—people, not numbers—at the top of his priority list. He believes that maximizing shareholder value and the well-being of stakeholders are not mutually exclusive goals, and in fact are well aligned.

Humana is a successful company by financial measures, but it is also ranked number one among health-care providers on *Forbes*'s The Just 100 list for its treatment of customers; is on DiversityInc's list of the top companies that promote diversity and inclusion; is in the top fifteen percent of its industry in sustainability performance; is included in the *Sustainability Yearbook 2020* by S&P Global; and has been similarly acknowledged by the Human Rights Campaign Foundation, the Hispanic Association for Corporate Responsibility, the National Organization on Disability, and Military Times. Broussard himself was named a Fortune Businessperson of the Year in 2020 and is a past recipient of the RFK Ripple of Hope Award. It can leave you breathless to see how compassion plus action can make a powerful impact.

When the pandemic hit, like all leaders, Bruce had to react and readjust to the quickly changing world we all were living in. He had to ask himself how to best support his employees and members. He also felt a responsibility to help his community.

He told me, "I was reading the *Wall Street Journal* and saw that Doug [McMillon] at Walmart was opening his parking lots for movie theaters for his customers. I said, 'Wow, that's a great idea.' So, I thought about what we have that's not being used right now that can help our local community. I thought, *We've got a bunch of empty spaces in buildings with a bunch of Wi-Fi in Louisville very close to under-resourced communities in the Jefferson School District. We've got empty office space, and the community has a problem with unstructured schools as a result of schools going virtual.* So I thought, *Let's provide space in our offices to be used as a school and community resource center.* I called my colleague Tim Huval, chief human resources officer, and said, 'Tim, this is what I want to do. I know everyone's going to tell me that we can't do this. I need you to get to yes.' Sure enough, we did it! My team set up a community center that has social services, a medical clinic, special education access, a virtual training area, a place to bring computers to be fixed. It's a great thing. It's an amazing little feat."

Bruce went on to tell me that he thinks business leaders need to take more responsibility for societal issues. He said, "I hear a number of my colleagues really taking this on. They see the need to be much more oriented to a holistic view of their responsibility as opposed to maximizing shareholder value only. Now that defies the Delaware law, it defies corporate governance, defies all the things that I have been trained to do. But I think there is a movement to do this, and the biggest influencer, I feel, is the employer. The employer has the opportunity to bring alive a much more thoughtful view on action." That was music to my hearing aids!

Bruce made sure Humana was following through on their mission to help improve people's health. They sent twenty-four million masks to members and employees, made sure there was access to tele-health, shipped one million meals to homebound individuals' homes, and more. My life partner's mom and dad, Penny and Jack, were recipients, and Penny can attest firsthand to how this gesture gave her a sense that her Medicare Health Insurer had empathy and took action for seniors who may not have had access to a mask at the onset of the pandemic.

He also made sure employees were supported fully in their work-at-home environments, and he increased the frequency of communication with them to provide transparency and a sense of community. Business metrics showed the positive—and quantifiable—impact. Their net promoter score (a measure of how likely customers would be to recommend them) and their employee engagement scores skyrocketed. Again, more amazing outcomes that compassion plus action produces.

In an interview with JUST Capital, Bruce said, "Happy employees and happy customers are going to be with you for a long time, and that will deliver long-term stakeholder value. We wrap arms around employees, they feel supported, they support customers, and that shows up on the bottom line."[4]

Bruce is what I would consider a highly evolved compassionate leader who exemplifies that empathy plus action completes the compassionate leadership equation. I've seen him demonstrate this for as long as I can remember. I asked him a question that I would go on to ask all the leaders we interviewed. Was he always this compassionate, and if not, how did he master this leadership approach?

He explained that it was an evolution for him. "As I entered my career, I don't think I had that empathy," he said. "I think I had more selfishness in my motivation and was more ego-driven and money-driven in my actions. But, as I matured, if I do have a 'compassion gene,' it became more evident in what I did, whether it was maturity, whether it was the business I chose. Maybe it was learning that one person doesn't have to lose for the other person to win."

Bruce explained further that compassionate actions build on each other, saying, "There's this reinforcing. When you do something for somebody else it comes back to you. Whether it's in confidence, whether it's in someone coming back and doing something on your behalf, or just knowing that you've been able to impact others. I think there is a reoccurring or reinforcing aspect to it. Once you start, that wheel gets bigger and bigger."

Compassion Is Stepping Away from the Rule Book

When I was promoted in November of 1993, I reported to Diane Munson, who was president of Caremark. Diane was brilliant in many ways, particularly when it came to getting the best from her employees. In many respects, many other executives felt somewhat conflicted about Diane's abilities to assume such an important and visible role with Caremark at that time. After all, the Caremark Physician Practice was growing significantly during the late 1990s, and with "Hillary Care" having failed, many companies were looking for new and innovate ways to address the escalating costs of health care.

I was not one of those naysayers, as I had seen Diane in action. While one would instantly see her compassionate and caring side, I knew she could also address tough situations in a way that led to solutions and productive outcomes. Our business at that specific time was tough and challenging. The company was under investigation from the Office of Inspector General, and a day would not pass without us being in the news, either through written reports by the *Wall Street Journal* or the *New York Times* or through our work with HIV/AIDS. Many grassroots advocacy organizations were furious with the billing practices conducted by Caremark. All this made compassionate leadership like Diane's even more important.

During that time, I was devastated by the loss of both of my parents less than a year apart from one another. It was a horrific time for me, thirty-five years old and suddenly an orphan. Diane heard the news that my mother had died suddenly. She said, "You are going to go to Italy and heal," and I said, "No, no, no, we've got a lot of work to do." She insisted. She told me that she knew that I loved Italy and then she gave me the time to go. My partner Jeff and I went soon after that call. Diane didn't just say, "I'm sorry you lost your mom and now get on with it." I've seen a lot of people do that. She took action and insisted on helping me heal. That experience shaped my life—it may have even saved my life! That was compassion.

Diane's leadership helped to reinforce for me that compassionate leadership was the right approach. That compassionate leadership could serve many purposes, such as increasing employee morale, strengthening the sense of community, and yes, bringing personal success.

Compassionate-Driven Initiatives

I was delighted to get to know Thasunda Brown Duckett through the RFK Human Rights Foundation, on whose board we both serve. At the time of this writing, Thasunda is the newly appointed president and CEO of TIAA, a Fortune 100 provider of secure retirements for people in higher education, health care, and other nonprofits. In her new role, she leads a company whose mission is defined by financial inclusion and opportunity—goals and values that she has pursued throughout her career.

Prior to this new role, she was the CEO of JPMorgan Chase Consumer Banking, where she oversaw more than $600 billion in deposits, 50,000 employees, and ultimately helped serve more than 25 million households.

Thasunda is one of the best examples of a leader who combines empathy with action, compassion with mission. She has used her compassion to promote her vision of inclusion and empowerment for all in the financial world. I was excited to talk with her to better understand what drove her to be such a passionate and compassionate leader.

I asked her how she defines compassion, and where this compassion comes from. Her words illustrate how her empathy not only fuels specific actions but also an overarching, ongoing mission in her work and in her life. For her, it's all intertwined and comes from a deep place in her heart and in her history.

Thasunda explained: "It's not just what you do that embodies compassion; it's how you do it. It's the place from which it comes. When I think about compassion, it's an action, but it's an action that's rooted in your inner core and your spirit. And then it shows in the way in which you move throughout this world."

For her, seeing financial hardship firsthand gave her the ability to relate to anyone struggling to make ends meet. "I think my compassion comes from a place I was able to see firsthand growing up with my parents," she said. "My dad worked for Xerox in a warehouse, and when they closed the office, he lost his job. We moved to Texas and had to start over in a small apartment without any furniture. But my parents taught me about the power of humility and compassion. My mother is a retired educator, and she would always tell us that if you are at school and someone does not have lunch, you give them your lunch, and you don't say anything about it. Because when you come home, you'll have a meal. Mind you, I came from very humble beginnings, and I know what it's like to open up the refrigerator and only see baking soda. But somehow, some way, my parents made a meal.

"Compassion comes from watching my parents do the very best that they knew how even when their best was insufficient," Thasunda continued. "I remember one of my most memorable Christmases as a child. It was like the biggest Christmas we ever had. I remember seeing my parents late at night talking and writing. And what I've learned to realize as an adult is that they were figuring out how to pay rent, how to keep the lights on." Thasunda also remembers, much later, when she had to tell her dad that he didn't have enough money to retire. When she posted an announcement about her new job at TIAA, she said, "I'm grateful to lead a company that has helped millions of people retire with enough to live in dignity."

Remembering her own family's economic hardship has allowed Thasunda to have empathy for the close to half of Americans who don't have even $400 for an emergency, who don't have access to banks or credit, and who suffer from inequality and injustice. She sees her role as one of bettering other people's lives, and she does this through her work in the financial industry.

For instance, she helped create the JPMorgan Chase Advancing Black Pathways program. The program assists black Americans in achieving wealth creation through educational outcomes and career success, while simultaneously closing the racial wealth gap. She was also a member of JPMorgan Chase's Women on the Move initiative, which helps women advance in their careers and businesses.

Before leaving JPMorgan Chase, she was working on the largest branch expansion into low-to-moderate income areas. This initiative was not only a growth opportunity for her bank but also a way to integrate her mission of helping people by giving more access to banking services to lower-income individuals. She knows that opening new doors for the bank also opens new doors in the lives of the people she works to serve. She also sees her employees become more engaged when they see how their work is making a positive impact on others. Her leadership is a powerful example of how both work and life can be fueled by purpose and compassion.

Compassionate Acts Can Change History

One of my personal heroes is the late John Lewis, the former seventeen-term Democratic Congressman and civil rights activist from Georgia. Lewis dedicated his life to taking actions to fight injustice and racism. He said, "When you see something that is not right, not fair, not just, you have to speak up. You have to say something; you have to do something." His life of courage and action in the face of the harshest forces became one of my earliest inspirations that still helps me stand up for what I believe is right. His life is also a testament to how one man can take actions that make an impact on many others—and even on history.

Many compassionate acts have begun with someone fighting for another whom they've seen suffering deeply. I've gotten to know former Republican Senator William Frist, MD, who represented Tennessee, serving two terms as the first practicing physician to be elected since 1928. Bill Frist and I have worked together on health-care initiatives over the years and probably formed a quick bond in part because we both have suffered from hearing loss. I've observed him performing many acts of compassion, even heroic acts, in his career as a surgeon, including performing heart and lung transplants and, when a gunman wreaked havoc on the US Capitol in 1998, aiding the victims and resuscitating the gunman. Or, when he played a leading role in the passage of the 2003 Medicare Modernization Act, a memory that's near and dear to my heart.

Some of his most compassion-driven actions were his efforts to improve medical care around the world. He has gone on medical missions to Africa and other third-world countries almost every year for decades. He was also integral to the passage of the PEPFAR legislation, an emergency plan for AIDS relief that provided life-saving treatment globally to millions of people and reversed the spread of HIV/AIDS worldwide. This legislation, supported by a bipartisan group of senators and President George W. Bush, was one of the most impactful in history, resulting in what is estimated now to be more than seventeen million lives saved.

Senator Frist described its impact in his book *A Heart to Serve*: "This progress was unthinkable when I was a surgical resident in training in the 1980s, studying the latest medical literature and tracking this mysterious new virus. On my annual medical mission trips to Africa, I saw the virus at scale. My clinics overflowed with AIDS patients. I watched the virus hollow out entire societies, taking first the most productive members at the prime of their lives—teachers, police, civil servants, mothers. I knew there was not much a surgeon could do for a patient dying of AIDS. But in the late 1990s, I wasn't only a surgeon. I had a new set of colleagues who wielded different tools. I shared stories and photos and data with my fellow senators. I found allies on both sides of the aisle who grasped the scale of the problem, but also saw—with hope—an opportunity to help. Joe Biden, Barbara Lee, John Kerry, Jesse Helms, and others shared my concern."

Eventually, President George W. Bush began formulating his plan to combat the HIV/AIDS pandemic, his actions also fueled by compassion. With only several other people in the Red Room of the White House, Frist heard President George W. Bush explain his plan to eradicate AIDS in Africa, committing to life and hope despite the various objections. Because of his medical knowledge and leadership, Frist not only helped pass the PEPFAR legislation but also presented it to the US Senate.

Frist stated at the vote, "History will judge whether a world, led by America, stood by and let transpire one of the greatest destructions of human life in recorded history—or performed one of its most heroic rescues." Because of this legislation, antiretroviral therapy is available to more than fourteen million (fifty-nine percent) of people living with HIV, and more than two million babies have been born HIV-free (as of 2018). PEPFAR has been reauthorized through 2023, emphasizing how the fight against HIV and AIDS is not over. With new infections every year, PEPFAR is just as necessary now as it was in 2003. Frist's compassion has led him to become engaged in medical, humanitarian, and philanthropic communities, ultimately making a substantial impact on innumerable lives.

I'm so inspired by these stories of leaders whose actions have far-reaching impact. But I think it's important to remember that not all compassionate acts need to be bold, heroic, or wide scale. Much of the time, compassion is most powerful when offered from one to another, without fanfare. It can be a daily practice in which many small acts over a career or a lifetime add up to a big impact.

Decades ago, I termed a quote that has served as my guiding light: Giving back is not about doing one great thing, rather it is about doing a lot of little things that have the capacity to drive great change. If I woke up every morning thinking the only way to address a need or a problem is by doing something great, I would not get up!

END-OF-CHAPTER EXERCISES

ARE YOU EMPATHETIC OR COMPASSIONATE?

Think about the following questions.

- Think back to a time when you observed an employee, a coworker, or a friend who was upset, ill, or suffering. Did you feel concerned for them? Did you feel tender toward them? Or, did you feel irritated or unconcerned?

- When you see someone treated unfairly, do you feel upset or protective of them? Or, do you feel unaffected or say to yourself, *It's not my problem*?

- When you see or hear about people suffering, even if reading about it or watching it on the news, do you feel upset about the suffering? Or, do you feel it's not for you to worry about?

- When you see someone suffering, do you experience their pain or suffering to the point where it affects your own mood or well-being?

- When you witness someone struggling or in need of help, do you think about how you can help? Do you take steps to help?

Reflecting on where you fall on the empathy-compassion continuum can help you figure out where you're starting. If you find yourself annoyed or nonplussed in the face of others' pain, you may not be in a place of empathy. As you read on, consider steps you might take to move toward that. If you feel very deeply about everyone else's pain to the point that you are upset by it regularly, you may be on the unhealthy side of empathy. Gaining a deeper understanding of compassion will help. If you find that you can feel for others but keep enough distance from their pain and suffering to be able to help, you are in the compassion zone!

Chapter 3

Lead from the Heart

W HEN LEADERS AT ALL LEVELS have endless items on their to-do list, constant pressure to deliver, and not enough time, does the seemingly warm and fuzzy topic of leading with your heart matter? Should it be a priority? The answer to that question is a resounding "Yes!" In this chapter, I'll tell you why.

Compassionate leadership is driven by a desire and a commitment to better your people, your customers, your stakeholders, and your community. It's about understanding what touches the hearts of others in order to bring out the best in them and allow them to feel connected to their work and see it as part of something bigger than themselves.

Having a sense of mission and communicating that to employees or team members gives them a sense of meaning in their work. Communicating how each individual's role connects with and contributes to a broader purpose allows everyone to feel part of the bigger opportunity to help people or make the world better. As you'll read in this chapter, when employees feel they are contributing in meaningful ways—whether big or small—they increase their engagement, commitment, and job satisfaction.

When leaders take time to acknowledge that their employees' health—mind, body, and spirit—matters, they help their employees thrive and deliver. And when leaders nourish their own spirit, it allows them to be the best they can be and sustains them over time. This is what I call holistic leadership!

People Aren't Just There for the Paycheck

My friend Congressman Joe Kennedy has always worked toward a bigger mission. Living that mission and seeing it fulfilled on a daily basis defines his leadership. Most people on his staff are there not for the paycheck but for the mission fulfillment. To me, Joe is an amazing example of a compassionate leader, in part because of his qualities of authenticity, vulnerability, and humility. He is a leader who listens and can walk a mile in other people's shoes.

I met Joe Kennedy through a mutual friend in Massachusetts who knew that Joe and I were like-minded about many issues. That friend also knew that one of my influential heroes was Joe's grandfather, Senator Bobby Kennedy. I am always struck by the commitment the senator made to a more compassionate society following the tragic loss of his brother in 1963 when he could have instead retreated, and no one would have criticized him for that decision. One of the stories about Bobby Kennedy that moves me most is when, after listening to a testimony about conditions of poverty in Mississippi, he traveled to the Mississippi Delta in 1967 to observe the situation for himself. While there, he embraced the children he met with empathy and understanding, and when he returned home that evening, he shared with his own children the perils of those living in Mississippi and the responsibility we all have to make better the world we live in. However, he did not stop there. He brought the issue to reporters, to his colleagues, and to strangers he met along the way, passionately pleading, "If you want change, you must be angry enough to want it." Robert Kennedy acted! He recognized that the promise of a great society by President Lyndon

Johnson was not fully realized, and he spent the last year of his life addressing action steps.

Joe Kennedy III comes from a long lineage of political leadership. He is the son of US Representative Joseph P. Kennedy II, grandson of US Senator and US Attorney General Robert F. Kennedy, and grandnephew of US President John F. Kennedy and US Senator Ted Kennedy. In office from 2013 to 2021, Congressman Joseph Kennedy III represented Massachusetts's Fourth Congressional District as a Democrat. The highlight of his career as a congressman was when he delivered the Democratic response to a Republican State of the Union in 2018. He was the youngest person ever to deliver the Democratic response, at just thirty-seven years of age.

Joe spoke to me about how conveying a mission results in people wanting to follow your lead. He said: "The mark of a successful leader is the ability to convince others to follow you. Anybody can try to lead you, but some of us go for a very long walk in the woods by ourselves if there's no one behind us! Followers actually make the choice to follow; leaders can't make that choice for them. Good leaders inspire followers to believe awfully hard in their mission."

What Joe describes here, in part, is the concept of followership. Understanding that a leader cannot force others to genuinely follow is very important. That is a choice made by those who are led. This nuance is key because it reminds us that, as leaders, we need to earn the followership of our people. It's not an entitlement or a given just because we take on a senior or supervisory role over people. Having a well-stated mission, communicating it regularly, and aligning actions to it touches people and helps them *choose* to follow you. In our research, we saw that this is especially important to younger generations, which make up around half of our current workforce.

Joe Kennedy has had plenty of young people on his staff and sees this as even more important for them. "There's been a lot written about this for the younger generation," he said. "They're not as motivated, necessarily, by financial reward, but want to be part of something that is mission-driven and mission-oriented. I think there's an awful lot that can be done around motivating a younger generation and a rising generation of Americans to say, 'Look, we can structure companies and incentives around the fact that, yes, we want to make sure you can stay and you hit benchmarks and you'll continue to succeed, and all the rest of it, but we're also going to structure this by mission. We hope that you're going to be willing to dedicate yourself to this.' I'm certain that anybody who worked on my campaign would tell you that they weren't there for a paycheck—because there's not a big paycheck! If they do it, it's because they believe in the mission of the organization, being part of something that is far greater than just the sum of its individual pieces. I think that is most effective, and it is the easiest sell for a leader to make when that initiative is dedicated in service to others and people understand that and believe it."

I've seen what Joe describes in every organization I've been involved in. Where there's purpose, there's passion. Where there's meaning, there's motivation, and where there's compassion, there's commitment. But that's not all. Purpose pays big dividends that show up on the bottom line.

Purpose Pays

Purpose doesn't just add to an employee's well-being, it adds to a company's bottom line, according to a Korn Ferry survey of executives. The vast majority of respondents (ninety-six percent) agree that there is a long-term financial benefit to companies that make a strong commitment to purpose-driven leadership, with seventy-seven percent agreeing "to a great extent."[1]

I believe this is true, because all people have a deep need to feel purposeful, to connect their own actions, work, and lives to a greater purpose. It's an essential drive that makes us human and makes us happy. I think of it as a person's "why" (and I know it's been a business buzzword for quite some time, for good reason). Having a "why" behind a job, career, or task fills it with meaning and gives us motivation. Asking people, "What is your why?" is one of my favorite questions when I first get to know someone and when I interview someone for a job.

Although people often say they resign or leave a job because of misalignment with their direct boss, they also leave due to the absence of a "why." They have no feeling that their job has any bigger purpose. Purpose matters so much that the majority of people would leave one job for another if they could go to a new job that has more purpose.

Having a strong mission and culture is business-critical when it comes to attracting top talent, with the wider employer value proposition becoming increasingly desirable in today's competitive jobs market. A Glassdoor Mission & Culture Survey found that more than three-quarters (seventy-seven percent) of adults across four countries (the United States, United Kingdom, France, and Germany) would consider a company's culture first, before even applying for a job there. Seventy-nine percent would consider both a company's mission and purpose before applying.[2]

It's about Engagement

My friend and compassionate leader Mike Valentine is the epitome of a successful leader who imbues work with meaning, and his employees embrace the mission and are motivated by it. Mike is the CEO at Baxter Credit Union (BCU), a financial institution that serves as an in-house bank for employees at companies like Baxter Healthcare, Boston Scientific, Cardinal Health, Target, UnitedHealth Group, and GEICO, among many others. I asked Mike how he managed through the pandemic. His answer was compassionate leadership in action.

"As a CEO, it's probably the most challenging year I've ever been through," Mike said, "but it's been very rewarding. I'm lucky. Because of the connections that I've had with our employees, there's a high level of trust, so right away we can communicate quickly and move into action.

"We were fortunate to have about ninety-five percent of the people working from home," Mike continued. "The first thing I was always concerned about was, I have my wife and three kids at home.

But all of a sudden, I'm thinking we have more than seven hundred to take care of. I asked myself, how do we keep them safe, keep them out of harm's way? Then it was, what can we do to make life easier for them? We started to do things like buy out their vacation days. We've never done that before. But we were able to give them cash in that way. We added a day as employee appreciation day, when everybody could take the day off and unplug. It's about putting the employee first. Then, we had to make sure that members were taken care of. So, we started to waive interest on loans. We also had emergency loans for our members.

"I told my employees, 'I think we have the greatest job in the world because look who we are helping: your mainstream American,'" Mike said. "'We're helping people every single day, you know, whether it's helping them make a payment, helping them get a car loan or refinance their mortgage, or helping them get through to the next two weeks.' I think that's making a difference. That turns the employees on a little bit, and that's pretty cool. I called them the 'financial first responders.' I do believe in engagement, and feeling purposeful drives engagement. We strive as an organization to operate in the seventy-fifth quartile of our peer group. We ask, how does BCU rank against them? And we were consistently at the seventieth to eighty-fifth percentile. As a leader, it's one thing to say you're leading the organization with compassion, and I think it's a positive, but it's important that it gets the results. That's the way the board of directors holds me accountable—if they look at the results of the credit union and see engagement and compassionate leadership quantified with real numbers."

Meaning Matters

Although nonprofits are better known for "mission" than most for-profit companies are, they, too, might not always communicate it or deliver on it. But when the connection is made, the sense of purpose and meaning can run deep, as Ash Roger's story illustrates. Today, Ash is co-director at the Lwala Community Alliance that I told you about in chapter 1. When she got the phone call offering her this job, she was having a baby, literally—she was on the way to the hospital! What happened from there resulted in a dramatic, deeply emotional connection to the work the alliance was doing, the result of which made Ash take the job without hesitation.

She tells the story: "I was living in Nairobi at the time with my family, and I was pregnant with our first child. I was in the interview process when I was very far along in pregnancy. I actually got the call with their job offer from the board while I was in labor. I was in an Uber on my way to the hospital in Kenya. I told them, 'Yes, yes, good. I'll get back to you.' And several hours later, I gave birth to our son. I hemorrhaged postpartum, which is the leading cause of maternal death in Kenya and in much of the world. I needed an emergency blood transfusion. I must say that I received fantastic care from a team of Kenyan doctors and midwives. It's pretty profound that that experience came on the same day that I joined this organization in which prevention of obstetric hemorrhage is a key program. Serendipitous to say the least! I do think that sometimes we have experiences in our lives particularly to teach us how to serve better, and I think that was certainly true for me. I was able to fully feel the terror that our clients, our community of ladies, go through, to personally experience that level of blood loss, being hypothermic, watching my baby being held by my partner, and feeling like I was fading away from my new family. That's a feeling that too many women in Kenya have and that too few recover from. I feel like that experience has been really fundamental and guiding for me in my role with the organization." This deep sense of meaning is what drives her every day.

Ash experienced empathy in a very strong, specific, and personal manner. Not all leaders will, of course. That's why a company's stated mission is so important, and why communicating to each employee how their specific role connects with the broader mission is so vital. It also means a great deal to employees, especially to the younger generations in the workforce, when they know that their company takes a role in bettering society.

For many, this element of purpose engages them more deeply in their work. Others, including most of the compassionate leaders we interviewed for this book, view their entire jobs and careers as acts of service.

Work as Service

My own commitment to service started initially with a calling to the priesthood but became a broader mission to help people through my work in the business world. I see this mission as my lifelong ministry.

I've always had a calling to help others, particularly those who are ill or in pain, probably because I both experienced and observed the pain of my mother and father and others in my family. My parents suffered because of the loss of my brother, who died tragically in a car accident at a young age. My mother was very faithful. If anyone should have been a nun, it was her. She loved children, so rather than being a nun, she got married and had a family. But she always had the notion to serve and give back. She lived the idea that life is bigger than what you get out of it. It's what you give, not what you get.

Our next-door neighbor's husband died at age forty-one. Just months after his death, she was diagnosed with terminal cancer. She had four children. We were a family of six kids with little resources, but every Sunday my mother would make extra food to take next door. This was one of a continual number of such quiet acts of kindness and compassion that I observed throughout my childhood.

When my parents died, all they left was the house. They had no wealth at all. And yet, they were always helping others. That's what made their lives rich. Observing their service to others made an enormous impact on me.

I was also deeply touched by the model of service and compassion shown to me by my sister-in-law Rosemary. Rosemary was a remarkable individual who helped me when I was trying to recover from my hearing loss. I was nine years old, but I talked like a two-year-old. I couldn't pronounce *W*s; I couldn't pronounce my name. Rosemary was a speech pathologist going for her doctorate at a local university so that she could serve people like me. She took me under her wing and helped me regain fluency. She took the time to help me understand that it wasn't an intellectual deficiency that I had; it was a disability. When she died in childbirth, it was a horrific loss. But in her short time with me, her compassion and service left an indelible impression.

You Don't Have to Be *in* Service to Be *of* Service

When I went on to the seminary, I learned so much about my own values and about the value of service. There, we started our day in prayer, and we ended our day in prayer. We prayed in the middle of the day between classes. So, we were developing academically and spiritually. I think that was the unique part about my development, that I had spiritual training along with intellectual training. We had a brilliant faculty and an enormous amount of time to reflect and think. It shaped how I looked at my life.

I learned the importance of ministry and that you can define your work and life as a ministry regardless of what you do for a living. You don't have to have studied for the priesthood to think about service in this way. And you don't have to be in a service job, such as public servant, doctor, or therapist. Any job can be viewed as an act of service. Ever since I learned this lesson, I didn't look at my work as just a career. I looked at it as a platform to do good and help others.

There are many ways one can think of their work as service. In my case, I gravitated to the field of health care, no doubt influenced by my own struggle with hearing loss and my witnessing of many medical tragedies in my family. President and CEO of Humana Bruce Broussard, whose leadership I described in chapter two, views helping his employees thrive so that they can offer health-care plan members exceptional service and support and helping his community all through the lens of service. He sees his role of CEO as one of service. He describes this as "maximizing the interests of those you're serving, versus maximizing your own interests," or "serving others versus serving yourself."

I think any leader can think about the work they do in this way. As a by-product of this, you can see how keeping your focus on those you serve—your employees, your customers, your stakeholders—can naturally lead to more success.

Katie Couric, multimedia journalist, television personality, and founder of Katie Couric Media, has a similar view on helping others while simultaneously finding business success. She started her own company with a goal to work with other companies that share her company's values. She explained: "We realized that the business model was changing and advertising and media were both changing dramatically. When it came to trusting new information, there was this gravitational pull toward companies and business leaders who stand for something. Consumers, especially millennials, want companies and brands to care about more than just the bottom line. We saw companies getting increasingly involved in storytelling. And we thought, *Why not team up with some of these companies?* I know how to tell stories, and they know the stories they want told. I'm interested in a lot of the things they're interested in, like gender equality, racial justice, environmental sustainability, loneliness and connectivity, and other big social issues that I can help them understand better. The first thing you need to do to solve problems is to understand the problem, and we can help with that. So, we started this company with a very diversified media portfolio—a newsletter, social media channels, podcasts, documentaries, scripted projects—that allows me to dip my toes into all these different media outlets and avenues because there are so many different ways to tell stories and to get important issues out in front of people." Katie described a perfect blend of work as helping to solve big societal problems, enjoying creative work, and finding business success—all in a way that helps make a positive impact on other people.

Bettering the Lives of Others

Some leaders, such as Dr. Sandro Galea, choose to do work that is more specifically in service to others, and even to the world. I worked with Dr. Galea, Dean of Public Health at Boston University School of Medicine, on issues concerning social determinants of health, focusing on improving the conditions that help all people have a better chance at health and wellness and quality of life.

Dr. Galea spent many years overseas with Doctors Without Borders, during which he worked amid conflict and mass-trauma events. Dr. Galea views compassion as not just helping someone with a problem or a challenge, but also optimizing the lives of others and creating a better world—as he strives to do in his work every day.

He describes it this way: "I see compassion as envisioning a better world and acting accordingly so that it's a better world for everybody. My favorite perspective on compassion comes from Martin Luther King, who believed that compassion is not just flinging a coin to a beggar, it's seeing that the underlying conditions that produced the beggar need restructuring, and then doing something about it. I think compassion is different than empathy, different than charity. Empathy requires that we understand and feel the suffering of others because we see the world through their eyes. I think compassion is distinct from empathy in that it says that you don't need to fully understand the world through other people's eyes, only that it is the right thing to do to minimize other people's suffering, whether you can understand the world through their eyes or not. I think it's the harder perspective. It's a harder and a higher hurdle to overcome. So, I think in the context of leadership, what compassion means is seeing the mission of leadership as the unrelenting effort to improve the conditions of people within an organization, not just because you can imagine what it's like when you're in the situation, but because it's the right thing to do."

Sandro makes an interesting distinction about it not being necessary to completely understand the needs of those you serve in some situations or have an emotional connection to the issue in order to do the right thing. In the case of compassionate leadership, it's my belief that if a leader can connect with their own heart and with others, and have empathy for others, they have a strong driver of leadership. But I also believe that those who may not naturally feel that connection right away can still address the needs of others because they know it's the right thing to do and will lead to better results over time. This is a good place to start.

We Can't Talk about Spirituality in the Workplace, Can We?

Many leaders don't see a place for spirituality at work or in their organizations. But, yes, I think we can think about spirituality in the workplace in a way that works for each individual and respects the needs of all. I believe it's part of the focus on addressing the whole person you are serving, and in my mind, that includes mind, body, and spirit. I think this is critically important for a leader to cultivate in themselves as well so that he or she can stay grounded, healthy, and aligned with their values, and sustain it over time. It's believed that Nicolas Chamfort said, "A day without laughter is a day wasted"; however, the same type of logic can be applied to an organization and soul. A day without a soul is a day wasted in advancing one's corporate agenda. It is almost impossible to move any company forward without a soul serving as the basic fabric of the organization.

In any workplace, organization, or community, I believe a culture that nourishes a spiritual side, a dimension that needs as much attention as its physical and mental counterparts, is necessary. I personally spend a lot of time in prayer. I don't necessarily pull out the Bible and read it every day, but prayer, to me, is as much reflection as it is meditation as it is reading the Bible or reading scripture. It's about spiritual nourishment, and that spiritual nurturing can look different for everyone. It might come through prayer, meditation, open discussion, or quiet reflection.

When I was in the seminary, I was in the chapel every day, praying and meditating. I did that for six or seven consecutive years. When I left the seminary for the world of business, I had to establish a whole new sense of how I would continue to fill my spiritual bucket. One practice that has remained constant for me is daily self-reflection. Every night I spend time reflecting on that day, analyzing things that I could have done better. It's a practice that allows me to accomplish something fundamental: "Know thyself." I think this is essential for a leader. I'll talk more about that in chapter ten.

Spiritual practice is also important for remaining committed to your values as our daily activities occupy and sometimes overwhelm us. One of my favorite books is *The Seven Storey Mountain* by Thomas Merton. Merton was a monk. If you want to find hope, especially in difficult times, this is a great book that had a huge influence on my thinking. In it is a line that has guided me my whole life: "You must be in the world but not of the world." To me it means that you're forced to be in this world, but you don't have to be *of* it. This speaks to the balancing of the business world or the material world with your own spirit. You don't have to adapt to the materialistic. You can have material things without them defining you; you can still maintain a connection with spirit.

I worked to address my employees' whole selves, including their spiritual side, when I was sales training manager at Boehringer Ingelheim. I made efforts to help optimize their work life and help them deliver results, two things that are, in reality, quite intertwined. At first, my trainees found my methods a little untraditional, even strange, but they came to love my approach because I was addressing another appetite, one not just for money or success that came from a much deeper place in the soul.

Dare to be a different kind of leader. Dare to be a little weird! I used to think being called weird translated into being a misfit, and then I realized one day that being weird means you are willing to do things differently, take risks, and not conform to traditional ways of thinking.

Imagine this scene: The room was dark except for candlelight. Everyone's eyes were closed. The soundtrack to *Don Quixote* was playing in the room. As you read this, you might not be envisioning a corporate training session in an office building, but this was, in fact, how I started sales training sessions. When I became training manager at Boehringer Ingelheim, I would bring everybody together, turn off the lights, and we'd meditate. I played *Don Quixote* because, to me, those lyrics conveyed a dogged determination fueled by passion and courage and a connection with your own spirit. This led to talking about the importance of finding inspiration in our work to help motivate the team to achieve our goals. I also talked about the importance of taking care of ourselves. And I meant our whole selves—body, mind, and spirit. We bring our whole selves to work every day, after all. Again, this is holistic leadership! Mind you, this was back in the mideighties, when no one was talking about holistic health.

Though I had trained as a priest, none of my motivational efforts were about being a religious fanatic. They were about recognizing that we all need to take time to provide sustenance to the spiritual side of who we are. Why is this important at work? Because it's the only way you can recognize right from wrong, your own shortcomings, or what may have been left out in a decision you made. Taking time out of a day to relax and reflect also helps prevent burnout.

During this time, when I was sales training manager, I worked with a guy who was having the opposite effect on the team. He is what I called a leadership bully. I remember riding in an elevator with him and overhearing him making jokes about the LGBTQ+ community and about women. I just had to keep my mouth shut. And I realized that in order for me to get ahead, I would have to adopt a focus on results, which I did. But I also felt that, if I maintained my compassion and integrity and focused on my people, over time, a better, more positive culture would push out the negative. A big part of this was my commitment to helping my people help themselves.

Fortunately, my results and the way I led the team were noticed, and I was soon promoted from training manager to district manager. Then I had an even bigger platform from which I could spread positive culture. I believe that within the company, there was a sense that I was different, that I "did" a different kind of leadership. In this role, I saw how instilling a team and a culture with values, purpose, mission, and a focus on nourishing the whole person could make a team happier and more productive. I acknowledged individual team members and treated them like whole and complete people.

Born of Compassion

I interviewed someone for this book whom I have known and admired for a long time, but until this interview, I hadn't realized the role that compassion, faith, and a belief that he should be of service played in his work. They are factors in what is arguably his great success.

Scott Minerd has been called a "formidable figure" on Wall Street. As a bond trader early on, Scott amassed enough wealth to retire at thirty-seven, but he has since rejoined the financial industry and now holds the position of managing partner and chief investment officer of Guggenheim Partners, where he oversees assets of $275 billion at the time of this writing. Scott is an amazing example of someone whose core driver is not financial reward, though it no doubt comes to him. His philosophy is to treat people well and be a good steward of what is under his control or influence, knowing that rewards will follow.

Like every leader we interviewed for this book, I asked Scott how he thinks about compassion and service, and the role spirituality plays for him. But first, I asked where he thinks these things came from. He told me that he was shaped by the world in which he grew up and was influenced by a family story.

"I grew up in Appalachia," said Scott, "where I saw poverty firsthand, people living in tarpaper shacks. When I was a child, my father's parents still didn't have running water in their home. My father actually put the plumbing in our house when he became successful enough to afford it. We lived in this world, but because my father became a successful businessman, we lived in a modern house. I can remember in the early sixties we had a dishwasher and a swimming pool. These were things that were incongruent with the world around me. I always noticed that my family would do quiet acts of generosity and compassion that nobody was ever to know or see.

"My brother had a friend in junior high school whose father was shot in a mass killing near our home," Scott recalled. "A person went insane and sat in the front window of his home and shot people in the cars as they drove by. My father ended up paying that boy's tuition so he could go to college. He didn't pay for mine. I'm not being critical that he didn't, but that fact was striking. I remember I said something to my father about it, and he became angry. I wasn't saying, 'Hey, you ought to pay for mine because you paid for his.' He was angry because he had done it secretly, and he didn't want anyone to know. So, that kind of selfless giving was modeled in front of me."

Scott told me another story that explains even more how his role in the world was defined. "Many people don't know this," he told me, "but my first name is actually Byron. And my father, who was born in 1933, his first name was Byron. He was Byron Kendall and was always called Kenny. I'm Byron Scott, but I'm always called Scott. I didn't find out that I had this name until I was in the second or third grade. I asked my parents about it, and the story that my father told me influenced me greatly.

"In the Depression, my father's parents lived up on a small farm with seven or eight acres, just enough to have a couple of cows and some chickens and to grow some corn. When the Depression hit, they lost their life savings in the bank. They had a mortgage on a house but they had no work. They had a neighbor who was a rich industrialist. His house next door was his weekend house. My grandparents would do neighborly things for him. They picked up the mail, mowed the lawn, and made sure his house was looked after while he was away. He would come in on the weekends, and my grandmother always insisted on baking him a pie or having him over for dinner. They finally realized that they weren't going to be able to keep paying the mortgage, and the bank was going to eventually repossess the farm. And they just waited. It was 1931. But the bank never showed up. The reason the bank didn't show up was because that man next door paid the mortgage. His name was Byron Parks.

"My father was the youngest of five kids. I don't know that my grandparents would have ever had my father if Byron Parks hadn't saved their house. So, I might not be talking to you today if it weren't for Byron Parks. Hearing that story as a child taught me a lot. Somewhere in me it registered that I wanted to be like Byron Parks. So, that motivated me."

Hearing his stories shed more light on why Scott views his life as he does, having literally been born of compassion. It has shaped how he lives in this world, and likely strengthened his foundation of faith, which drives his daily actions.

He quoted from the Old Testament prophet Micah: "'What does the Lord require of you, but that you love kindness, that you seek justice, and that you walk humbly with your God.' So, you have to ask yourself the question, 'Do you seek justice?' *Seek* means you're hunting for it, that you're not just sitting back. You go out there and find places where you can do justice, where you can do acts of kindness. Many of us don't go out looking for that. We are just laying back. I live by that scripture, so I must always have my eyes open for an opportunity to advance justice, and I have to really in my heart love compassion and kindness and mercy. Those are things I actively try to always keep in front of me." Actively looking for ways to lead from the heart is, indeed, compassion in action.

END-OF-CHAPTER EXERCISES

WHAT'S YOUR PERSONAL PURPOSE?

Think about what drives you personally, what motivates you and brings you the most satisfaction. What do you consider your special skills, strengths, and best contributions? Think about how these tie together and form a sense of purpose for you in life and work. For example, I mentioned earlier that my own illness as a child and the loss of my sister-in-law Rosemary made me sensitive to the needs of the ill and needy. Working as a hospital chaplain reinforced this. In the business world, I chose the health-care industry, another opportunity to help those who are ill. Putting this together, I have clarity on my personal mission and purpose—that of helping others, particularly the sick, needy, or marginalized populations, through compassionate action. Connecting my everyday actions to this bigger purpose adds meaning to everything I do, whether it's holding the hand of someone who is ill or doing paperwork. It makes it all mean more.

Think about your experiences and what you most care about and write your own purpose statement.

What is your work mission?

Whether you are a CEO or a midlevel manager, it's important to know and communicate your business's or organization's mission to all who work with and for you. If you have such a statement, terrific! If not, write one up and then share it.

Chapter 4

Compassion Is Strength

Some people think that a compassionate leader is a weak leader, or that compassionate leadership is not strong, powerful, and results-oriented leadership. That could not be further from the truth.

After many decades of learning and practicing compassion, coupled with the recent survey research and in-depth interviews I conducted for this book, I understand compassionate leadership's power well. I've seen it again and again, and I believe that once you understand it and understand how it's applied (and how it's not!), you'll see it in its true light. You'll have a new vision of compassion that is strong, courageous, and kind. You'll understand that by the very definition of the term, compassionate leaders are necessarily strong and tough leaders. Compassion isn't weak; it's the power skill for the next generation.

Interestingly, though we saw that sixty-seven percent of the most senior respondents (CEO, president, owner, etc.) in our workplace survey said that compassionate leadership is often viewed as weak, they also said that it's important. And, on the flip side, when asked if this type of leadership is weak, the majority of the group of compassionate leaders we interviewed for this book said the opposite: Only twenty-three percent strongly or somewhat agreed. That to me is an important difference. It tells me that once practiced, its power and effectiveness is clear.

Throughout this book, I'll be highlighting leaders who integrate toughness, decisiveness, the ability to make hard decisions, and the fortitude to execute on them—and do it all with compassion. Toughness and compassion are not mutually exclusive. Combining them is an essential part of making compassionate leadership effective.

The Real Face of Compassion

Those who believe that compassionate leadership is weak have the mistaken impression that a compassionate leader is someone who is kind, outwardly caring but not particularly tough. They might see them as yes-men and yes-women, people pleasers, distracted, or nice but ineffective. Jeff Weiner, former CEO of LinkedIn, who was consistently ranked one of the Top 10 CEOs on Glassdoor, is well known for his compassionate leadership style and his passionate advocacy for compassion. He once said, "The strongest people I know are compassionate. True unconditional compassion requires almost superhuman strength and self-confidence." I agree.

Compassionate leadership is not new. It's been an approach that leaders have used throughout history. These leaders are anything but weak! Think about Nelson Mandela. He lived much of his life under apartheid. He suffered intense racism and endured violence. He spent twenty-seven years imprisoned only to campaign for peace and reconciliation upon his release. Think about Martin Luther King Jr. fighting for civil rights in the face of violence, being the subject of a brutal FBI investigation, having his home bombed, only to keep fighting to make the world a better place through peaceful protest.

Think about Princess Diana, who in 1987, at the height of the public's fear of HIV, visited with AIDS patients and shook their hands—without gloves—changing people's perceptions on this disease around the world with one quietly courageous act. Or Abraham Lincoln, who battled through bitter and divisive campaigns, fought to abolish slavery, and navigated the country through the Civil War and its aftermath. Or Pope John Paul II, who visited his would-be assassin Mehmet Ali Ağca in prison and then later requested he be released. There's nothing weak about these compassionate acts by famously compassionate people. And the list of these leaders goes on and on— Malala Yousafzai, Gandhi, St. Francis of Assisi, Jesus!

The toughest and most courageous compassionate leaders don't only come from the realms of politics or human rights, and they don't only show strength in times of war or social unrest. There are leaders everywhere taking actions every day that require commitment, courage, endurance, and strength of will. All of the leaders in this book have done powerful work that models these values and characteristics.

It's Not a Question of Whether, It's a Question of *How*

The question today is not whether a leader should be compassionate. That's a given based on the proven positive impact it has on people and profits, and because today's workforce and world are increasingly demanding it. The real question is *how* to practice compassionate leadership so that it's *effective*.

Practicing compassionate leadership effectively does not mean ignoring or setting aside the tough issues. It doesn't mean that you let people off the hook if they need constructive feedback. It doesn't mean that people who don't perform or who do something to damage your culture or your company shouldn't be held accountable.

All leaders know that the tough decisions still need to be made, the conflict still has to be addressed, the challenge still has to be overcome. But executing these with compassion protects your organization's culture. Executing with compassion builds and sustains the trust of your team, stakeholders, and community. It helps a leader get things done. It produces results.

Being Nice Is Not the Same as Being Compassionate

Leaders should understand the difference between being nice and being compassionate. There is often confusion around this. I'll give you a very simple example.

I'm being nice when someone walks past me in the hallway and I say, "Hey, Joe! Good afternoon! How are you doing?" with a smile on my face and my eyes looking right at Joe. I'm not expecting anything back from Joe, really. Nice is saying please and thank you and following expected traditional conventions of politeness—and meaning it.

Being compassionate is pushing that envelope a little bit further, to really hear that person. That takes more effort—just a little more—and it's called listening. Listening allows you to know how to then take action if the situation warrants it.

I'll never forget the time I walked into an elevator, and there was an associate who reported to one of my executives. I asked, "How are you doing today?" and he started crying. Just burst into tears in front of me. I said, "What's the matter?" He told me his mother was in Iraq and her brother was killed and she had gone to learn how it happened. His uncle was dead, his mom was gone to investigate, and he was devastated. I immediately said, "You come to my office," and we raised the funds that helped his mom and family get through the financial part of an emotional issue. Nice was "How are you doing?" but compassionate was going deeper: "I hear you. *What do you and your family need right now that we can help you get?*"

It's two different approaches, and both start off with being nice. I have long lived under the notion that whenever you see someone, you should rest assured they're having a tougher day than you are. That's compassionate leadership: recognizing without question that somebody will be having a tougher day than you, then asking yourself how you can really connect with that person in a way that can bring them out of the challenging moment that they might be having so that they know they are not alone and so that you, with the resources you can muster, can help in a relevant manner.

This is not to say that as a leader, you are responsible for seeking out all of your team's personal challenges and trying to fix them. However, when a challenge comes to you and you see your employee suffering, by all means help if you can. It not only forms deeper bonds in relationships but also sets an example that ripples out and trickles down.

Leadership Is Tough Work

Leadership is not for the faint of heart. It involves addressing conflict and resistance, pushing new or possibly unpopular ideas (resistance and rejection is our first, knee-jerk reaction to change), saying no when it might disappoint people, firing people, and even fighting to end isolated or systemic corruption or injustice. This is all tough work, and every last bit of it is essential in getting work done, making progress, meeting goals, and protecting your culture and people.

Toughness, when combined with compassion, mitigates the potential for being walked over, assumed weak, not listened to, or taken advantage of.

Compassion doesn't mean allowing people to break rules or make your culture toxic, as I learned firsthand in my role at Caremark, when I had to address illegal activity. I had to take one of the toughest actions I've ever taken when I became a regional vice president.

I had suspected that my general manager in Buffalo was stealing. He was confiscating the copayments from the HIV AIDS patients who we served during a time when many of these patients simply could not afford the copays, and we had a policy to let them go. This particular GM was indeed collecting the payments and diverting the dollars into an account which had only one benefit—his own!

I called a mock executive meeting in Boston, which meant he had to come out with the other leaders and meet with me, and I sent my CFO to Buffalo to look into it. Sure enough, I was absolutely correct. He was embezzling hundreds of thousands of dollars.

In that situation, it wasn't hard to see what the right thing to do was. I had to fire him. The hard part was doing it. In a case this dramatic, it can be scary to confront someone who might react violently. There's also a fear that if you fire someone who is very popular among his peers, there might be a landslide of people walking out the door.

The day I let him go, I made sure I had a security guard with me. He was so angry he came at me wanting to choke me. He said, "You did a number on me!" And I remember my response to this day: "No. You did a number on yourself." Anyway, he paid the price for his misdeeds. And even though I worried that people might be upset with me because I let someone go who was popular, no one on the team walked out as a result of his firing. I made sure to communicate what I could to the team while continuing to work with them toward our collective goals. I think people trusted me even more knowing I was willing to do the right thing even when it was very tough. I believe they understood that addressing an issue that put us all at risk was an act that was protecting all of us.

I think it helps for leaders to think about the bigger picture to find the appropriate mindset from which to find the strength to be firm or do things that are hard. For example, I think the compassionate side of me is full of ethics and discipline that give me the strength to follow through when faced with a challenge like this one. My ethics and sense of justice gave me the fortitude to take action. Leaders can find this resolve in many places, often in their devotion and commitment to excellence and to helping their team work to their highest potential.

Compassion: Driven by the Pursuit of Excellence

Craig Samitt, the former president and CEO of Blue Cross and Blue Shield of Minnesota, who I introduced in chapter one, speaks about toughness as something driven by the pursuit of excellence, or a high standard that he pushes people toward.

Craig described his outlook this way: "You hear the expression that nice guys finish last, especially in the business world. I've lived my career hoping to disprove that perspective, or that paradigm. To be part of a book about compassionate leadership, and to sit shoulder to shoulder with other strong and successful leaders who have been compassionate on their way to success means so much to me. I have long believed that in folks who do not lead through compassion, their approach has been a learned behavior in its own right, that the behavior has been reinforced, that they've been encouraged or incentivized to be incompassionate."

To rephrase Craig's thought, incompassionate leaders may be who they are because they were previously rewarded with results, promotions, or successes when they reached their goals but weren't compassionate in the process. I think we need to rewire leaders for compassion. I think we need to promote, encourage, support, and nurture those who are compassionate leaders, and remove the misconception that compassionate leaders are soft. There is a difference between having the so-called soft skills and being a soft or weak leader! You come to recognize that compassionate leaders are the strongest, most steadfast, long-lived, and successfully purpose-driven leaders that you can possibly find.

Craig continued, "I've been told that my leadership style has been described as 'an iron hand in a velvet glove.' I think what people mean by that is that it's a combination of a strong focus on getting stuff done. I set goals. I do as I say. I set high standards, and I support people to achieve them. I hold people accountable to their part of the goal achievement. That is the 'how' of being a leader who might wield an iron hand. I have high dreams and hopes and expectations about what's possible in health care, but the velvet glove is how I can inspire and support and how I can be respected. With an iron hand in a velvet glove, I combine the hard metrics of doing and achieving (the iron hand) with the people-influencing, people-supporting approaches that get it all done (the velvet glove).

"I can help people get to a tremendous result and look back and have them be thrilled and amazed with how fun, enjoyable, or inspired they could be in the journey to get to a very big, measurable, tangible result. I think you can be hard and soft. And frankly, I would say that I probably can go further and faster by leading with compassion than by leading with fear. I seek to combine the iron hand and the velvet glove as the best of all possible leadership styles that an executive could have."

Craig's compassionate leadership is so well honed, he makes it look easy, but certainly it's not. Leaders will always have tough challenges, decisions, and conversations that they need to respond to.

Tough Conversations Are ... Tough! Have Them Anyway

One of the most difficult parts of a manager's job is giving feedback. In a survey of 7,631 people done by the leadership development consultancy Zenger and Folkman, when asked whether they believed that giving negative feedback was stressful or difficult, forty-four percent of leaders agreed. When talking with managers about giving feedback, they heard comments such as, "I did not sleep the night before," "I just wanted to get it over quickly," "My hands were sweating and I was nervous," and "They don't pay me enough to do this job." Because of this anxiety, some managers resist giving their direct reports any kind of critical feedback at all.[1]

My favorite line from the Broadway play *Camelot* is "Honesty is fatal, it ought to be taboo." It's true, honesty can be brutal. But sharing important information with an employee that can help them improve is critical, and employees want it.

If you have to address a tough situation from a compassionate place, what does that look like? A common case might be having to deal with an employee who isn't performing. You might be considering some tough talk or worse, letting them go. The first thing to do is to commit to having the hard conversation, if you're certain it's the right thing to do. As we know, many managers and leaders drag their feet in these situations because they're so difficult. Kicking the can down the road in these cases makes the situation worse.

The next thing to consider is how to have the conversation. Many leaders get frustrated, and often the more command-and-control-style leaders will address things punitively or with anger. Regardless of the outcome you want, this is never the most effective way to deal with these situations.

It helps to think about the feedback you need to give as something being offered in the service of bettering the employee and the company. It doesn't necessarily need to be viewed as negative feedback or constructive "criticism." It can be viewed as guidance that can help an employee grow. Remember, employees *want* feedback! Most would prefer negative feedback over no feedback. (I'll explain in chapter six why you might consider getting rid of the word *feedback* all together!)

It's also helpful to offer the person on the receiving end of the feedback a chance to feel some sense of control or participation in the conversation. When I deliver difficult or sensitive information to an employee about their performance, I tend to be very direct and clear in my comments, and keep them tightly focused on a specific example. I do it in a way that gives the person an option first. I ask them, "Can I give you some thoughts on how the meeting went?" If they say no, then I'll say to myself, *Fine, the person doesn't want it.* If they say yes, that allows them to feel more ownership in the process. It also means that we just built a compassionate relationship and that they're interested in growing. And they're going to keep paying full attention and get a dialogue going with a willingness to learn and grow (and maybe give me some constructive and honest feedback in return!).

Compassionate leadership is about choosing the right words and delivering them with the right attitude and in the right spirit. How you have difficult conversations matters, because it impacts culture and sets a tone for how you communicate in the future. I'll go into more detail on the critical topic of communication in chapter six.

Being Liked versus Being Trusted

A word of caution on a common pitfall among aspiring compassionate leaders: You don't need everybody to like you! As I contemplated how people would feel about me after I let one of their team members go, I had to remind myself that being liked was not the goal. You have to know that you will make decisions that some people will like and some people won't. Some people will not like you. It's inevitable. So, you have to accept this fact as soon as you can so that it doesn't delay or prevent you from taking tough actions or making decisions that might be unpopular but necessary.

That is part of what comes with being tough as a compassionate leader. Not everyone is at ease with not being liked by everyone. I came to an understanding a long time ago that people liking me was not essential. This was liberating, even though it's not a pleasant thought.

Trust is a different matter. You have to have a majority of people trust you in order to get things done. And leading in a way that develops trust is likely to also result in plenty of people liking you. But to be a strong and effective leader, you have to be willing to let go of *trying* to be liked. So, embrace this fact, and then go ahead and make the decisions you need to make, and have the tough conversations you need to have.

Be Willing to Fight for Your People

One of the common characteristics of compassionate leadership is a willingness to fight for your people and for the bigger goals of bettering your organization, your community, or the world. Fighting does not have to look negative or angry; what I mean is that you are willing to do what it takes to get things done that are important for the greater good.

Earlier in this chapter, I mentioned great leaders in history who were both compassionate and strong. One of the common themes in these stories is the enduring fight to solve a problem, to right a wrong, or to improve things. This applies in the business world, in politics, in education, really in any arena a leader finds themselves.

Envisioning your role as a leader who fights for your people, your customers, and your stakeholders is another source of strength and gives a leader another motivation. It adds to a leader's personal mission. It doesn't take a rough and forceful personality to fight for others. It can be driven by quiet courage, fortitude, and a little grit.

Interestingly, one of the toughest leaders I interviewed for this book was a nun.

Compassion Takes Grit

I was introduced to Sister Mary Scullion through colleagues at St. Joseph's College in Maine, where I am currently a Scholar in Residence. St. Joseph's was founded by Catholic order The Sisters of Mercy, to which Sister Mary belongs. Sister Mary Scullion is a notable advocate for the homeless and was included among *Time* magazine's 2009 100 Most Influential People for her work.

Sister Mary has spent much of her time in downtrodden neighborhoods on the streets of Philadelphia. She has taken on fight after fight, including taking a fight to the Supreme Court and winning. She has been jailed multiple times. When you talk with Sister Mary, it's clear she is one tough nun who is unafraid to get her hands dirty, to fight the fight she believes in to improve the lives of those she serves.

She is currently codirector of Project HOME in Philadelphia, which is a community of people from all walks of life who are committed to ending and preventing chronic street homelessness in Philadelphia. Their vision statement is, "None of us are home until all of us are home."

Sister Mary spoke of how Project HOME started: "We started Project HOME in the locker room of a swimming pool thirty-one years ago. And over the past thirty-one years, Project HOME has developed more than 900 units of housing. We have another 150 in predevelopment. We have developed an integrated health-care center with a couple of sites. It includes primary care, behavioral health, dental, and wellness services. We have the Huntington Learning Center Comcast technology labs, a state-of-the-art technology center located in the second-poorest neighborhood in Philadelphia, to expose our residents and people within the community to technology for education and employment. That means it's for children in the neighborhood as well as adults.

"We have the Hub of Hope, which is located in the sub-basement of the Suburban Station transit hub and provides showers, social services, medical care at a health-care center on-site in the train station where people are homeless. And then we have outreach and coordinate outreach, street outreach for the city of Philadelphia, and outreach teams out on the street every day, every night. We house more than 1,000 people every night and provide thousands of people health care each year. The Learning Center serves more than 1,000 adults each year and a lot of kids. We are just working with people to hopefully bring them home."

Sister Mary has moved mountains. In the late 1980s, she took on the fight to allow homeless people the right to vote, a right that up until that time was not given to them. Her most recent court battle involved the right of fair housing. When Project HOME was looking for a new location in Philadelphia, they were blocked from a location because the neighborhood did not want lower income people to live there. "When we first started, the city of Philadelphia tried to unfairly block us from coming into a neighborhood," she explained. "We got the United States Department of Justice to sue the city on our behalf for the right of federal fair housing. We actually won after four years. It was the most intense struggle and went to the Third Circuit. We were even in jail a couple times."

I was intrigued by the strength Sister Mary exuded, and her deep compassion. When asked about what moved her and gave her strength, she said: "There are times when we are touched by the compassion of another person for others, as witness to that act. I think it's really a gift. And I think it's about being truthful, living your life truthfully, speaking truthfully. The more that we can witness what is true and what is compassionate—that really is humility. Someone once said that the most courageous thing you can do is own your own story. And I think that in life there is so much pretense, people saying, 'No, no. We're all fine; we're all good,' instead of going out, not shying away from what's real—which is often very tough—and then truly making it all fine and all good or at least better."

I loved hearing about Sister Mary's perspective on being real and not shying away from what's difficult. That is very common: when something is particularly hard, perhaps deeply uncomfortable, many of us instinctively avoid it. Think of passing a homeless mother on the street. It's easier to ignore a truth like that than to confront it. But not only does reality need to be confronted, it sometimes needs to be looked at more clearly, because that lets us see a beauty in the fragility. Sister Mary told me a story of how she once witnessed something beautiful as others hurried by. "When I was working at Mercy Hospice there was a woman who was called the 'Duck Lady,'" she said. "She had Tourette's Syndrome, and it would appear to people that she was quacking, but really, it was her affliction. She lived on the street, and no doubt people walked by her and judged her. But she actually had a Social Security check, and she got a little room. She found this other lady who was on the street, and she invited her into her little room to stay there out of the cold. And I'm thinking that Duck Lady is one of the most compassionate people I ever witnessed." That's just one example of her compassion.

Sister Mary is proof that you can take on the role of a steadfast fighter while also living the life of a compassionate member of your community—all the while remaining able to see the beauty, vulnerability, and acts of compassion of others.

Compassion *Creates* Courage

Some people think that they have to have some kind of outsized amount of courage in order to take on big efforts like Sister Mary does, or to stand up to those who might not agree with them, or to fight for what they believe in day to day. They believe they need to summon courage in order to take action. That may be partially true or true of certain situations, but the interesting thing I learned about courage is that you don't always need to first find or summon courage to take a strong compassionate action. In fact, compassion can *create* courage!

I believe that adopting and living from a strong, steady foundation of compassion actually gives you courage, as stated in a quote from the *Tao Te Ching*: "With compassion one becomes courageous. Compassion brings triumph when attacked; it brings security when maintained." In my life, embracing compassionate values and ideals provides a source of strength that can be tapped when needed. Compassion creates courage, courage drives compassionate acts, and participating in compassionate acts builds more courage and compassion. A powerful virtuous circle indeed.

The Dalai Lama put this in more general terms when sharing what he sees as the path to happiness (which is all about compassion!): "The more we care for the happiness of others, the greater our own sense of well-being becomes. Cultivating a close, warmhearted feeling for others automatically puts the mind at ease. This helps remove whatever fears or insecurities we may have and gives us the strength to cope with any obstacles we encounter. It is the ultimate source of success in life."[2]

END-OF-CHAPTER EXERCISES

TRY THIS AT HOME—AND AT WORK

The next time you have to give someone tough "feedback," before you do, step back and replace the word *feedback* with *respectful dialogue*. Then, to help take away anxiety about the conversation and make it more productive and compassionate, break it down into a few steps:

1. Be clear on what you would like to change or improve, and why. Will the respectful dialogue help the person do a better job or improve relationships? If it's a petty grievance, drop it. If it is valuable, go to step two.

2. If you're feeling angry about the issue you are going to discuss, pause for a moment before you jump in. This may be a moment to think about empathy. There is likely a reason for the person's actions or lack of performance. Start with an open mind and some empathy.

3. Frame the respectful dialogue as an opportunity to improve or develop. For example, if you need to tell your employee that they are monopolizing meetings, instead of saying, "You are talking too much," you can frame it as, "You offer great input, and your thoughts help others think of great ideas, too, so make sure to leave others time to share as well. It will help us all get the best ideas on the table."

4. After you share your ideas for how they can improve, ask them if they have any respectful dialogue for you, or any follow-up questions. If they have tough comments to share with you, be open and model the behavior of someone who values respectful dialogue.

5. End on a good note. Thank them or acknowledge them for something they've done well, or for their openness and effort.

6. Take the time to write an email—or even better, a handwritten note—thanking them for the interaction.

Part II

Secrets of Successful Leaders Who Win Hearts and Deliver Results

Chapter 5

Earn Trust First

MANY MANAGEMENT THEORISTS AND LEADERS believe that culture comes first when building a successful organization. I've heard many say that "culture eats strategy for lunch." I disagree. Trust eats strategy for lunch every day of the week. Trust is a precondition to building positive culture. Trust has to be established first to lay the groundwork for effective leadership. Everything else follows.

Trust is essential in all relationships. Positive, trusting relationships drive productivity, creativity, change, and growth. As a leader, you can put any program out there, you can communicate your vision, mission, and values. But unless you have your people's trust, these critical things won't be universally embraced or put into action at the highest level possible. I think many leaders do it backward. Those leaders come into new companies and immediately start sharing their vision and dictating goals before they have begun to earn the trust of the team. Vision and goals are embraced faster and more fully with an investment in trust first. This is especially true in difficult times, or when attempting to launch challenging initiatives or make big changes. Trust is the glue that makes it all work.

It's also the only way you can get things done in the long run. If you look at what our job as leaders is, after all, it's all about getting things done. You can either get your team moving by going in with a sledgehammer, which can create resistance or anger, or you can use what I call a velvet hammer and get it done quickly in an environment where trust is fundamental.

George Shultz, former Secretary of Labor, Treasury, and State, died while I was writing this book. He was known for many things, one of which was managing high-stakes negotiations, such as a nuclear missile treaty with the Soviet Union and a plan for peace in the Middle East. I read an essay in the *Washington Post* that he wrote to mark his 100th birthday. In it, he reflected on his life, and his thoughts about trust powerfully expressed its fundamental nature. He wrote: "I've learned much over that time, but looking back, I'm struck that there is one lesson I learned early and then relearned over and over: Trust is the coin of the realm. When trust was in the room, whatever room that was—the family room, the schoolroom, the locker room, the office room, the government room, or the military room—good things happened. When trust was not in the room, good things did not happen. Everything else is details."

Why Trust Is Important

Trust should be at the top of every leader's priority list, in part because it is at the top of every *employee's* priority list. In our research for this book, when we surveyed 1,500 people in the workforce at all levels and asked them what characteristics were most important in a compassionate culture, the two with the most affirmative responses by far were commitment and communication. This is compelling, because communication and commitment combine to form trust. When messaging from leadership is clear, regular, and honest, and when it is directed toward and accepted by everyone in the organization, team members feel like involved contributors, and they feel safe to share their thoughts.

Trust should be addressed with urgency because, aside from being essential, it's also in decline.

Trust in organizations, companies, and institutions has deteriorated in recent years. In a 2016 CEO survey from PWC, fifty-five percent of CEOs said that a lack of trust poses a threat to the ability of their organization to grow. Trust in institutions and companies has only declined since then. In the 2020 Gallup: State of the American Workplace survey, more than half of millennials (who currently make up half of our workforce) did not believe that corporations behave ethically; this was an increase from thirty-five percent in 2017.[1]

Lack of trust in an organization leads to serious issues, like lower engagement, less innovation, decreased productivity, and higher turnover.

Paul J. Zak, Harvard researcher, founding director of the Center for Neuroeconomics Studies, and professor of economics, psychology, and management at Claremont Graduate University, has invested decades in researching the neurological connection between trust, leadership, and organizational performance. His work shows a direct correlation between the amount of oxytocin in the brain and the level of trust they feel in any situation.

Over his two decades of research, Zak discovered that "compared with people at low-trust companies, people at high-trust companies report seventy-four percent less stress, 106 percent more energy at work, fifty percent higher productivity, thirteen percent fewer sick days, seventy-six percent more engagement, twenty-nine percent more satisfaction with their lives, and forty percent less burnout."[2]

The other quantitative results of a trust-based culture were remarkable. Zak concluded that those working in high-trust cultures:

- Enjoyed their jobs sixty percent more

- Felt sixty-six percent closer to their colleagues

- Had eleven percent more empathy for their workmates

- Experienced forty percent less burnout from their work

- Earned an additional $6,450 a year, or seventeen percent more than those working at low-trust organizations

His research suggests that trust can be built with specific actions that increase oxytocin in the brain. This reinforces many of the key behaviors I've observed and our interviewed leaders discussed: giving positive, immediate feedback for positive performance; giving employees a voice in designing their own job; communicating thoroughly and frequently; facilitating other people's growth as both a person and an employee; and showing vulnerability.

The Practice of Trust

When I was CEO at public health-care company Healthways and its later iteration, Tivity Health, I did my best to connect with as many of the company's nearly 2,000 employees (in 2015) as I could, as quickly as possible and before I did anything else. I wanted to understand their roles and their motivations and challenges to ensure that I understood them and that they knew I cared about them. I had frequent town hall meetings to communicate with the entire team. In the first six to eight months of my tenure as CEO, I started a weekly practice of making a list of twenty employees from all over the company whom I would either call or meet in person for a one-on-one talk. After those calls or meetings, I would send them a handwritten note. Once I understood my team's views, had asked for their input, and had secured their trust, I started to more strongly establish the culture, put a vision in place, and share it widely.

What I was working on was building trust. In fact, on my first day as CEO, we had a town hall meeting that was like an inauguration. I was before 2,000 people. And I said to them, "I do not expect you to trust me today. I need to earn your trust." I got a resounding applause for that. I said, "I am committed to restoring bonuses, I'm going to restore performance reviews, and I'm going to restore open communication." I think every leader feels that, because they've been canonized or appointed as a CEO or chief marketing officer or other leader, they're immediately the king or queen. As if you get the trust automatically. No, you have to earn that trust. And, yes, you'll know when you've earned it.

I knew six to eight months after my first speech, when the stock moved from $9 to $20 a share. I started to pay bonuses. We began to get a better reputation in the community. I had started to earn their trust.

Trust is the critical driver when you try to get the big things done. Consider, for example, if I had announced one day that we're going to acquire another company, and I had *not* built the trust. Then, I would have had 1,000 employees creating 1,000 different stories about that decision. And those stories would have taken on lives of their own. Some of them may not have been correct, and some may have been damaging. That would not get everyone on the same page. That would not get agreement or buy-in from my team.

The Three *T*s

It was in that job that I instituted what I call the Three *T*s, which represent the sequence of building leadership relationships. The Three *T*s are

- Tenderness

- Trust

- Toughness/Tenacity

First, approach people with tenderness, with empathy. Show that you care, and make an effort to understand their experiences. Once you've established that caring relationship, you can open up and connect on a deeper level. You can communicate openly and with transparency, delivering on what you say you're going to deliver. This builds the trust.

After you have the trust, you can more effectively lead. Sometimes that means leading with toughness or tenacity, but because you have built a foundation of trust, tough feedback can be given and received, hard decisions can be made and communicated, and people will be more likely to respond positively or at least with understanding.

I used this approach with a very senior leader I hired at Tivity Health who posed a management challenge. Scott was on my executive team. He was a high performer who was clearly skilled but not compassionate in his role as an executive. He was tough on his people but had done nothing to lay the groundwork that would allow him to be demanding of them. His employees were unhappy, and it was creating a negative environment that bled out into other areas of the company. He was exceedingly direct, in sometimes disrespectful ways, to his colleagues. He may have been doing it from a sense of trying to get things done, but it was having a negative impact.

It was obvious that the situation needed to be addressed. Scott was in a role that directly impacted the growth of the company. He was delivering results, but because of the negative impact he had on his team and his fellow executives, those results would be unsustainable. It was also clear that the results could be even better if the problem was fixed.

I knew I had very tough messages to deliver to him, but before I did, I laid a trusting foundation for us to work from. I supported Scott in his role, and I invited open communication between us. I listened to his experiences and tried to get to know his motivations and stressors. I got to know him as a person, inviting he and his wife to my home and learning about who he was outside of work.

It wasn't easy sitting down with a fifty-eight-year-old man and pointing out where he needed to change. But after working with Scott for a while, it was clear that a tougher approach was needed. At one point, I had to tell him that his days were numbered if he didn't make a change. He could have told me to take a hike, but because I spent so much time building the trust first, he was open to feedback, and he listened. Since I also took the time to get to know his wife, she agreed with my assessment and told Scott, "Donato has your best interest in mind. Listen to him."

Scott rose to the challenge and underwent a transformation. And after this change, he and his team delivered even stronger, sustainable results. When I last connected with him, he was interviewing for a new CEO job, and he credited it to the investment I made in his development. Scott also shared with me the number of emails and letters he received after his departure from employees, praising him for his sense of compassion and acknowledging that they had underestimated his ability to change.

How to Build Trust

If you want a successful culture, it goes back to what Harvard Business School concluded a number of years ago about health care: It wasn't cost, it wasn't quality that was the problem; it was a lack of trust. And if you can build trust in health care, then you can correct the cost and correct the quality. You have physicians, however, who don't trust health plans. You have the pharmaceutical companies that the consumers don't trust. So, how do we get trust back into the organizations of this industry?

First, you have to understand that trust is not a one-way street. Employees have to trust their direct boss and their business's leaders. Leaders have to trust their employees or those who they lead. Leaders also have to cultivate an organization that allows employees and peers to trust one another.

Trusted Leaders Show Up Authentically

There are many components to building trust as a leader. There are many processes and actions that can be taken. But, fundamentally, trust is built at the human level. *Authenticity* is a term that is very trendy these days, and not everyone gets what *authenticity* means. For me, there are three key things a leader needs to do to earn trust, and they are all versions or aspects of authenticity: be honest, be vulnerable, and be yourself. And perhaps a fourth—accept the fact that you do not have to be the smartest person in the room.

Honesty Is Not Just a Policy

Honesty is about communicating openly and truthfully, and not shying away from tough questions or using obvious spin when answering them. It's about aligning your actions with your words.

I think a lack of honesty is where most of the relationship fractures begin. The unwillingness of somebody to be open to honest feedback is an example. And a fear of being honest is why leaders don't give feedback. I think they are too afraid that the person with whom they share honest observations and advice will be defensive or angry or will shut down. They presume people aren't comfortable with truth.

As someone who focuses a great deal on relationships, I've thought a lot about why people are uncomfortable with honesty, especially in the form of feedback that might be hard to hear. I've developed a basic mindset going into conversations that considers the lifetime of experiences the other person might have had that may result in them being afraid of the truth or defensive about hearing it.

Someone's life experience is like a package or a box. All throughout your life, you are throwing things into that box. Well, the box eventually becomes heavy. Sometimes it becomes stressed or damaged as it's shipped from one place to another.

I think that's what our lives are like. The heavy load carried place to place can leave a person feeling damaged and vulnerable, which can lead to that person protecting themselves, shutting people out, or reacting defensively. I've learned to try to recognize when a person's box is heavy, or when it's damaged, and why I sincerely commit to working to build trust with that person and to helping them open up to honest dialogue to get beyond that point.

I think a leader has to be willing to treat a person's experiences honestly and with great reverence. In fact, it's critical in working relationships. A leader needs to model respect for honesty, and this runs both ways.

A leader should make their employees or team feel comfortable when they are sharing candid views or opinions. And a true leader is someone who will ask the question and not be afraid to receive the answer. This type of communication has to be modeled throughout the organization. The more you make it safe for honest conversations to be exchanged, the more honest feedback and interactions you will have.

Vulnerability versus Strength

Life has taught me a heck of a lot about vulnerability, and I didn't fully embrace those lessons for a long time. These are tough lessons for many of us. Growing up with hearing loss, failing fifth grade, and then having to wear hearing aids throughout my life made me feel very vulnerable, but I did not share that for a long time. Not only did I not share those feelings of vulnerability, I did not even share that I had a hearing problem at all. I never wanted anyone to know I failed fifth grade while my twin brother advanced to sixth. Instead, I kept that to myself, hiding it so that I could show what I thought was a brave face. I told myself it was important to appear strong as a leader to assert my competence. That meant hiding what I thought could be perceived as weakness.

I was wrong on all counts. What I learned was that having challenges and failures, or, in my case, a disability, did not make me seem weak. It made me seem human. People trust others who are not afraid to show in some form or manner that they, too, experience pain and have imperfections. Embracing and owning my imperfections took courage and strength. And that is what comes across when people share themselves openly with others.

By the way, the first time I shared my childhood tragedies, my hearing loss, and the challenges of being gay as a CEO, someone said, "Donato! We thought you lived a boring life!" A lot of this is a creation, a mirage made up by people who feel that they have to convey the image of a perfect leader. It goes back to that box analogy. You have to be willing to unwrap it like the gift it is and share it with others. Like any gift, it will most likely be well received.

The Path to Freedom

I finally fully embraced vulnerability in 2014, when I received the RFK Human Rights Ripple of Hope Award from the matriarch of the family, Ethel Kennedy. For years, I had hidden my life partner, Jeff, from everyone. As I was getting up to receive the award, I suddenly felt in that moment that I could not receive a human rights award if I was not willing to introduce my partner in front of 2,000 people. So, I introduced Jeff for the first time after nearly two decades of being in a very supportive and loving relationship. Until then, I had really left out an important part of my life.

That moment was very redeeming. I felt free. I felt that I no longer had to hide. It was one of the best moments of my life, and I finally understood that the fear of vulnerability occurred in the hiding. The freedom and strength occurred in the sharing with many familiar and unfamiliar people and in their recognition of my humanness. In that one instance of being myself, I garnered trust from family and friends that has been transformative in all of my encounters since I received that prestigious award.

It is probably the most touching moment I've experienced. I got a standing ovation, probably because it was clear that I was embodying that it's okay to be who you are.

Vulnerability and Trust

Vulnerability is a key to building trust because showing vulnerability is a way to say to others that you trust them, that you're willing to share your real self with them. You're human; your box is damaged. I'm human, and my box is beat up pretty well, too.

You're willing to reveal parts of yourself or your experiences that are deeply personal, perhaps painful or embarrassing—or that you imagined were so. You're willing to say that you don't have all the answers. You're willing to drop the tiring effort of appearing perfect.

I recently read a quote from Wharton Professor and psychologist Adam Grant that expressed this well. He said: "Projecting perfection protects your ego but shuts people out and stunts your growth. Revealing struggles shows humility and humanity, opening the door to new sources of support and strength."

Essentially, this expresses to people that you are human. You are imperfect. You are not trying to hide, to pretend, or to be above those human qualities. This in turn allows others to feel safer opening up about their own imperfections. It allows them to ask for help if they need it or to give feedback. And it offers opportunity for deeper bonds to form.

The Key to Any Human Endeavor

One of the most compassionate leaders I interviewed for this book is Dr. Mark Pochapin, a gastroenterologist and department vice-chair at NYU Langone Health in New York City. He was introduced to me by journalist Katie Couric, with whom I have worked on several projects that focus on improving health care. Mark was the doctor of Katie's then-husband, Jay, who had cancer. Mark's compassion helped Jay and Katie through this difficult time and helped Katie after Jay passed away. He is a true believer in the power of vulnerability and trust.

Mark told me that trust is central to his leadership philosophy and is, in fact, key to any human endeavor. When we first started speaking, he showed me something that perfectly symbolized his perspective. It was a lapel pin that he called his Leadership Rocket. On the core fuselage is the word *trust*, and the two wings that allow it to fly are excellence and compassion. He explained: "I have to trust my colleagues, patients have to trust their doctor. I have to trust that a patient is going to listen to my advice and be a partner in their care. Trust is key in any human endeavor, in any relationship. Trust is a critical component for human bonding."

Mark expressed how he sees vulnerability in the context of leadership, saying: "I think that for a leader to establish trust right up front, vulnerability is a critical component. You can't trust someone who doesn't really exist. We're not superpeople, we're human beings. One of the things I know as a physician is that we're all mortal, we all get sick, we all get old, and we all die. I've taken care of kings and queens. I've taken care of celebrities. And you know what, when I have an endoscope in their stomach, we're all identical on the inside. So, the point is that for us to build trust we have to say, 'Look, we're human, too.' We have to say, 'I'm here with you, we're in this journey together.'

"I was taught early in my career that you need to have a tough exterior, that you shouldn't show emotion," Mark continued. "However, I see it differently. Connecting with your patients emotionally is important as long as you set boundaries. We all need boundaries, and creating boundaries is very important for everything we do in life. How wide the boundaries are is part of the art of medicine. Physicians need to show compassion but not get so involved that they can't move on to their next patient. Yet a boundary must still be wide enough to allow doctors to provide comfort to the hundreds of patients who have such difficult stories in their own right.

"But on the other hand, compassion can be very uplifting, because out of the difficult stories we are inspired and uplifted by the beauty of human connection, kindness, and love. Now, I think about the tough decisions I have to make, both as a physician and as a leader, and I know that these decisions must be made with compassion, too.

"I think compassion demonstrates courage. It's easy to put up the wall and say, 'Not my business. I don't care; that's their issue.' But it's hard and takes courage to show compassion, because when you're showing compassion, you become vulnerable. Being able to speak up and say, 'I'm going to be here with you and hold your hand if you need it,' takes courage and commitment, but it also demonstrates compassion and unleashes the power of human kindness, a key ingredient for healing and comfort."

Be Your Whole Self—It's a Lot Easier Than Being Someone Else

Vulnerability is part of authenticity, of your humanness. Saying and showing, "I'm ready to show my flaws, failures, and foibles" is one of the fundamental pillars to building trust. But authenticity is not just sharing your vulnerabilities; it's showing up as who you really are, your whole self in your full glory! An authentic leader is one who speaks from the heart, shares their best gifts with their team and organization, speaks the truth, and lives their own truth. When leaders show up and bring their whole selves—their real, unvarnished selves—to work, they build trust and allow others to feel safe to do the same.

Leading from an authentic place means that a leader acknowledges their imperfections and is okay with not having all the answers. Living and leading authentically means you have self-awareness and an ability to be real about who you are. This is a key component that is very tightly tied to compassionate leadership because allowing people to be themselves and then investing in helping them be their *best* selves brings the best out of the entire organization.

In an earlier chapter, I shared part of my conversation with RFK Human Rights Foundation board member Thasunda Duckett about how leading with mission inspires her actions. She told me that what allows her to be driven by that mission is owning and embracing who she is. She explained, "I do believe that my titles are rented, but I own my character. I can say unapologetically that I show up with my ownable assets because I understand where my purpose comes from. And if my purpose is to inspire and to make impact, I have to do that with my ownable assets. In order to make impact and in order to inspire, you have to be okay with your story. You have to be okay with all those highs and lows you have.

"I show up every Monday for my staff meeting, asking people about their weekend and asking them how they're doing. There were moments where we spent that whole meeting time talking about George Floyd or talking about someone's life. When you do that on a consistent basis, what you're showing people is that first and foremost you care about them. If you're not good, and I can't see you, I can't see your stress, can't see why you're underperforming, can't see why you're on edge. But if I understand that, I create space for people to talk in an authentic voice, in a vulnerable voice. Think about the magic that provides in business. During the George Floyd and COVID-19 crises, leading a business in a pandemic with 50,000 employees who had to show up to work every day to make sure that Americans had cash in their ATMs, to make sure that they could deposit checks and had a place to go, that was the hardest thing in my life. To be a mother, to be a black woman, and to be an executive leading people who are navigating a pandemic and wildfires and social unrest, I was not okay. And I publicly said to my team, 'It's okay to not be okay.' And what I was modeling was that we can no longer compartmentalize our lives. It's all fluid. And that unlocked so many employees to send me notes and say, '"I cried, Thasunda. Thank you for giving me permission.' That means so much, because when you can lead with vulnerability, you can lead in your own truth, you can unlock the truth about others. And that is how you model compassion. That is how you impact the world as a leader."

Two-Way Trust—Trust Your Team

Trusting your employees is part of building trust culture. A leader can't only focus on how to earn the trust of others. A leader has to allow employees to earn his or her trust as well. It's a two-way street.

I mentioned Sharecare CEO and great leader Jeff Arnold earlier. One of the things about Jeff that I have been most impressed by is how he trusts and empowers his team. It's clear that trust has benefits.

I asked Jeff to tell me more about his thoughts on this. He said: "I've got great peers. It's like having ten sets of eyes and fifty sets of hands. We have such great cadence, and there's such trust between me and many of my colleagues that it allows us to create something that's very authentic. You know, it's not manufactured. I mean, we look out for each other. We trust each other. We believe in each other's amazing capabilities. We believe that we can do the mission, and that we can actually have an impact. What you start to find is that the community starts to govern itself."

So how does a leader work to show that they trust their employees or members of their organization? For one thing, it's important to have clear communication about what is expected of any employee. You have to establish the goals. And the goals have to be not just the business goals but also personal growth goals. Then, you learn to trust your employees by their ability to enact the goals. I used a tool I called a scorecard. During performance reviews, my employees and I talked about their development and about what I could be doing better. I took the time to demonstrate to them that I cared about them. But I also took the time to understand why they may or may not have achieved certain goals.

Another critical element of building two-way trust with employees is giving them more voice in how they shape their jobs and how they practice them. Letting employees share in their job design shows them that you trust them to know what they need to do, that you acknowledge the professional that they are.

Two-way trust is critical when making major transformations. Involving and empowering your team when making changes that affect a group or the whole organization is key to building trust. My good friend and Tramuto Foundation board member Dr. Mary Jane England shared an example of this with me. Dr. England has had a rich and varied career. She studied psychiatry in medical school. She has since had roles that include heading the Massachusetts Department of Social Services, working on health-care policy in the private sector, and ten years as president of Regis College. She shared how she applied lessons she learned while training as a psychiatrist to building teams in corporate, government, and educational settings.

She explained, "One of the things psychiatry taught me is that we first need to listen. Then, importantly, we have the patient be the one to solve the problems. So, you empower the patient, and then they work with their strengths to solve their problems or overcome their issues." When Mary Jane was invited back to Regis College, her alma mater, to become president (the first woman president), she had to overcome major challenges, and she facilitated important transformation by listening and empowering her team and earning their trust.

She described the situation: "When I started, I found the college was having terrible financial difficulties," she said. "My decision was to involve everybody on the campus, the faculty, staff, and students, in solving the problem. We had a process that went on for a number of months. They came back to me with some very difficult but critical information. Then I was able to make the decisions, but only after I first involved and empowered the team and school community. The good news was we were going to survive, but we had to cut majors, we had to cut faculty and staff. All of it was traumatic, but everybody was involved in the decisions. To allow people to be productive in their own rights and to come up with the suggestions that I followed is something that I think is really important. If we're going to act, we should never act alone. We definitely have to involve others in doing it, or they won't buy into it." In other words, trust your team, and in doing so, you'll earn their trust in return. This will go a long way in laying the foundation for a high-trust culture.

END-OF-CHAPTER EXERCISES

SELF-REFLECTION: ARE YOU BRINGING YOUR WHOLE SELF TO WORK?

To build relationships and earn the trust of your peers, colleagues, and employees, it's important to be yourself, to *be human*, to drop any facade of perfection. Think about when you might have opportunities to do this.

- If an employee or colleague comes to you and admits that they are struggling, can you share with them that you have struggled with that issue or something similar too?

- If you're having a hard day, and you're not yourself in a meeting, consider opening up about that. It doesn't mean you have to share all your sensitive, personal information, but letting people see your human emotions gives them permission to do so too.

- Do you feel that you have to have all the answers? If so, consider flipping this to having all the questions instead. Sharing that you don't know something—or everything—builds trust and allows for others to step up.

- Own up to mistakes and errors and make it safe to fail. Generation Z wants a "safe" environment. Many colleges are now providing a safe learning environment, in which they involve parents as partners to better understand the needs of their children. Consider providing a safe working environment and perhaps a designated safe room in which anyone can feel comfortable and safe expressing their feelings.

Chapter 6

Build Compassionate Culture

I USED TO SAY THAT CULTURE COMES FIRST when developing a successful and sustainable organization. But, as I explained earlier, I've since revised that to say that trust comes first. Trust is a precondition for a positive culture, as it's the very foundation of healthy, sustainable relationships among the people who collectively make up any organization. Healthy and productive culture is built on trust and powered by compassion. These elements are interlinked. A compassionate and trust-based culture is the strongest foundation from which an organization can grow and thrive over time.

Strong leaders from successful organizations know this. But some leaders and corporate boards view culture as a lower priority, something that you might devote time to after focusing on hiring the best people you can afford or find, delivering your best product or service, or (especially from the old model's perspective) hitting your numbers. Others see it as a separate entity, distinct from the main activities of the organization. Many address it once in a while or sporadically during the life of the organization when perhaps external changes arise to challenge its survival. While the notion of hitting numbers first may sound appealing, it is a short-term focus.

You may deliver on your numbers for a year or two, but sustaining them without a culture built on trust is like someone saying, "Let me develop the space shuttle to take you to the moon, but you need to find me the instructions to craft the engines." The person might wing it to get the engines working, but sustaining the engines will be a miracle at best.

In fact, strong culture is integral to success when it comes to achieving any of those things. Strong culture makes workplaces more productive, more engaged, and more profitable. This has been shown in study after study and is articulated repeatedly by workers themselves in workplace surveys all over the world.

Strong cultures attract talent. In fact, forty-six percent of job seekers cite company culture as very important when choosing to apply to a company, and eighty-eight percent say that culture is of some importance.[1] On the flip side, employees who don't like their organization's culture are twenty-four percent more likely to quit.[2] On a related note, employees are twenty-six percent more likely to leave their jobs if they feel there is a lack of respect among colleagues. Disrespect is a sure sign of an unhealthy culture.

Top drivers of culture include trust, respect, collaboration, commitment to employees' wellness and growth, a sense of purpose, and a mission that acknowledges and commits to things beyond the company walls, like healthy communities and a healthy planet. Compassionate leadership includes every one of these components, and compassionate leaders, naturally, develop all of them.

And just as a healthy culture needs compassionate leadership, compassion can be cultivated more successfully if the underlying environment or culture is conducive to it. Compassionate leadership creates compassionate culture, and compassionate culture creates compassionate leaders and coworkers throughout an organization. It's a virtuous cycle that allows organizations to flourish.

What Leaders Get Wrong about Culture

There are many different ways to articulate the definition of culture. In the context of a business or organization, you can think of it as the sum total of the employees' or members' shared values, beliefs, and practices. The key piece of this definition that leaders get wrong or miss entirely is the notion that culture is *shared*. The idea of a shared culture includes a nuance that leaders often miss, which is that by its shared nature, it must also be created by the whole organization. In other words, culture isn't just *shared* by the people, it's also *created* by the people. This includes the CEO, executives, board members (yes! As you read this section, ask yourself if any of your organization's board members have actually gotten involved in developing and understanding the culture you are creating), senior leaders, and, ideally, everyone in an organization.

It's especially important for new leaders to understand shared culture. And the only way you can understand the existing culture when joining a new organization is to be willing to understand the people, to understand what drives them, what they believe their company or organization stands for, and what they care about. This really connects with the whole notion of empathy. As a leader, listening to and understanding what your people are feeling and what they believe is essential to understanding existing culture. And if the culture needs improvement, tapping into their underlying motivation for the work that they do will help motivate your team to participate in strengthening the culture. Listening to your employees, acknowledging them as co-owners of your culture, and empowering them to participate in its evolution are all parts of an empowering and compassionate process.

Culture Is Not Created in Isolation

I went through a process when I became CEO at Tivity Health, which was called Healthways at the time. When I started at Healthways, there were nine corporate values defined. The company printed them on the back of employees' business cards.

I realized intuitively that these were not right, not aligned with the actual culture being lived out in the business day to day. I decided to collaborate with folks to understand what they thought about these stated values.

First, I discovered that no one could remember them or come up with them when asked. This was the first eye-opener for me. Values have to be ingrained in the very fabric of the culture you're developing. People shouldn't have to think hard about the values or have to guess at what they might be if asked.

Everyone agreed that we needed to narrow it down to the right values and then communicate them more effectively. I created a committee with members from all over the company and involved my leadership team.

I asked a lot of questions of the committee. I realized that they were afraid that I was trying to develop a culture just like the one at my former company, Physician's Interactive Holdings. I had just come out of Physicians Interactive Holdings. It was a company that I founded with Perseus Private Equity, so I was pretty partial to those cultural values. But the team, quite frankly, came back and told me they didn't want that culture. Transferring my former culture to this new company would have been a big mistake. It was hard for me, to be honest! As a leader, you get attached to certain things, especially when you believe they have worked. Ultimately, the company created its own set of values with my facilitation and guidance, and that was the only way to do it.

So, it's important for leaders to avoid defining the culture on their own in a vacuum or from an ivory tower. Culture is not developed in isolation and then handed down. This can lead to a team feeling that their leader isn't listening. It can lead to a lack of trust, a lack of empowerment, and a lack of alignment. Alignment is lining up and being in sync or on the same page as the whole of your staff. You cannot share a vision without alignment. There is no alignment without conversation.

Certainly, it can frustrate a leader when the cultural values they are trying to convey are not being adopted or even known. Your job as a leader is to question, listen, push the team's thinking, and empower people in the process so that you come back with the right values that everyone can adopt.

Culture Is a Journey, Not a Destination

Another misperception about culture is that it is a one-and-done exercise figured out in a two-day workshop by four of your people. Some leaders articulate their company or organization's values, maybe post them on their website or hand them out on a card at a company meeting, and then call it a day for culture-building! The reality is that culture is a living and evolving process. This means it is likely to change over time.

In many cases, culture can change because a new leader joins a company or organization. Culture can be changed or strengthened in times of shifting contexts (markets, laws, consumer expectations, and so on). Thus, new leaders are brought in specifically to change the culture in a crisis, or when the organization has taken a wrong turn. The example of Uber comes to mind. Its board asked the founder to step down and added women leaders to its board after allegations, then company-wide revelations, about its misogynistic culture.

As I just hinted, there are many triggers of change that don't have anything to do with a CEO. The most front-of-mind example as I write this book is the COVID-19 pandemic, an external crisis affecting all businesses in their internal operations. There has not been a time during my career when so many companies had to shift their focus and invest time and resources in their very survival, including taking a new look at their culture. If the prior culture did not live and breathe these values, suddenly things like compassion, flexibility, and adaptability had to take priority for companies to weather the storm. To remain relevant, a lot of old ways of doing and thinking were either thrown out the window or repositioned to address the times. Some, to be sure, already had a compassionate culture to build on; those companies quickly responded in a way that let them navigate the crisis with a united team and less discomfort. The companies that did not have a strong culture in place faced tougher headwinds.

This might lead you to think of the strategic, long-term advantages of a strongly compassionate, values-driven culture. And you'd be right!

Societal trends can push a company to make cultural transformations as well. For example, as society evolved to have a greater awareness about the food we eat, where it is sourced from, and how it is grown and brought to market, food company cultures were impacted. This societal awareness didn't only happen outside the companies, but also inside them as well. Big chains with an existing cultural awareness, like McDonald's, changed how they sourced their food to address how the cultural values of their employees and customers diverged from the company's decades-old practices. And it communicated those changes clearly to all.

Walmart is a great example of a company that continually adapts its culture to respond to outside forces that impact its employees and customers. I remember that, years ago, Walmart was viewed by many consumers as The Evil Giant Retailer that trampled its way into neighborhoods and put small businesses out of business. Since then, Walmart has become a global leader in social responsibility, pushing through big changes that positively support communities and the environment. When there was a shooting at one of its stores, the company changed its practice regarding selling ammunition. Most recently, it changed its management model in stores to a team approach, and it has made big changes to invest in its workers' financial well-being, career development, and futures.

The important lesson in what Walmart has done to protect and evolve its culture is that it not only acknowledged the things its customers and employees care about but also took action that aligned with that new awareness. It modified its practices accordingly.

CVS is another great example of a company that's stepped up, terminating all sales of cigarettes in recognition of their toxic effects. With that one decision, the company forfeited billions of dollars of sales yet won the trust of many, including customers, health-care providers, and employees, particularly millennial workers who value the commitment to social causes over profit.

Now, there is no doubt that many of the actions companies like Walmart and CVS took under the heading of culture were also good for business. That's part of the point of this book. Compassionate leadership is a leadership that recognizes and delivers on growth and sustainability, strong performance, and profitability. It delivers strong double bottom line results.

Words and Deeds Have Power and Value

The most powerful tools any leader has are their words, and taking into account the trust factor, their deeds (actions, behaviors, processes, lifestyle) must echo their words and vice versa. This makes them an "aligned" leader of the culture they are building and supporting.

Once a leader and an organization have articulated the essence of their culture, values, and mission, these need to be communicated effectively. The core statements used to express the culture will ideally be adopted, embraced, and practiced by all those in the organization. Teams will identify with these values and feel good about them. They will refer to them when faced with certain types of decisions. These ideas or statements will act as a company's North Star.

In reality, there is often a big gap between the existence of these stated values and an employee's awareness and understanding of them. In fact, in our workplace survey, more than eighty percent of senior leaders said that their organization has established and updates its mission statement regularly. Yet only fifty-nine percent of entry-level workers thought that was so! Somewhere along the line, two or more internal groups disconnected. Communicating culture well and often, and living it with every action and decision every day, is the only way to make sure it is understood and sticks. It's just as important to reinforce it as it is to articulate it in the first place.

Among the compassionate leaders I interviewed for this book, I was struck by the unwavering focus on compassionate culture that is demonstrated by Samer Hamadeh, founder and CEO of Zeel, an on-demand booking platform with a large network of health professionals—including massage therapists, nurses, physical therapists, and behavioral health specialists—who will come to your home or office. I've gotten to know Samer well working within the health-care industry and through my position as an advisor on Zeel's board. He has an impressive practice when it comes to communicating and reinforcing culture.

Can You Have Too Much Transparency?

Something that Samer and I agree on is the power of transparency. I've always believed and have told my employees that if anyone asks me a question, I will answer it openly and honestly as long as the information is not confidential or does not violate anyone's privacy. Transparency is the fastest way to rid a culture of false narratives or unfounded rumors, or prevent them in the first place. Samer agrees, even in the face of some who disagree with his approach.

Samer told me that he is so transparent, he even shares his private company's profit and loss statements from time to time to let every employee see the financials in full, including how much cash the company has on hand and how the company is performing. For managers of traditional leadership models, this openness is tantamount to treason!

Samer explained, "I've been showing the P&L since my first company in the nineties. I decided early on that people would understand what we're doing better if I told them everything. Sometimes saying too much comes back to haunt you, especially in lean times, like during the COVID-19 pandemic, when people can get scared. But if you're saying too little, they start to make things up."

I asked Samer if he thinks there is such a thing as too much transparency. "Some of my executives caution me about telling people too much," he told me. "But I'd rather trust the team and have them disappoint me than go it alone and not have people behind the mission truly knowing everything we're trying to do. People appreciate it. I get emails and texts all the time saying things like, 'I love the transparency' and 'I'm glad you're including us in these discussions.'"

Celebrate Your Values Often

Samer communicates cultural messages in a way that employees can understand and relate to, and he reinforces these messages relentlessly. He told me that he had a customer service agent who didn't see her hourly job as important. He helped her and others in the unit understand that their jobs are some of the most important in the company. He explained to his employee, "We have massage therapists who depend on us for income. If they're lost and can't find a client's location, they're calling you for help. You have to help them. If you help them keep an appointment, they get paid. Or, consider that a customer is in pain and is counting on the service we provide. That's primarily why people use our services; sixty-two percent get massage therapy because of pain."

He continued, "We have so many stories that come in through our customer service agents. Like the story of a female provider who sent Zeel a video last Christmas of her daughter screaming with joy as she's opening presents because the woman had been unable to buy presents for several years but then could because of the extra income she made through Zeel. Or the story of patients, too many to count, who say things like, 'Your therapist was massaging my hip and found a little lump. She said it didn't feel right, and it turned out it was stage one cancer. Thank you so much for the empathy you show us in your appointments.' So I told those agents, 'Your job as a customer service agent is critical. It is to listen to those stories, show empathy to our customers, and make sure that the appointments happen; it is critical.' Then I tell these stories every week. My job is to keep telling the stories that I hear, because the employees forget about them again a month later. That's why we meet every week, and I'm always telling the stories. Sometimes our teams say, 'You're so repetitive. You keep repeating our values at every meeting.' So, fine. I'll repeat them every other meeting, but I'm going to keep repeating them because I need to just drill them into the team's DNA."

Samer is clear, "You create a set of values to guide people. I didn't create values right away. I was indirectly but intentionally helping to create them, but after a couple of years, I saw that we had a culture and values, then I wrote them down. There are six of them. So, in our case, we wrote them down to spell a word that everyone could remember. A lot of companies do mission statements and values, and nobody ever remembers them. So we not only wrote them down so that they were memorable, we posted them all over the walls. We also talked about them at nearly every town hall. Moreover, we have a monthly newsletter that celebrates somebody each month who exhibited one of the six values. For example, one of our values is empathy. So, we rewarded an employee in the call center who demonstrated the empathetic value. We explained what she did. Then we gave her an award, a $100 American Express gift card."

Values and culture must be brought to life and nurtured no differently than a newborn. Think of how happy a parent is to show anyone a picture of their new baby. As time goes on, though, they stop showing the pictures, and perhaps innocently forget that the evolution of their child builds from the past. This practice is no different than building a culture. Once it's crafted, you need to bring it to life, show pictures of what it looks like during each cycle of its evolution. To do otherwise is to support the old adage, "Out of sight, out of mind."

That's key to building culture: writing down the values, posting them everywhere, and then celebrating them quite regularly with awards and gatherings. That's how each value is brought to life and kept top of mind for all your team members, who are otherwise so busy every day doing the tasks involved in their jobs. It's all part of building culture. And you have leaders who are propagating the same values you want to see in others.

"The focus on culture has paid off," said Samer. He told me that Zeel has seen engagement rates much higher than the industry average. The retention is great, too. Even millennials, believed to leave positions quickly, stay longer at the company than they typically do at other companies.

Live and Breathe Your Culture

Bruce Broussard, the CEO at Humana, whom I wrote about earlier, is a believer in this idea of consistency and repetition when communicating culture. To him, that constant communication is one of the keys to building culture and is intertwined with building it.

There are many ways to do this, but two important themes, repetition and modeling, are essentials in Bruce's playbook. He explained: "If you keep on saying it, people are going to listen at some point in time, so part of it is just the reinforcement of it. You do that through how you set your priorities, what you measure, storytelling, or rewards—you pick the lever, but you have to be consistent. The second thing is you've got to be an example of it yourself."

Whether building culture or protecting it, compassionate toughness enters as Bruce's third key. "The third component is that you have to make tough decisions," he said. "There have been a number of people I've had to change out because they were not an acceptable cultural fit. I have nothing against them. I just tell them directly and with compassion and respect, 'Listen, you're just not on the bus. I'm not saying you're wrong, you're just on the wrong bus.'

"To protect a culture," Bruce continued, "my fourth component is recruiting. You could recruit somebody who has the right attributes, but when they're put in an environment that doesn't reinforce those traits, you're not going to get that out of them. One person doesn't change culture; it is a group that changes that. That group is no different than any other community; that community has to stand for something. There has to be a reinforcing aspect of it. We recruit for it, but there are probably people we've recruited who have gotten on the bandwagon, but if we hadn't reinforced the culture, probably wouldn't be in that same mindset."

Communicating Expectations

No one would follow a rule that they don't even know is a rule, so it is important to let employees know what your expectations are about your company ethics, code of conduct, values, and mission—everything that you call your culture. Giving them the Employee Handbook is not quite the same as communicating culture to them.

To get the best from employees, it is essential that a leader spend time making sure his communication is expressed clearly and in a mutually trusting and compassionate way. And as I described in chapter five, having first laid a foundation of trust and compassion should create an environment of openness for people to speak freely and really listen respectfully to one another.

It's been proven in organizations that poor communications can have disastrous results. One pitfall of old-school, transactional leadership is that it leads to poor communication. This type of leader expects their followers to obey out of faith, from a void of information and communication. It doesn't happen. A lack of clear communication negatively impacts productivity[3]: Twenty-eight percent of employees cite poor communication as the reason for not being able to deliver work on time. Again, an employee who is guessing what your expectations are (rather than knowing them in a clearly articulated way) simply cannot meet your expectations!

Miscommunication costs companies with 100 employees an average of $420,000 per year.[4] I'd say that a loss of $4,200 per employee each and every year should be motivation enough for leaders at all levels to optimize healthy and clear communication when delivering assignments, conveying expectations of behavior, setting goals, and collaborating in teams.

When asked, most leaders will agree that communication is indeed important. They are aware that a lack of it causes problems. In fact, eighty-six percent of corporate executives, educators, and employees cite ineffective communication and poor collaboration (the latter of which is just another form of communication) as reasons for failures in the workplace.[5]

Communication needs to be open to allow employees to understand and deliver on goals, receive and act on feedback, keep processes flowing, and optimize results. Compassionate communication is critical to highly functional teams, as it creates an environment of encouragement, support, respect, and a sense of safety, which allows for sharing of ideas. The imperative starts at the top and needs to be modeled and shared throughout the management ranks. And if there is a skill that merits training, this is it. It's fundamental, critical to success, and widely understood to be important, yet many don't know how to practice it.

How Communication from Compassion Looks

Compassion plays a bigger role than you might think in effective communication. Remember, essential components of this style of leadership include things like empathy, trust, willingness to commit to the development of others, and a desire to act to alleviate pain, suffering, challenges, or obstacles.

I'll give you an example of a management situation and how it might be addressed with and without compassionate communication. Let's say there is a manager, Dave, who has an employee, Ross. Ross's performance has started to decline. Ross showed up late several times, and Dave is worried that Ross will miss an important upcoming deadline. Without a compassionate leadership style, there is not a lot of openness or trust in the relationship, so Ross does not try to talk to Dave about it. Dave feels frustrated; maybe he assumes Ross's behavior is a result of laziness or a sense of entitlement. He might think that because Ross didn't explain the lagging performance to Dave, he must not have a good explanation. Dave becomes stressed over it; he's upset, but he doesn't want to address it. In fact, sixty-nine percent of managers are uncomfortable when communicating with their employees,[6] so we know this happens every day. When Dave finally decides to address it, he reprimands Ross. Then, he tells Ross that he's letting his team down, or simply says, "You can't be late anymore" or "If this keeps up, I'll have to bring the human resources department into it." Ross says nothing and leaves upset. The result: Dave remains frustrated. Dave and Ross's relationship deteriorates. Ross becomes further disengaged, and his performance declines even more. Ross's disengagement makes a negative impact on the team and is shared by some of them. The deadline—many deadlines—are missed.

Let's take the same situation and apply a culture of compassion. Ross is late to work. Because Dave has laid a foundation of trust and openness and has showed his employees that he cares, Ross asks Dave if they can talk. Ross explains that he has a sick child at home and a spouse who has been having to work overtime, so it's been a struggle to get to work on time. Dave is glad to hear the reason from Ross and thanks him for sharing the situation. They talk about how to deal with the situation together. Ross might tell Dave that he has time to make up his work at night after their child is asleep; this offers Ross some needed flexibility about the time he gets to work. Dave might also look at other short-term solutions to support Ross, like getting others on the team to help with the big project that's due soon.

Because it's a compassionate culture, other team members are happy to jump in to help; they know it will be reciprocated for them if they are in the same kind of need. The result of compassionate leadership: Ross is supported and able to care for his child without the stress of work making the situation worse. Dave has given Ross a reason for trust. Dave has proactively made a closer bond with a valued member of his team. Ross feels even more engaged and committed, because he feels the boss has his back. Dave feels good about supporting Ross, because he feels the team has their backs. Dave, the manager, headed off issues before they affected business results. Dave did his primary managerial job, which is to help his team get things done by providing them the ways and means to do so.

The bottom line in the above scenario is that if a leader is compassionate, it creates a sense of safety and trust that allows employees to come forward with issues and challenges before they become problems. Compassion results in more relaxed, more all-in, more effective employees. Understanding and working in this type of culture gives a manager tools and skills that help take the stress and anxiety out of talking about difficult issues.

It's Time to Get Rid of the Seagull Model for Performance Reviews

One of the most anxiety-provoking conversations for both leaders and employees is the annual performance review. Leaders dread the time it takes away from their other work. They also dread the potential pushback, resistance, and conflict that real feedback might evoke. Employees pick up on this dread and fear for their livelihoods (mostly unnecessarily, because termination of an employee rarely happens at performance review time). Everyone dreads the reviews because the current model supports the notion that, like a seagull, the leader is flying in, dumping, and then moving on.

I am all in to discuss an employee's performance, but what I'm suggesting to you is a different way to look at performance review time altogether.

A better approach is to hold a series of both planned and impromptu performance conversations throughout the year. Just as we eat pieces of food that are small enough to chew, swallow, and digest, individuals need to take in observations about performance in frequent, short encounters. That way, when you give the entire review, there are no surprises or misunderstandings. While some of these discussions might be well-prepared, others are check-ins or follow-ups.

The idea is that you have regular, periodic conversations with your employees during the whole year about skills development, performance, outcomes, attitudes, engagement, work ethic, or whatever is on the table for each employee. Mine are weekly, but biweekly or even monthly will do. During these meetings, you and the employee talk about how things are going. Importantly, these are two-way dialogues, covering things like how expectations are being met and whether there is something you and the employee can work on together to help them grow. It's an opportunity for employees to give you feedback. Are they getting clear enough instructions from you? Did you not have their back at a crucial moment, and some resentment or distrust is building up? Are you sharing enough information and ways and means for them to do their jobs? These meetings are a way to give constructive feedback, reinforce good work, and collaborate to solve issues that may be preventing the employee from doing their best work. And always ask, "What am I *not* doing to support you?"

Most important, it shows your employee that he or she is a vital member of the team and that you're willing to take the time to listen, to get to know them better, to help them grow in their skills, and so on. It is a moment for offering support for their overall well-being. It shows a real commitment to that employee and their development.

Sixty-five percent of employees in one survey stated that they didn't get sufficient feedback about their performance or work from their boss.[7]

In our workplace survey, commitment was the component of leadership that ranked highest among employees. Eighty-two percent of respondents said that "committing time and resources to the mental and physical wellness of an organization's members or employees improved productivity and profitability."

You see the disconnection. Managers say, "Yes, it is a viable bottom line–building tool." Employees say, "Give us that feedback!" Yet it doesn't happen.

The beauty of a series of performance reviews being a continual conversation is that once you get to the final annual review, it takes only minutes to put together. You have the notes you made throughout the year in that employee's file, so you know exactly what the top points are you need to check in on or reiterate. You can then spend the majority of your time focusing on developing plans for the upcoming year.

Please Stop Asking, "Can I Give You Some Feedback?"

Think about it. When someone asks, "Can I give you some feedback?" how do you feel? Do you assume it's going to be positive or negative? Most people wince a little inside and steel themselves for negative feedback or constructive criticism (which is often just another term that stresses people out because they expect the worst). I don't like to use the word *feedback* anymore. I prefer to think of it as a constructive dialogue, and to refer to my ongoing meetings as weekly check-ins. Or I'll just get to the point: "Let's chat about that skills training you wrapped up last week," "Tell me how that new customer service script is working," and so on. Notice the absence of the word *feedback*. You haven't asked the employee for feedback on his training workshop or about the data measuring the new script's effectiveness. You've framed it all as a conversation about specific things that are important for the overall performance of the individual, or the team, or both.

I think this practice has become more prevalent in the time of COVID-19. With so many of us working remotely, these more frequent check-ins have become an essential tool.

When you do have input to offer that is about a performance issue, I suggest approaching it by saying, "May I give some observations?" If you get rid of the word *feedback*, it can change the whole nature or tone of the conversation. If you've described it as *feedback* up front, when you're talking to the person all they're thinking is, *Am I going to lose my job? What am I doing wrong?* And they go to a dark place. You want to start the conversation by not taking them to that dark place. That's your responsibility as a leader. So, call it a *constructive dialogue*, and start the conversation: "May I share with you a few observations that I have? I would like your input."

Don't take the approach of what the employee did wrong. I try to reinforce the positive behavior first. Catch people doing something right as often as you can. Praise has enormous value. A culture of praise can raise productivity and profitability in a firm by twenty percent.[8] It's actually what you might call a *brain hack*. Praise releases dopamine, which improves memory and allows the brain to work more efficiently and creatively. This reinforces the behaviors you want to continue and puts some trust in the bank for when you need to share something negative. Mark Twain said it well: "I can live for two months off of a good compliment."

Let's Talk about That

At Tivity Health, I put a big emphasis on open communication lines. I believe it's something leaders model. The leader has to show the way. This openness makes sure any dissenting opinions or negative feedback are shared and is a way to take the pulse of your employees.

Every Friday, I instituted an open meeting called "Ask Me Anything." Those became the best cultural check-in calls that I have ever done in my career. The meetings were set up so that anyone could come, anyone could ask a question, and they didn't have to give their name. This practice started when we took a survey of our employees and discovered that sixty-five percent did not feel empowered. Opening up a forum for total candor and input was a step toward allowing the team to be empowered. And, by the way, I did get some tough feedback, yet my job as modeler was to always acknowledge it, and I believe I did that. It's important to avoid rejecting any feedback out of hand. It should serve as a starting point for more information collection, greater understanding, better communication, and all sorts of improvements in challenging situations.

One of the most open and caring people I know is Dr. John Seibert. John is assistant professor of otolaryngology—head and neck surgery—service chief, and director of education at Vanderbilt University School of Medicine in Nashville, Tennessee, and he is a practicing physician in a community practice there as well. I know John because he is one of my doctors. When I thought about who to talk with for this book, he came to mind immediately because his compassion is tangible.

I've witnessed firsthand how pleasant and caring his team is at his practice. I've seen their open communication with each other, and I believe it is key to the success of his practice. He described culture as what attracts people to want to work there. "I think of it like, you build the ship, and people start coming," he said. "People realize this is a place they want to be part of. It's a 'How can I serve you?' culture. It's the servant attitude we've been trying to focus on. We're trying to get away from this big institutional medicine feeling. I think our employees were saying, 'Hey, I want to be part of this, because actually, it makes a better work environment.' I mean, you can have this strong, authoritarian kind of system, but people don't want to be part of that. And I think corporations and businesses and hospitals realize that we want people to be invested. It makes a difference for our patients. So we have people who are genuinely happy to see the personnel, saying things like, 'Oh, Mr. Jones, so good to see you again.' They love that they can have that relationship there. And then I think our nurses and our medical assistants, they love that environment."

Candor with compassion is one major focus in the culture John and his team have created. Candor is distinct from the transparency I also use. John described monthly meetings during which his team gets together for real conversation. He explained: "If we have issues, we talk about these things. My mantra always was, be part of the solution, not part of the problem. Let's talk about these things. Let's do this now. We have a small office here. I think a lot more people feel like this is where they want to be because we have that culture of 'I really should talk about that.' And when people were hurting, we addressed that, saying, 'Hey, I know talking about this is helpful. How can we take it a step further and *help* you with that?'"

END-OF-CHAPTER EXERCISES

DO A CULTURE CHECK

As I mentioned, company culture may not always be what a leader thinks it is. Take some time to do a culture check. You can check in with your own small team or direct reports and ask them how they would describe your company culture. Or, if you're a more senior leader, open it up to a larger group or the whole company in the form of a survey. Then, compare the results to what your stated culture is, or what you want it to be. If there is a meaningful gap between what a senior leader describes as their culture and what employees say, there is some work to do on defining and reinforcing your organization's cultural values.

TAKE STEPS TO REINFORCE CULTURAL VALUES

When you have stated values, find ways to share them—often.

1. Casually but intentionally mention or give a shout-out to a colleague or employee when you see them doing something that embodies one of your organization's values. For example, in a team meeting, you might say, "By the way, I want to give a shout-out to Mary for going the extra mile to help our customer solve her problem. She even went beyond her job scope. Thank you, Mary." Everyone likes a pat on the back, as long as it's authentic. I keep a notebook with me to note these things as I see them happen.

2. Give prizes or awards to people who take actions that are in line with company values. You can do this many ways. Set up a nomination process and have people nominate others when they observe an action that they appreciate. Or, build these moments into larger meetings.

3. State them, over and over. As many of our leaders describe in this book, they repeat themselves—a lot! They know repetition works.

SET UP CHECK-INS

If you have employees reporting to you, set up periodic, ongoing check-ins rather than waiting until there is a problem or an end-of-year review to sit down and talk about how things are going.

Talk with your employee about the process. Decide if this will occur every week, every month, or sometime in between. Set the tone for these meetings by defining them as opportunities to share information with each other, to give each other any updates or feedback. As a leader or manager, you can make quick notes from each of these meetings to allow more detailed reviews. This is also an opportunity to reinforce when the employee is doing something that supports your culture.

Chapter 7

Work Better Together

I F THERE'S ONE THING that the year 2020 taught us, it's the importance of having a trusted network or community to rely on in a crisis and strong teams to get us through challenging times.

In addition to the COVID-19 pandemic, we witnessed political division and social, economic, and racial inequalities. On top of that, whole generations are experiencing another kind of epidemic in parallel to the public pandemic: loneliness or a sense of lost relevancy, made worse by quarantining and often accompanied by depression and/or anxiety. There has been the shift to remote work, unfamiliar to many and thus perhaps a further cause of anxiety. All of these changes have led to an even greater need for building unity and cultivating community at work and in life.

We've long seen the power of strongly collaborative, unified yet diversely composed communities and teams. Studies have shown that people working in such groups innovate faster and are more successful at finding solutions to problems. Members of teams are also more engaged and satisfied in their jobs.

For companies or organizations to excel, and for communities to prosper, people have to work well together. If communities don't make the effort to do so, people stay divided and isolated, and their progress stifles. If companies and their leaders don't commit to working well together, they risk losing ground to those who are unified and collaboration-conscious, diversity-wise.

We know that well-knit communities prosper and strong teams excel. But what makes them excel? In my decades of experience working in leadership positions in the corporate world, community groups, and my foundation and nonprofit organization, as well as in study after study, I have observed that the fundamentals of great communities and teams are consonant with the fundamentals of compassionate leadership. Compassionate leadership cultivates the essential components that drive successful groups and teams.

Communication, Commitment, Collaboration

Compassionate leadership's essential components include the practice of listening to others, exhibiting empathy, actively caring about others' well-being, supporting the team with resources to do the job, and showing respect.

Compassion means you are building openness and trust so that others aren't afraid to offer ideas or critiques.

In our own workplace survey, *communication*, *commitment*, and *collaboration* ranked as the top three keys to compassionate culture and collaborative teams. These keys of compassionate leadership combine to help the people involved form a strong sense of community, which is the essence of successful teams.

Employees or members of a community want to know that their leaders have their backs during difficult times. Teams want to know that their leaders are doing their best to provide all available resources when they are collaborating to achieve a challenging goal or make an unfamiliar shift in direction together. When leaders do demonstrate their commitment to their people, what will happen? People will go the extra mile to reach a goal. They will feel safe enough to share ideas that just might move the team, the organization, or that important project forward. They trust enough to ask for help.

Emotional Investment

My good friend Steve Woods is CEO of TideSmart Global, an experiential marketing firm. As such, he is something of an expert on what creates human connection. He believes that to connect in ways that make one person want to work for or help another, there needs to be some emotional investment. Years ago, he taught a marketing class at the University of South Carolina. He told me about how he taught this to his class. "I was trying to explain how marketing worked, explaining that it's all about psychology," he said. "To demonstrate, I went into the hall outside and called a kid named Jimmy who I had never met before into the classroom. After establishing that he and I had not met before, I told him I had two questions for him. The first was, 'Is there any chance on Saturday you can drive me to the airport?' This was an out-of-left-field question, so he said no, he was busy. I asked the next question. 'Two weeks from now, my wife wants to repaint our dining room, would you mind coming over and helping paint?' But Jimmy said a quick, 'No, I'm busy,' and then escaped the room.

"One of the students said, 'Hey, Professor Woods. What was that about?' I said, 'If I asked you to drive me to the airport, would you?' And he said yes. That led to me explaining this concept of levels of emotional investment. We use that with every client program; we create a metric where we quantify levels of emotional investment. So, in the class, I use the experience with Jimmy to demonstrate that the natural state of emotional investment when individuals first meet each other is typically zero. That also applies to companies and brands and our coworkers. On the other side of the continuum is what we feel for family members. We feel 100 percent. I have three kids. If my kids needed anything, kidney, bone marrow, heaven forbid, I would give everything. So, when people meet and have live exchanges, they make an emotional investment in each other. Creating opportunities for people to work together in teams, over time, raises the collective emotional investment and therefore helps to motivate team members to help one another."

Does Community Matter at Work?

We were born into communities, because what is a family but a small nuclear community living within a larger one? Community is an essential component of a society. The family unit is where we start our learning. The peer units at school are where we find ourselves and our place in the outside world. The team units at work are where we test our skills, our ability to produce, innovate, and make a difference. And outwardly spiral our communities to cover the globe! When the smaller communities thrive and operate harmoniously, so does the larger society.

But many doubt that the concept of community fits in a commercial company. Does it? Does it even matter in the world of business? Emphatically, yes, to both questions. Building a community within your organization is more than just a nice-to-do.

When asked in a 2018 LinkedIn workplace culture study what would keep employees at their company for the next five years or more, the number one answer was a sense of belonging, having people at work they can be themselves around.[1]

In other words, community keeps people in their jobs!

Think about when you move into a new neighborhood. For most, the level of enjoyment of that neighborhood will be highly dependent on the sense of being part of the community. When you walk down the street, do your neighbors say hello and know you by name? Does one of your neighbors ever stop you or stop by to ask you for help, or offer to help you? Are you invited to the neighborhood block party or holiday gathering? Do your kids play with neighbors' kids down the street? The more people feel they belong and are part of something, the safer, more comfortable, and more willing they feel to turn around and contribute as a full-fledged member of the community and collaborate, too.

If you are checking your organization off as just a place to visit for the day with very little sense of belonging, there is not much investment or engagement. This applies whether you are one of its leaders, a staffer, a volunteer, a contractor, or a temporary worker.

For leaders, it is very hard, if not impossible, to get a consistently turbocharged level of performance when employees don't feel invested or connected. I'm not saying you're going to get nothing. But we all have levels of performance within us. When we feel like we're part of a greater mission, when we feel we are an acknowledged and valued part of the team, when we feel like we're part of a respectful and respected culture, then we naturally want to (and will!) go beyond our standard ho-hum performance into higher gear.

This is especially true since the COVID-19 pandemic and quarantining. With its imposed remote-work-or-no-work and remote-school-but-really-no-school, millions of all ages have been thrown into an environment of isolation and loneliness. The dominant mental disorders, depression and anxiety, have afflicted people of all backgrounds, and many of them had never dealt with such states before.

People who complained about going into work or the dreaded commute to the office shifted their perspectives dramatically when they were suddenly not going into work and not able to get behind the wheel to grumble about other drivers. Despite surveys that find that "about half" of the people value a community atmosphere,[2] the COVID-19 requirement of distancing has made us realize that we all value that face-to-face, live-and-in-person interaction, feedback, and collaborative give-and-take.

Five Compassion-Driven Keys to Building Community at Work

There are five main elements to creating a community that increases employee satisfaction, loyalty, and retention while driving innovation and productivity.

1. Espouse an Engaging Mission

Research conducted by Shawn Achor showed that "work altruists were ten times more likely to be engaged . . . and forty percent more likely to receive a promotion."[3] These people are the ones who are so connected to the mission of a company that they increase social interaction during a crisis rather than decrease it.

To encourage this sort of perspective in the workplace, you will need to create an environment that relies heavily on a strong mission. A positive workplace culture is another way to achieve this goal.

2. Encourage Respectful, Inclusive Communication and Empathy

While you may not literally have an open door all day long, make sure your team knows that you are available. Make sure they know—by your actions—that you listen closely and with care, understand, won't crush ideas, won't make people afraid to speak to you or in a group. Your team also needs to know that such behaviors are expected of each of them when communicating with you and with each other. I went as far as providing all of my employees with my mobile number, and it was refreshing to see how many actually took me up on my offer for them to call me.

3. Give Everyone a Voice

All people need to be seen and heard to feel they belong. It is important for a leader to understand the communication style of all team members. When another's style is radically different from your own, you'll need to step up and shift to their style—if only for a moment—to permit each member to speak up in their own manner. It's critical for leaders to encourage each person to speak up, and then equally critical to be prepared to listen to them when they do. This reminds me of a quote from Matthew Henry: "There's none so deaf as those who will not hear."

Some individuals have a reputation for not speaking up or for being shy, but it actually might be that they fear the wrong words will come out of their mouths, or that they simply will not find the right words, or that they fear mockery for any thought or idea they might suggest.

Some people speak 100 miles an hour, while with others it feels like you'll fall asleep before they finish one sentence. Patience and understanding are basic requirements of a leader to make sure that each team member is both seen and heard.

Community-focused leadership, or what some have called *communityship*, does not make use of the egocentric kind of leadership that is quite common in the business world. The exercise of top-down authority without engaging your teams isn't working anymore. Communityship requires a lighter touch or a humbler leadership. A community leader is personally engaged in order to engage others, so that anyone and everyone can speak up and exercise initiative.

4. Empower All Levels of Management to Share Values and Co-Own Community

Managers at all levels should recognize the power they hold in creating a valuable work environment that has at its forefront— empowerment! In fact, researchers found that middle managers were especially important and valuable aspects in building community, not only because of their knowledge of the organization but also because of their level of commitment to the company.[4] We also know that middle management is sometimes the level at which a gap forms between the top layers of leadership and the rest of the group. Staying in sync with middle management and every layer throughout an organization is critical. No one owns anyone in an organization!

5. Communicate Community Values from the Top

Commonly lived values, mission, and corporate goals are what the top echelon of leaders are actively living daily. Their job is not only to define, articulate, and reinforce them, but also to allow people to feel fellowship around common goals, mission, expertise, and interests. They must "walk the walk" in addition to "talking the talk" to model and embody these values.

Community Is the Vehicle for Compassion

I've long admired Reverend Becca Stevens for her ability to create community. Becca is the founder of Thistle Farms, a Nashville-based community organization and global movement for women's freedom that helps to heal, empower, and employ women survivors of human trafficking, prostitution, and addiction. She is also an Episcopal priest, speaker, entrepreneur, and author. I was the recipient of Becca's wisdom and compassion for years when I attended the church where she serves as a priest, and she has since become a cherished friend. For her, building compassionate community is a passion, a calling, and an expertise. She has a beautiful view on compassion and community that she expressed as she told me the story of Thistle Farms.

Becca started Thistle Farms with one house and five women in 1997. Its history is a journey of what a community looks like when it comes together. "It was never only about helping a subculture of women who were deemed survivors of addiction, trafficking, and prostitution," she explained. "It's always been about engaging a whole community to say how can we work together to make our whole community safer and more loving. This includes survivors, but it's not exclusive to survivors. It's also about everybody being able to tell their story without shame or fear. It's about challenging language and legislation that's detrimental to people. It's about freeing people up so that they don't have to turn a blind eye to childhood sexual abuse and trauma. It's about compassion toward refugees, a big population of whom gets trafficked. It's about all of that."

An important component of her organization is Thistle Farms Social Enterprises, which was started to create entrepreneurial income streams for the residential program and to provide gateway jobs for the program's participants. She described the why behind this: "Early on, we started in the enterprise world, because we knew that poverty was also a huge part of why women continue to stay stuck where they are, whether it's in an unjust prison system or a really unhealthy relationship. The easiest definition of compassion for me is that I'm willing to enter another story and stay in that story." This means not just helping or having empathy, but taking action.

"Compassion, when a woman joins our community," Becca continued, "may be giving her a really beautiful bed with a new comforter and a sheet that no one else has slept on. Help her feel safe and clean, maybe for the first time in a long time. But a year down the road, compassion for her might look more like access to a car dealership that's willing to help her with a bad credit rating so that she can get a car.

"You're walking with someone. You're walking down their road. You are helping them cross the stream. Compassion is practical. It's a journey, and it definitely involves action. It's also a remembering. I think compassion is remembering your own brokenness and how it made you feel. This is how you are able to transform that into compassion for others. You take your own broken openness and turn it into a broken openness in your heart.

"Community is the oldest entity for healing the world knows. So, it is the entity for doing whatever your work is with compassion. It's the entity that, as I understand it, holds us up. And it holds us together. And it holds us accountable. Somehow, when we all do this together, there will be some other magical quality because of the work together that none of us could have achieved by ourselves.

"So, at Thistle Farms, it means we're all doing this work of healing individually. But when we come together in community, there's another entity in the room, you know, the sum is greater than its parts, right? And so, when you see Thistle Farms, it is so not my vision. And I don't even care about vision that much anymore. I have a very, very strong community. And that is what will move us farther than we could ever imagine. So yeah, I definitely think community is the entity by which compassion happens. It's the transportation device."

Becca's words and her approach to leveraging compassion for community building can be applied in any organization, both not-for-profits and for-profits. The outcome is the same—stronger teams, collaboration, unity of action, and better outcomes.

Collaboration Is More Than Teamwork

Collaboration, or "laboring together," is the act of working together to create or achieve something as a group, typically (but not always) something that one individual alone cannot achieve.

It is more than teamwork in your business or community. In fact, it never starts there at that level of worldliness but rather in the heart of a family unit. A parent can do things alone and certainly does so over the years the family exists. But more meaningful education, engagement, understanding of self and others, and (let's face it) chores are achieved when the parent gets every member of the family involved in a shared project. The shared project could be as simple as dinner cleanup: clearing a dinner table and cleaning up every evening as a family team. It could be more complex, inviting even the youngest of children to give suggestions about where or how the family should spend their two-week vacation together next summer. Collaboration gets each individual doing something that is meaningful to the end result.

There is no doubt that collaboration is essential to making a group of people into a successful team. Collaboration is essential for pulling together members of any community—whether it be a family, a department of a corporation, or a community nonprofit—into any endeavor.

A recent joint study between the Institute for Corporate Productivity (i4cp) and Rob Cross, the Edward A. Madden professor of global business at Babson College, found that companies that promoted collaborative working were five times as likely to be high performing.[5]

Take this a step further as Becca Stevens has and move into compassionate collaboration. In our workplace survey, eighty-five percent of all levels of workers said a compassionate workplace encourages cooperation (aka collaboration), which in turn leads to greater productivity and profitability.

Since collaborative cultures are proven boosters of productivity and performance, it's no wonder many leaders and companies study the components of what makes great teams. Google undertook perhaps one of the best-known of these studies.

What Google Taught Us about
Compassion and Collaboration

Google's two-year study, called Project Aristotle, was an effort to define what made the best teams work compared to those that didn't. Prior to this study, the company believed that assembling the best people was the key to creating the best teams. They found that they were wrong.

This widely reported study yielded important keys to strong teams. Perhaps the most talked about was the idea of psychological safety, which I will get to. But to me, the biggest learnings were about compassion.

What Google discovered after studying 180 teams was that there weren't clear answers arising from the mountains of data. As described in an article in the *New York Times*,[6] Google struggled to figure out what made their teams successful until they came across literature on group norms and behaviors and insights from a research study on collective intelligence (also known as abilities that emerge out of collaboration) by a group of psychologists from Carnegie Mellon, MIT, and Union College.[7]

Project Aristotle's researchers then went back to look at their data to find any team behaviors that magnified the collective intelligence of the group. Google outlines their conclusions, which honed in on five key characteristics of enhanced teams:

1. Dependability

   - Team members each get things done on time and meet expectations.

2. Structure and clarity

   - High-performing teams have clear goals and well-defined roles within the group to help the team reach those goals.

3. Meaning

   - The work has personal significance to each member.

4. Impact

- The group believes their work is purposeful and positively impacts the greater good.

5. Psychological safety

- Their environment is one in which everyone is safe to take risks, voice their opinions, and ask judgment-free questions, and managers protect the people and create safe zones so employees can let down their guard.

Google found that the latter point, psychologically safe environments, had the added effects of less staff turnover, a higher likelihood of diverse composition (where *diverse* meant all genders, mixed racial backgrounds, and mixed educational and experiential backgrounds), and leverage of that diversity to achieve greater or faster outcomes.

The most interesting insight to me about what makes successful teams was a finding that didn't show readily in the data. It was the link to compassion. After the data was in, the researchers shared the results with Google managers.

The *New York Times* article described how one of their managers, a man named Sakaguchi, was surprised by the results, as he had thought his team was strong; however, the survey showed him otherwise. He was concerned enough that he gathered his team to discuss the results. On his own initiative, he took a step that proved to be revelatory: He opened the meeting by asking everyone on his team to share something about themselves that the team didn't know. This is not something that happens in most workplace meetings! He went first. He disclosed that he had stage four cancer, which had been growing very slowly over his years at Google, and that recently his doctors had found a new spot that was more serious. No one on his team, no one in the room, knew this before and would never have guessed that he was going through this challenge. After Sakaguchi spoke, another teammate stood and described some health issues of her own. Then another got up and revealed a difficult personal breakup. Eventually, everyone had shared a personal, previously unheard story.

The team then focused on the survey and on what was happening in their workplace. They all found it easier to speak candidly about the things that had been bothering them on the job. As the article states, it was easier to reveal "their small frictions and everyday annoyances." Sakaguchi got the feedback he needed about his management style, and the team's level of compassion and collaboration skyrocketed.

There was nothing in the survey or in his hierarchy's instructions that called for Sakaguchi to share his illness with the group. He seemed to do this intuitively. To him, psychological safety was related to openness, trust, and empathy. The more the team bonded emotionally, the better they worked together.

We versus Me Culture

I've been inspired by every conversation I've had with Don DeGolyer, a long-time industry colleague and compassionate leader. Don is senior advisor at Koch Strategic Platforms, and has had long and successful stints at major health-care companies like Pfizer, Johnson & Johnson, and Novartis. Don is also the founder of an amazing nonprofit, the Strong Women Foundation, whose mission is to help single moms during times of need to propel them, their families, and their communities forward. Don is known for his ability to create and lead strong teams, so I asked him about how he does it.

He gave me an example of when he was asked to run the generic drug business at Novartis pharmaceutical company. "When I first joined the division, we needed a major cultural transformation," he told me. "The existing culture was a 'me' culture that was very competitive. They needed to learn how to collaborate with our internal partners, who they perceived as the competition, but, to me, were part of our team! I asked one of the people who reported to me for a report that he had. I waited and got nothing. I asked again, and then I got a hard copy. Finally, I got a PDF, when all the while he knew what I needed but resisted, holding on to information as if I was a competitor. I finally said, 'Come on, let's stop playing this game. This is not your information. It's the company's, it's *ours*.' He didn't last very long. He didn't fit the culture that we were creating.

"Simply put, it was a 'me' culture, as opposed to a 'we' culture," Don continued. "So, we needed to go from a group of individuals to a high-performance team. People were very guarded with information and suggestions. I needed to demonstrate that this behavior was not going to be acceptable and would not be supported. Some people saw this, and they got off the bus. Others moved up to the front of the bus, and we needed to bring in other people who were going to complement the folks that stayed.

"Then, one by one, I needed to make sure that we really got to know each other on a very personal level and what was important to each individual before we even set forth with the strategic imperatives and the values that we were going to follow. We got to know each other and appreciate the differences that each other brought, the styles and motivations. Once understood, we could come together and establish what our strategic imperatives were going to be. We put the mission ahead of any individual's needs.

"We were able to do that over four years. In the first year, we had strong double-digit organic growth. The second year, we were able to do the same and compounded that, and the subsequent two years we were able to do two acquisitions that helped to drive our industry-leading results. We were the fastest-growing generic company in North America. We delivered stronger results as a fully aligned team focused on one mission."

Collaboration Isn't Always about Achieving Greatness

Imagine a new CEO going to his board soon after joining the company and saying, "This division that you want to sell, in which you invested nearly a billion dollars over many years, you're not going to get a penny for it. What we're going to do is pay somebody to take it." I did this very thing in May 2016, a mere six months after moving into the CEO role at Healthways (now Tivity Health), following nearly two years as the chairman of the board.

This is not just a story of a very untraditional deal; it's a story of a different kind of collaboration.

When I started in my role as CEO, there was a division that was not successful. Losing millions, it was a drag on our profit and loss. The company aspired to sell it for $300 to $500 million. But after numerous inbound inquiries that didn't go anywhere, it was clear that no one wanted it. As a public company, I was getting pressured by the market to just shut it down to stop the losses. I couldn't sell it, but shutting it down would have meant that nearly 1,500 people would have lost their jobs, and customers who supported both divisions would have faced uncertainty with the services they were purchasing for their members.

I resisted the urge and expectation as a new CEO to move fast to get rid of it. I didn't want to rush in and do something stupid. It reminds me of a Yogi Berra quote: "You don't want to make the wrong mistake." You're going to make mistakes, but don't make the wrong one! So, I approached this situation with care and a more collaborative, thoughtful approach. Collaborating is best approached like carpentry: measure three times and cut once.

After I realized that I couldn't sell the company because it showed such an enormous loss on the P&L, I started to talk with Jeff Arnold at Sharecare about a very different deal. The important message in this is that the way we came up with a solution demonstrates some of the most important parts of collaboration.

It's about looking at all areas. It's about listening to people. And I listened to the bankers. I listened to the tea leaves that were telling me, "You're not going to be able to sell the business." I listened to my customers who said, "Don't shut it down!"

It's taking a more careful approach and collaborating with input from multiple sources, and then being able to say, "It's not going to be all my way. There would need to be give and take."

It wasn't going to be easy for Jeff to say yes, because what he was about to acquire was a business that was losing money and had out-of-date technology. We started to talk about the need to collaborate with all the players involved, the need to keep all the employees, the need to continue serving all the business's long-time customers. We negotiated with Jeff Arnold the opportunity to give him the division that wasn't making money. Yes, give it to him, plus $25 million! In return, we got what was highly speculative stock and a commitment to keep our people and our customers.

There were detractors, and some who wanted me to push my own agenda only. Others thought I should be doing a better, more heroic deal. But collaboration at its best is recognizing that if you present your idea and then just listen to the thoughts and insights of somebody else (like a Jeff Arnold and your team), you can come up with ideas and solutions that are going to be absolutely powerful. You don't let yourself be driven by other people's biases or false conclusions; you remain open, learning and listening throughout, until you come to what may not be (and in this case, was not, at least in the beginning) an obvious conclusion.

I felt great about the outcome but nervous nonetheless about announcing it. I thought that the public markets would crucify me because a billion dollars had been wasted. But you know what? There wasn't any big reaction.

By the way, this story has an important postscript. At the time of this writing, the company announced it is going public on the NASDAQ at an estimated enterprise value of $3.9B, and Tivity Health will undoubtedly realize a significant gain from what everyone thought might be speculative stock in Sharecare. I knew Jeff, and I knew that, in time, he would turn the company around—and he has! I also knew that, in time, that stock we took, which my board felt was most likely worthless, was probably going to realize a genuinely nice gain. When Sharecare goes public and continues to grow, it could mean a pretty healthy return on the $25 million, especially considering that on day one of the deal we eliminated all losses from the company's P&L—there will be an actual gain on the stock in Sharecare.

Are You Laying the Right Foundation?

Compassionate culture and collaboration are not just a foundation for teams getting more work or better work done on a daily basis. They lay a foundation for greater creativity and innovation.

Similar to Project Aristotle, a study done by researchers from the University of Michigan in Ann Arbor found that empathy and kindness create psychological safety in sharing information, highlighting that the spirit of experimentation and innovation flourishes in a work culture of safety. Many of the topics covered in this book relate closely to why compassionate teams are more innovative.[8]

Let me be blunt: If you, like pre-survey Sakaguchi, are unaware of the realities your teams are living on a daily basis in the workplace, you need to ponder the following statistics and commentaries.[9]

Only twenty-nine percent of workers strongly agree that they are expected to be creative or think of new ways to do things at work, and only fifty-two percent of the twenty-nine percent say that they are given time daily to be creative.

If creativity is expressly required, workers will step up; otherwise not. Thirty-five percent of workers say that they are only given time to be creative a few times a year or less. Few managers schedule time for creativity, but scheduling it is what ensures that it happens. It is what shows that creativity is a cultural value to the organization and gives managers something tangible to measure.

Only eighteen percent of employees, or fewer than one in five, strongly agree that they can take risks at work that could lead to important new products, services, or solutions. First, risk aversion can make a company less competitive in the market and slow to adapt to operation innovations that boost productivity, increase profit, aid retention, and improve recruitment. Second, companies that discourage risk can create a climate of insecurity for their workers. Employees feel safe to reach further, and are more emotionally positive, when their managers encourage constructive risk-taking. Risk-taking is far more common in high-trust, compassionate cultures. People are more likely to go out on a limb and share what might be new or different ideas, and others will feel safe offering feedback that may make them better.

People who work where creativity is supported report higher levels of personal, team, and organizational performance, and they are less likely to say they're looking for another job. Pixar has long been mentioned as an example of creative culture. It achieves innovation and creativity through a compassionate culture, as its former president Ed Catmull explained in a 2008 *Harvard Business Review* article, "How Pixar Fosters Collective Creativity." He attributed the studio's success in creating a string of highly popular animated films to its "vibrant community where talented people are loyal to one another and their collective work. Everyone feels that they are part of something extraordinary, and their passion and accomplishments make the community a magnet for talented people coming out of schools or working at other places." Pixar is a great example of how trust, community, and shared mission result in greatness.[10]

Like Compassion, Art Is Best Cultivated in Community

One of the compassionate leaders interviewed for this book was Noah Greene, a similarly passionate artist and teacher. He expresses a beautiful view of community, creativity, and art.

Creative endeavors are often born of community or inspired by shared experience. Compassion allows trust, openness, vulnerability, and connectivity. As an artist, Noah explained: "Compassion, connection, and community can't exist in a vacuum. You have to be able to engage and to interact. This needs to involve more than one. Art is similar. I tell my students that art can't be made or expressed in a vacuum because there is a connection that happens when I make art. There's a conversation or a story. There's communication happening."

Noah expanded on the importance of community. "As humans we crave it or we get lost," he said. "If we didn't have community or connection of any kind, we would go completely crazy or not develop normally. When you look at children who are born in isolation, they have no ability to use language, they have no ability to really engage with the outside world after that, and they're completely lost to us. It can't happen by itself."

Expressing and sharing art builds community as well. There is a give and take, a communion around shared feeling or experience that art facilitates. "I always hope that an individual who has either interacted with me or my art will feel that connection," Noah said. Like Pixar or a community like Noah Greene's, developing and nurturing a culture of compassion results in creative expression and innovation. Sharing a passion around creating, innovating, and finding new solutions to problems, in turn, creates community. A beautiful and very fruitful, virtuous circle.

Move Over, Innovators

In any community or in any team, you have to strike the right balance between the innovators, artists, or geniuses and the rest of the group. Putting too much emphasis on too few in the group can lead to suboptimal results—people feeling left out or unheard or as if they are in a culture of competition.

When my first book came out, I was invited to Switzerland to speak at a university. There were maybe 500 students in the room. And I asked, "How many in this room want to be known as an innovator?" How many do you think raised their hands? Nearly all of them. Then I asked, "How many of you want to be known as an integrator?" Only a few raised their hands.

I think we've lived for too long under the notion of Steve Jobs and Bill Gates and other tech icons who have created a whole new generation of folks who think that if you're not innovating, you're not contributing. The picture we hold in mind of innovation seems to still be that of a lone genius coming up with a new thing all by themselves.

I think we have to be very careful not to overlook the importance of the rest of the team and the role of those who integrate those ideas and advances, because the all-team collaboration yields even better innovations than solo geniuses. I think we have to say, "Quit just rewarding the innovators. We need to make room for collaborators, too."

Turn Collaboration into "Collabovation"

As a leader, you have to aim for a balance between collaborating and innovating. You may have high-performing, mission-critical innovators on your team, but they need collaborators—it takes a village—to make sure that innovative ideas get improved, shaped, vetted, and implemented. I don't think about the process as collaboration in this case; I think it's about *collabovation*. This is the art of cultivating the conditions in which teams use collaborative skills that lead to innovation. This includes avoiding the pitfall of elevating stars on the team while failing to recognize the power of the whole group.

As leaders, there are a couple of dangers here. First, you'll need to recognize that, at any given time, you're going to have some geniuses who want to go it alone and push their innovative idea forward. They won't fully acknowledge that they need finance, marketing, sales, or human resources involved. Another danger of this thinking is that you may let one person forge on under the (false) assumption that they have enough specialized knowledge to consider every component, every permutation, every potential weak point or market challenge.

In fact, in a recent study that retroactively reviewed thousands of published academic papers, researchers found that *teams* were more innovative than *individuals* almost every time.[11]

So, when you focus on your people and set up your team, you must make sure that you're balancing the individual contributors and their value with the value of the collective team. When it comes to successful teams, the result of the collaboration is often greater than the sum of its parts or any one contributor alone. There is great value in those in the roles of critic, contributor, brainstormer, and supporter. The creative people in the room who share ten ideas a minute might get more attention in a discussion, but the quieter people who are assessing and synthesizing what they're hearing, who might see even bigger synergies or fatal flaws, are just as important. They will be just the ones you need to pay attention to the details and the process and correct for slippage, such as budget excesses or fast-approaching deadlines.

It's similar to a sport played in teams: You have a small number of strong individual players, but without the rest of the team to build plays, carry out strategies, and see the hole through which one of the strong individuals can run the touchdown, the stars won't even get to play.

I'm not saying not to reward the innovator. I think you need to give them plenty of support and praise. But when you start to move to the notion of innovation as more of a team sport than a solo-genius endeavor, you'll get even better results. Teams can be, and often are, collectively the innovators. That happens in a culture of collaboration.

END-OF-CHAPTER EXERCISES

HOW STRONG ARE YOUR TEAMS?

Do a Google-like evaluation of teams in your organization. The strength of your teams equates to the strength of your results.

1. Does your team share one common goal, or are there competing people or factions within it?

2. Do your team members speak equally in meetings, or do one or two people dominate the conversations?

3. Do team members want to help each other, or is there an everyone-for-themselves feeling?

4. Does your team have clear goals that everyone understands?

5. Does your team celebrate the innovators and idea people but not the facilitators, supporters, synthesizers, and integrators?

6. Do team members feel and express empathy for each other?

7. Does your team feel that what is being implemented reflects collective input?

Chapter 8

Harness the Power
of Differences

GREAT LEADERS KNOW SOMETHING that gives them a strategic advantage and increases employee morale, retention, productivity, and innovation: Great leaders know how to harness the power of differences in their organizations.

In part, this practice includes building, respecting, and celebrating the diversity and differences among team members. However, great leaders go a step further. They intentionally cultivate diverse teams and optimize their performance. It is not just their internal teams that are built to be diverse. It is the whole organization, including the board.

Diverse companies have proven to be stronger across many key measures, profitability included. Cultivating workplaces that are rich with different types of talented people is not only the right thing to do and the compassionate thing to do, but also a beneficial thing to do to support your people and boost your top-line revenues and bottom-line profits.

Diversity Has Many Dimensions

One's success is not built on similarities. Success is built on differences, and, in fact, the differences create a very strong foundation for measurable business success.

In organizations, these differences, this diversity, can be defined quite broadly. They might include the characteristics you are born with. These are called *inherent* characteristics: age, gender, race, ethnicity, sexual orientation, and personality type. There are many other characteristics that are important for well-functioning teams called *acquired* characteristics: a person's life experience, workplace expertise, industry knowledge/skills, cultural or linguistic background, education level and/or degrees, personal beliefs, and personal behaviors/attitudes.

Those inherent and acquired characteristics make up two-dimensional diversity.

Looking at diversity through this broad prism allows a leader to form highly functioning teams. In fact, according to an article in the *Harvard Business Review*, "Companies with two-dimensional diversity are forty-five percent more likely to report that they captured a larger portion of the market and seventy percent more likely to have entered into a new market in the past year."[1]

How does diversity impact the day-to-day operations of a business? Consider, for example, if a team tasked with creating a new technology product meant to appeal to a (younger) Generation Z market consisted of only white senior executives who have done dozens of product launches, supported by seasoned engineers and research-and-development professionals in their fifties. This team makeup would have both advantages and disadvantages. There may be benefit from their depth of experience. They might move faster if they've been through the process many times before. They could potentially avoid pitfalls they've learned about in the past. Perhaps they have high-level industry contacts built over time that benefit the project.

But what about the downsides of no diversity, or not being able to match your team composition to the composition of your market?

This team will be lacking in perhaps even a basic understanding of the targeted generation of customers and their needs, wants, and budget. What motivates this generation of buyers? Are they well-traveled, ethnically aware, linguistically talented? The list of things you cannot or don't know is daunting when you have a one-dimensional perspective. The older, less diverse team might miss important nuances of this market, which is much more diverse than the product team itself. Generation Z is not all Caucasian and of a fifty-plus age!

To resolve the issue and meet your customers where they are, you need team diversity. Diversity that better mirrors your market, your buyers, your patients, and your customers allows you to give them what they need and want—and lots of it.

It's critical to stay conscious of this goal of curating teams made up of different types of people. It starts with sharing and implementing the values of diversity and inclusion company-wide and reinforcing them regularly over time.

From a hiring standpoint, you have to cast a wide net to find more diverse applicants. You have to conduct interviews that are multidimensional. You can ask about technical expertise and experience, but it's also helpful to also ask people how they might respond in various situations to get a better sense of their philosophies or personality. I like to ask people about their why, about what motivates them, and about their life history, not just their work history. It's also absolutely essential to be conscious of your unconscious biases in the hiring process and in promoting from within. Yes, we *all* have them.

The Numbers Don't Lie

There is a strong business case for diverse teams, workplaces, and communities, and there has been for decades, but not all leaders pay more than lip service to the concept.

If you don't believe that mixing up, as it were, the composition of your various work teams is a valuable way to spend your time, consider just one aspect of diversity's impact on the bottom line, as demonstrated by Kevin O'Leary of TV's *Shark Tank* fame. He believes having women in charge is profitable.[2] He states that his preference for investing in companies founded and operated by women (all else being equal) is because they produce superior returns. Out of more than forty companies he invested in, about ninety-five percent of the women-led companies met their financial targets, compared with just sixty-five percent for businesses with male leaders.[3] Get women into your teams and into your hierarchy of leadership! Organizations with higher representation of women in C-suite positions have a thirty-four percent greater return to shareholders compared to organizations in which less than half of the leadership positions are held by women.[4]

Workplace diversity is an important factor, whatever your team's composition ends up being—and for sixty-seven percent of active job seekers, it helps them stay engaged and alleviates the age-old recruitment problem called employee turnover.[5]

Companies in the top quartile for higher-than-average racial and ethnic diversity and higher-than-average gender diversity are thirty-five percent and fifteen percent more likely, respectively, to have higher-than-average profits compared to similar companies without such diverse teams.

The McKinsey study Why Diversity Matters found that companies in the top quartile for gender-diverse executive suites were fifteen percent more likely to generate above-average profitability than those in the bottom quartile of companies, whose executive teams were predominantly white and male.[6]

When it comes to staffing, companies with higher proportions of racially and ethnically diverse employees have a thirty-five percent higher performance advantage over companies relying on a "culture fit" that tends to trend white and monocultural.

Clearly, diverse workforces drive performance and innovation better than those that are more homogeneous. Companies that created teams with a mix of genders and a range of professional talents and skills, educational and social backgrounds, and ethnicities and races had nineteen percent higher innovation revenues, according to a 2018 *Harvard Business Review* study.[7]

Diversity at Work Needs Work

Diversity is proven to drive success, yet it's woefully underutilized. It is hard to train for diversity. You just have to *do* diversity. A lack of diversity or a lack of inclusion, meaning treating and including every member of the team or group equally with respect and dignity, creates a negative culture and certainly takes away from compassionate culture. Compassion means *do it*, and you are the one who must show others the way.

A quick look at where we are today shows us that we have a long way to go to adopt more diversity. In a *Harvard Business Review* study, seventy-eight percent of employees stated that they work at organizations that lack diversity in leadership positions.[8]

In 2020's Fortune 500, there were only thirty-nine women CEOs, and only three of those were women of color. Women executives have been on the list only since 1972. In that same 2020 list, ninety percent of CEOs were Caucasian men. Among all US companies with 100 or more employees, the proportion of black men in management stayed flat, only moving from three percent to three and three-tenths percent between 1985 and 2014. Frankly, lack of diversity exists because the leaders are predominantly white men, and they are the ones hiring and promoting other white men.[9]

A majority of companies are not fully embracing the power of diverse workforces and are no doubt underperforming as a result.

I remember an encounter with a fellow CEO at a Fortune 50 company who was the antithesis of respectful, tolerant, and inclusive. After I voiced support for another executive, something he saw as too nice, he screamed at me that the only reason I was so supportive was because I was Catholic, Italian, and gay. Without getting into how unprofessional the comment was, it was clear as a bell that this very well-known CEO did not embrace diversity. He was obviously more comfortable with someone similar to his own traits, and that was not me.

The Familiarity-Breeds-Liking Effect

There is a psychological phenomenon that is often used in advertising called the exposure effect. Also referred to as the familiarity-breeds-liking effect, it describes the tendency for people to feel a greater liking for someone who looks similar to themselves. The more familiar that person seems, the more they are seen as being attractive and intelligent. In hiring, this is a cognitive bias that leaders should be aware of. If you're not intentional and conscious about this, you will have a tendency to hire people who are just like you. This can result in decreased diversity and weaker teams.

There is a positive flip side to the exposure effect, however. This was demonstrated in a somewhat odd but telling experiment done by Charles Goetzinger, a professor at Oregon State University, back in 1968. The researchers asked one student to come to class every week in a large black bag with only his feet visible. At first, the rest of the students were suspicious of this strange behavior, treating the student in the bag with hostility. They avoided engaging with the student in the bag. But, over time, the student became familiar, even a little intriguing compared to the rest of the class, and eventually the students interacted with him in the same way they did with one another. What does this translate to in a company setting? The more a company or a leader hires for diversity, and the more different types of workers join their organization, the more the rest of the company will accept this as what a workplace should look like. You don't talk about diversity. You must *do* diversity.

Diverse teams and diversity among managers at all levels creates a wealth of ideas and a depth and breadth of perspectives and expertise. Hire your direct reports to bring competencies and perspectives that you don't have.

I am a huge fan of the Myers-Briggs personality test, but use any test (DISC assessments, EQ assessments, there are many options on the market). Administering such assessments disciplines me to make sure that I hire intentionally from a diverse personality standpoint.

We don't want to only hire people who agree with us or who approach decision-making from the same mindset. Regarding personalities, I come across as assertive, but that's usually a result of passion for what I do. Actually, and according to my Predictive Index profile, I am not a naturally dominant leader, so it helps me to have others on my team who are more outspoken or direct. Regarding skill sets, I know many CEOs, myself included, who did not come up from a deep financial background, so hiring a very strong CFO in those cases is essential. Regarding tech versus creative work, highly logical thinkers who excel as technical leaders may want some complementary personalities around them who are more intuitively creative ideas people. Then, as far as age and gender, someone like me, a white man in his sixties, certainly benefits from having people around him of different genders, generations, races, and even national origins. Not only does that bring many perspectives, it also better represents the nation we live in and our real customer base.

What about the People Who Don't Embrace Diversity?

Companies have to fully adopt the view that diversity is mission critical. The values and practices set from the top have to include and reflect this. Put the data and the statistics (which have not changed much over the past forty years—about how long most very senior executives have been in the workforce) in front of your all-white, all-male, all-one-generation leaders, and fill future senior openings with the highest talent available of any gender, any age, and any race and ethnicity with any varied and transferable industry experience who fulfills the criteria of the position. All it might take is your company's own black bag experiment. Again, it is a just-*do*-diversity exercise.

From an individual standpoint, in addition to the education and adoption of diversity as a value, it's a mindset change for us all. You cannot change an individual's mindset by decree, and that is often why today's diversity training courses and inclusion and diversity rules just don't work.

Leadership evolves, thus it does not follow a cemented blueprint for the rest of your life. If you're going to assume a leadership position, just like doctors and dentists, who frequently have to get continuing medical education, or engineers, who need to keep up with their certifications, all leaders, too, must grow. It's essential, as you're entrusted with the development and well-being of other people. I have a poster in my office in Nashville to remind me of this fact: "When you are through developing, you're through."

Your growth as a leader means you are not married to one plan, one way of doing things, one product for life, one type of personnel, one type of customer, one type of tool, or one style of management. Your evolution is dictated by outside change, but also by your willingness to undertake internal growth. There is a vast and fascinating world of people and talent out there: Bring it into your business!

What Starts at the Top Can't Stay at the Top

I want to share a big caution to senior managers. Make sure that the positive values shared at the senior level are flowing through the organization. I have said this elsewhere and that's because it is so vital to get right. Your company's values must be not just the values held by your C-suite, but also the values held by every single person it employs. The only way everyone shares values is to communicate them, talk about their meaning, live them daily, and keep demonstrating them in the organization.

I've seen time and time again how CEOs and leaders convey their values to those who report directly to them, and perhaps broadly at company meetings. Then they assume those values are being reinforced throughout the organization at every level. I invite you to assume, from now on, that they're not.

In our workplace survey research, we saw significant gaps between what leaders think they are conveying or what they believe the company is doing, what their middle managers are experiencing, and what their entry-level teams are experiencing.

I saw it in my own experience when I did a company-wide employee survey at Tivity Health. I asked if employees experienced any bullying in the company. I was honestly shocked to learn that twenty percent of our company's employees said they were being or had been bullied in the workplace. There I was, a CEO talking about respect and inclusion, while bullying was happening within my own teams! It was a sobering moment indeed.

I learned that many people were feeling the same way in companies all over the country. Close to thirty percent of adult Americans say they are bullied at work. *That's seventy-six million US workers.* This awareness led me to fund a workplace dignity program with the Robert F. Kennedy Human Rights Foundation. It was clear to me that this was an issue that needed to be addressed.

The Robert F. Kennedy Human Rights Foundation had already been a very big champion of ending bullying in high schools and had educated five to seven million students on what bullying looks like and how to stop bullying. I decided to partner with them and fund the creation of the RFK Human Rights Workplace Dignity Program through the Tramuto Foundation.

What triggers bullying in an adult workforce? Being gay when coworkers are not. Being brown when coworkers are not. Being a woman "in a man's world." Being foreign. Being outspoken. Being shy. Holding a degree. Not holding the right degree. Employees from underrepresented backgrounds and marginalized groups of society may be even more likely to experience treatment that compromises their dignity at work. The list could be endless—*if we let it be so.*

Bullying is the opposite of being respectful. Build respect.

Work is a key source of meaning in our lives, and it's where we spend most of our time. Therefore, it's a major lever of dignity. But despite the aspirational and value statements organizations may issue, what employees feel is often quite disconnected from what senior leaders believe to be true about their organization's culture. Often *dignity* is written into value statements or codes of conduct but is not put into action on most levels.

Dignity Is the Common Denominator

RFK Human Rights senior vice president Jeffrey Siminoff shared how dignity is an overarching concept when it comes to building inclusive, respectful workplaces. "Dignity is our inherent value and worth," he said. "It is our common denominator. It underlies human-rights work around the world. And human rights do not end when people enter the workplace, where most people spend at least one-third of their lives."

Dignity is foundational and needs to be expressed and honored through specific day-to-day actions and behaviors and through structural interventions from the hiring process to the moment the employment relationship ends. Ensure that all workplaces—whatever the type (office, manufacturing, service, etc.)—are, in the words of the United Nations Declaration of Human Rights, "just and favorable." If they are not, productivity suffers, employee engagement and retention drop, personal relationships are harmed, and polarization in the world around us can take unfettered root at work.

Organizations can close the gap by prioritizing the dignity of their employees—their inherent value and worth—both in the day-to-day actions and behaviors of their managers and other leaders and more structurally through organization-wide processes and policies (like recruiting, onboarding, communication, benefits, and more). Our work at RFK Human Rights provides tools for change in each of these areas, fostering a new understanding of the workplace in which all can thrive.

Jeffrey further explains how this concept evolves as our workplace evolves. "This goes for the physical workplace, the remote or virtual workplace, or the interrupted workplace for people on a leave," he said. "And while honoring dignity urgently matters during times of great stress and crisis, as the COVID-19 pandemic and repetitive cycles of domestic racism have taught us, its importance doesn't fade away during day-to-day experiences in more predictable times, for in those moments, we establish the anchors and roots of workplace culture foundations that guide us when we face deeper, unexpected challenges. In fact, it may even become more urgent as we see the ways in which long preexisting inequalities[10] (whether in the United States or elsewhere) can become more entrenched and exacerbated and come into sharper focus."

Compassion toward Those with Whom You Have Differences

Some of the biggest differences you'll find among people are not just the outward differences such as their age, race, gender, or foreign accent, but also their attitudes, opinions, and interpersonal styles. It's important to model respectful interactions and engagement around differences regardless of their origin. Compassion is key here. It lays the groundwork for respectful and open communication through empathy and trust.

A first step in respectfully navigating differences is making sure to be very conscious of the fact that there is a lot we don't know about other people. The first question we often have about someone is, "Why isn't he/she more like *me*?" That might make you laugh, but when we complain about someone else, the complaint comes from the perception that the other person is not like you and . . . should be!

Everyone has had experiences—good and bad—that led them to where they are now, to their opinions and reactions in any situation they face today. Approaching others with compassion and empathy allows us to understand that there is usually a reason a person is acting as they are or holding an opposing view. It's not up to us to try to change their view all the time, or immediately, but it is up to us to try to understand them. This opens the door to a conversation. It gives us the opportunity to learn from each other, find common ground, and then move forward together.

Look for Commonalities

As a journalist, an entrepreneur, and business leader, Katie Couric has a wide lens on differences and divisions in society, which show up in all of the environments in which we work together. Katie looks for ways to seek commonalities with people who disagree with one another. During our conversation, she said, "Somehow we've forgotten our common humanity and the things that we have in common. If you ask the average American, 'What do you care about?' I think they largely agree. They care about their families. They care about helping their neighbors. They care about health. They care about their children being healthy and happy and educated. Everybody cares about those things.

"We've never been quite this tribalistic, where we've gone to our respective corners. In a weird way, I think it has to do with our desire to connect, to feel a part of something. And so you pick the team you want to be a part of, or the ideology you want to be a part of. It's so 101, or basic, that you can't generalize about people, and yet that seems to now be our default position. I believe you find common ground with people by acknowledging them, by seeing them, by appreciating where they are, and maybe their disappointments and their 'dreams deferred,' as Langston Hughes would say. We don't seem to be listening, and we've lost our ability to empathize with people. So, I think the first thing for bringing people together is understanding, appreciating, and acknowledging other people's pain.

"After the shooting in 1999 at Columbine High School, I had an interview with a black father whose son was killed and with a young white kid whose sister was killed. They were brought together by circumstances and held hands during the interview, and it was profoundly moving to see such raw emotion. They reached out because they needed each other. They reached out to each other because of their shared grief. But the world has become so black and white, literally and figuratively.

"Why can't I care deeply about police brutality and the fact that black men are profiled and subject to traffic stops and shootings at a disproportionate rate but also have empathy and sympathy for police officers, who are trying to do their job but perhaps haven't gotten the right training? We feel like we have to choose between one or the other, have to be pro-police or pro–Black Lives Matter. Why can't I say both of these things? 'I want the police to do a better job, and by the way, I appreciate them, because they put their lives on the line every day to protect us. And, I want to make sure that black people in America are afforded every opportunity their white counterparts are.' I feel like we have to make these false choices, and I think we need leaders to help bridge that divide. I think that's where compassion comes in. You feel compassion for everyone involved in a problem, and as much as compassion, *respect*—we have to respect one another. I think that's where we need compassionate leadership.

"I'm writing a book now, and recently I wrote about the fact that I interviewed the Central Park jogger [the victim of the famous 1989 assault and rape case], but I didn't do a story on the boys who spent all that time in prison and didn't commit the crime. Through my own lens and my own circumstances, I'm drawn to stories that too often reflect *my* experience. And I think we have to get out of our comfort zones and understand other people's experiences much better, which is hard. You have to understand your own implicit bias. Why you have a certain reaction. I try to stop and step back and think, *Wait a second. Why am I reacting or thinking a certain way?* And I think that we all need to do that more to appreciate our own cultural conditioning and circumstances that have made us think and act a certain way."

There Are No Winners or Losers

One of the most fundamental and perspective-changing views that our compassionate leaders embrace is the idea that there are no winners or losers. So many of us view the world through a competitive lens that ends up pitting one against another. This is often the source of conflict or disrespect at work. Compassionate leaders understand that this view—a view that so many of us carry around, sometimes subconsciously because it is deeply ingrained in our culture—is wrong.

St. Joseph's College president Jim Dlugos, mentioned in chapter one, articulated this lesson well. "Too much of the world is organized into winners and losers," he said. "It's seen as a zero-sum game, in which for someone to win, someone else has to lose. You know that is a huge problem in terms of how we organize our understanding of things. There can be more joy. There can be more happiness. There can be more success in the world. We can actually grow the pie higher, to build on an old political phrase. This notion that we only have so much and we've got to fight for it is just wrong."

In our workplace research, we saw that eighty-five percent of workers believe that a compassionate workplace leads to cooperation, which in turn leads to higher productivity and profits. Yet a whopping seventy-three percent of senior leaders saw the workplace as more competitive than cooperative. This is a frightening finding. This means that this "truth" they hold becomes a lens through which they view the workplace. This lens may be unconsciously and negatively impacting how they react to or treat their colleagues and employees. In a dramatic contrast, our compassionate leaders had the opposite view. Only twenty-three percent saw their workplace as competitive. This is not surprising, as this view is closely aligned with compassionate leadership.

Leaders who act from a place of compassionate leadership more naturally cultivate a culture of cooperation among individuals of diverse experience and background. The top performer is not the only one on a team to get praise; entire teams get praise for staying the course to some great outcome. The person who is the most outspoken in a room is not the only one who is listened to; the quiet ones are solicited and also heard with equal attention.

Living these cooperative values every day tamps down the competitive forces that cause division and infighting and allows teams to be more collaborative and more supportive of an open exchange of ideas and information. Every member of a very diverse organization makes a contribution that has deep value and brings its mission to life.

END-OF-CHAPTER EXERCISES

DIVERSITY REPORT CARD

Get a baseline on where your team or organization currently stands with regard to diversity. After you have a baseline, set goals for moving toward more diversity where you need to—with specific goals and dates attached. This should include a broad set of metrics, such as:

- race

- gender

- age

- technical expertise

- experience/background

Chapter 9

Great Leaders Are Great Listeners

W E OFTEN USE THE TERMS *hearing, listening,* and *understanding* interchangeably. But compassionate leaders know the critical differences between these activities, and they behave accordingly. To make decisions based on complete information or data, to act on and not react to issues, to interact authentically with those around you, and to take appropriate and effective action, it's important to understand the distinctions between the three components of receptive communication and how they work together. Then, you need to put them into practice.

1. **Hearing** is the simple perceiving of sound. It doesn't take any action on the part of the person hearing. They just need to be within earshot of the sound. This aspect of the skill set is one-way only. It is passive.

2. **Listening** involves action. Listening is hearing something with thoughtful attention. A good listener is involved in conversation with committed participation. The difference between hearing and listening is the difference between a *versation*, or a one-way monologue, and a *conversation*.

Conversation, by definition, can never be just one-way or solo, but is necessarily two-way or multi-way. It is active.

3. **Understanding** requires thoughtful attention with some empathy and inquiry added. To understand, you must ask relevant questions and build as complete and accurate a picture as possible through reconfirmation of information shared. This is, again, a two-way or multi-way interaction. It is active and interactive.

From now on, when you are asked to listen or ask others to do so, incorporate these three components for better and more compassionate outcomes. There are significant benefits to learning to combine the three skills and to cultivating a team that not only understands the importance of them but also practices them with everyone.

Active, skilled listening makes employees feel respected. Actively seeking to fully understand makes people feel heard and empathized with, which allows leaders to strengthen relationships and drive engagement. When employees feel heard, they feel valued, which allows leaders to respond to employees in a meaningful, appropriate way and make employees feel cared for. It allows both leaders and staff members to build and participate in stronger teams that produce better ideas. Exercising these three skills will make leaders better decision makers, better problem solvers, and better at motivating and engaging their workers. This threefold practice builds trust among individuals, trust that they are heard and understood, and that you believe in their contribution and importance to the team.

We All Need to Be Understood

Feeling seen and heard, listened to, and understood is a deep and fundamental human need. It helps us feel safe, that we are in a safe tribe. It helps us feel approval, acceptance, and belonging. As social creatures, the act of someone listening and understanding us is validation, a recognition of belonging and of our value. Having someone take the time to really pay attention to us, especially if they listen with empathy and understanding, forms a connection called *membership*. We belong. We are part of a community and are valued and empowered.

However, I have long implemented the advice from Stephen Covey's book, *The 7 Habits of Highly Effective Leaders*, to "seek first to understand, then to be understood."

Listening seems like such a basic human skill. Shouldn't we all be doing it well by the time we join the workforce? You might think so, but in many places and interactions, the answer is no. In engagement surveys across industries, employees rate the feeling that they're not being listened to as one of the top reasons they become disengaged. In one poll of professional workers in the United States and Canada, sixty-four percent of those polled agreed that their biggest problem was "leaders making decisions without seeking input."[1] That translates as leaders who do not hear, listen, and understand those on their teams with the knowledge, data, concerns, resolutions, and innovative ideas.

Compassionate and conscious companies that have high engagement have mastered a culture of active listening, understanding, and taking the necessary time to understand the issues. In a recent study,[2] Salesforce Research surveyed more than 1,500 business professionals on values-driven leadership, and they discovered that a person is more than four times more likely to feel empowered to perform to the best of their abilities if they feel listened to and understood.

Compassionate leadership inspires compassionate listening. This starts with a willingness to hear and sincerely connect to the other person's story, and then really listening, which incorporates empathy and moves to true understanding. Understanding leads to aligned action, action that is informed by understanding and is in sync with the real, nuanced, and sometimes complex communication we're receiving or situations we're responding to.

Sometimes we're faced with situations in which we need to listen to those with whom we don't have a lot in common. For example,

I grew up in a household with athletic siblings; however, the only athletic ability I have is jumping to conclusions. All humor aside, I am not an athletically inclined person, yet my brothers definitely were. My older brother, who was killed in a car accident at the tender age of twenty-three, was voted one of the top ten best college basketball players in New York State. My twin brother and other older brother were both successful college basketball coaches. While I was not gifted in this sport, I took the time to listen to them talk about their passion, stories about winning and losing, and what skills were needed to become a great basketball player. This active listening kept us close, despite my lack of connection to their experiences. If we don't make these efforts, a diminishing sense of connection to the stories that make others relevant is indeed creating a generation of lonely people. No doubt distracting technology that prevents one from truly listening to the stories of others makes this worse.

Another study looked at how workplace culture in North America, Europe, and Asia-Pacific countries affected engagement. They found that fifty-five percent of respondents didn't feel their opinions mattered to their bosses![3] These statistics make it clear that an unwillingness to hear, a lack of listening, and a resulting lack of understanding is contributing to disengagement. Low engagement means weak performance.

There are serious downsides when this threefold skill is not adopted by leaders. Let's take one example that illustrates what can happen in a conversation if a manager is first, not willing to hear, and second, not fully listening. Perhaps the manager is stressed and busy and rushing through each day. If, when an employee describes an issue they are having on the job to the manager, the manager is a lazy or distracted listener, they may only hear some of the facts without understanding the full situation. To speed things along, the manager might quickly make a connection to similar situations they have recently experienced, make a few assumptions, and skip straight to forming their opinion on the right course of action. They might give guidance on how to solve the problem, but, because they stopped listening midway (or sooner!) through the employee's sharing, when the manager formed that quick opinion, the chances are good that they got part of it wrong. Or even all wrong. This will result in the employee not feeling heard, being given ineffective advice, or, worse, being directed to implement a solution that is either not the best way forward or even worsens the original issue. This can also undermine the trust or respect the employee has for the manager, and might I suggest that is probably the one clear outcome to not skillfully connecting with the employee!

This scene occurs millions of times a day in corporate America and in interactions among people everywhere.

From Hearing to Healing

A common example of not being listened to is one that many of us have experienced in a doctor's office. We've all had the experience of going to the doctor and feeling rushed out as fast as possible. Sometimes the physician doesn't even make eye contact. As someone who goes to the doctor frequently, I know what it's like when a doctor isn't listening. It doesn't feel good to interact with a doctor who doesn't fully see or listen to us, especially when we are already feeling vulnerable or worried about our health.

I mentioned earlier my doctor and friend Dr. John Seibert of Vanderbilt University School of Medicine. As a compassionate leader, he is another kind of physician. When I interact with him as his patient, it's like he is not in a hurry at all, like he has all day to listen to me. He understands the importance of listening both for the positive effect it has on human emotion and for better outcomes.

In our interview, he explained that listening can have special import in his profession. "I always try to make patients feel that I'm really listening," he said. "I do spend a lot of time with each patient and actually some patients get angry, because sometimes I end up an hour behind. The system is made to go, go, go. We have ten-minute slots for each patient. I look at my schedule and kind of laugh like, 'All right, well, we'll get done whenever we get done.' My nurses feel the same way. There is a quote, 'The greatest need for a patient is not to be healed, but to be *heard.*' I really believe that healing includes being listened to and acknowledged. When I was learning medicine, in my residency, I was trying to figure out all the science, the pathology, the technical side of things. And when I got into practice, I realized, 'I'll see patients, and really what they want me to do is just allow them to tell me about what's going on.' And for them, that was a healing process."

Listening and understanding also makes for a more skilled physician. "I think what happens then is I understand them," John continued, "and sometimes that will lead to a better diagnosis. For example, a patient will tell me, 'I had this pain for a little bit in my neck.' And in my mind, I might jump to the most common reason for the pain, something common, not very serious. But, when you really listen, you might realize something about what they're telling you makes you want to explore that further. I'll see ten patients with the same kind of pain that's not a big deal. And after a while, you're sort of on autopilot. But then you realize that maybe that tenth patient has cancer, and that is not uncommon. So, it's not only making an emotional impact, but a physical one. That makes you a better physician."

John also reflected on the benefits that come back to him. "It's getting harder and harder to find enough time with each patient with the demands that are on us," he said. "I don't want to rush through the day without the real human interaction. I would feel like a machine. Honestly, I go to work some days and I'm so tired. I look at my schedule a bit overwhelmed, and I think, *Oh, my gosh, this is a lot of patients.* But then, by the end of the day I think, *Wow, that was awesome. I got to talk to people. I had the privilege of being part of people's lives.* I get to ask questions that most people don't get to ask. I'm honored to be here. I'm honored to do that."

The connections that form with listening strengthen relationships and allow for better decisions. Participative listening and connecting also benefits the listener just as much.

There are several keys to active listening that I have long believed are critical. I categorize these into two types: best practices, and pitfalls, or red flags, to avoid.

The Best Practices of Listening

The best-practice category of these secrets to successful listening involves proactive things you can do to cultivate the discipline of good listening. These also include steps to take to make sure you turn that listening into understanding.

1. STAY FOCUSED AND PRESENT

First, commit to being not 100 percent present but 110 percent present when you're listening to someone speak, because it's easy to get distracted. The ten points above the 100 percent means you are practicing self-awareness, discipline, and intention. Aside from making that conscious commitment, one way to do this is to make sure to carve out enough time to have real conversations, especially if it's important. In a group setting, never rush the speaker. Allow them to finish their thought fully before moving on to the next person or giving your own response.

Leadership guru Simon Sinek takes it a step further and encourages leaders to "be the last to speak." This sets the stage for everyone to be heard, to get all the contributions from the group, and it models respectful listening. It's also an advantage in that you learn the opinions of others before you give yours.

2. ASK QUESTIONS—LOTS OF QUESTIONS!

Be curious. Approach listening as an opportunity to learn. Asking questions gives the person talking a chance to express themselves fully, and it should lead to better information and better understanding. Asking questions helps you get clarity, making sure that you don't walk away thinking that you know what the other person meant when, in fact, you may not. The questions you might ask often naturally evolve from the conversation, but even simple open-ended questions can help. For example, you might ask, "Is there anything else I should know that I didn't specifically ask you about?" While the answer to this is often no, I've heard some surprising things as a result of this question. Not only do the questions themselves yield information that can lead to better understanding, but also the process of asking them helps you be more engaged.

Stefano Lucchini, the RFK Human Rights Foundation of Italy chairman I mentioned earlier, champions the practice of asking himself questions in addition to asking others. He explains: "Before making decisions or speaking about the issues that I'm dealing with, I listen to others. Listening is central to compassion, as compassion involves doing others the service of attempting to understand. I anchor myself by thinking through a set of questions, such as, *What are they experiencing now in their life?* This helps with context. *How might they deal with the problems we are discussing?* This helps me understand what they might contribute. *Is it possible to do what we are discussing in another way?* This helps me think laterally. All of these questions place me in a position of using compassion, a sincere desire to understand how others are thinking. I firmly believe that doing so makes for better decisions, better communication, and better outcomes."

3. LISTEN WITH EMPATHY

One of the questions Stefano mentioned is, "What are they experiencing now in their life?" With empathy, you perceive information through that person's experience, in a more subjective manner. Do this in addition to hearing the information in a more objective manner. This is core to cultivating empathy in the listening process. The speaker will sense that you are being both objective to facts or data presented and subjective to her point of view about them. Combining both perspectives rounds out the understanding you end up with.

Empathy will always lead to better understanding for the listener in addition to making the speaker feel understood.

4. PAY ATTENTION TO BODY LANGUAGE: NONVERBAL ANALYSIS IS MORE POWERFUL THAN WORD ANALYSIS

My favorite philosopher, Yogi Berra, once said: "You can observe a lot by just watching." Listening involves more than just spoken words. Never underestimate what is being expressed by the body language that accompanies spoken words. Does the body support or contradict the words being spoken? Is the speaker saying yes while shaking their head no? Are their arms crossed? Are they tapping their foot with impatience, or are they leaning forward with open posture and making eye contact?

Reading body language is a particularly well-honed skill for me, after so many years of not being able to hear. I think this is why I've been so good with nonverbal listening, but I know anyone can learn to read the body's meanings. You can add immensely to your understanding of what is being said by watching a person's nonverbal cues, their movement, and the way they look at you (or do not). This is a much greater intensity of involvement, because now you are watching somebody as well as listening to their words.

5. CONFIRM WHAT YOU HEARD

Once you've done the work of points one through four, you still have to make sure that you got the speaker's meaning and information right, that you and they share the same understanding. If they say, "No, you got it wrong," ask more questions to clarify. If you fail to confirm, you may (and many leaders do) end up acting on incorrect assumptions. Repeat back what you think you heard often, to confirm it. This is a fundamental communication technique that will most often remove any chance that you get it wrong. Saying, "If I understood correctly . . ." also serves to bolster the other person's trust in you as someone they can speak to and be heard correctly by, and that you value their input enough to get it right. And do not be embarrassed to admit you got it wrong. You may discover your admission of missing the mark convinces the other person that you are actively listening.

Beware of Communication Red Flags

Untrained or hurried leaders commit three costly communication mistakes that can be avoided with a bit of awareness and practice:

1. PASSIVE LISTENING

Passive listening is listening half-heartedly—or worse, pretending to listen while your mind is really somewhere else. It is also listening as just one of several other simultaneous tasks you are performing. Then, it cannot be considered proper hearing, listening, and understanding at all, but rather only (if you are lucky) hearing.

We do this because we are distracted or have mentally and energetically checked out. We are only doing the first part—hearing—and not engaging in true listening and real understanding.

This leads to a lot of missed information and misunderstanding, and is certainly noticed as lack of interest and attention by the person speaking.

Put the phone facedown. Set it on "do not disturb." Close the office door. Adopt the mantra, "Do one thing at a time and do it fully." Make eye contact with the speaker. I have never been convinced that anyone can multitask by answering emails on their phones while attempting to actively listen. Try it! You receive an unwanted email during your conversation and immediately the disturbing news derails you from understanding what the other person was trying to communicate to you. This leads to one and only one outcome: communication malpractice!

2. DON'T LISTEN TO REPLY, LISTEN TO UNDERSTAND

Another common issue that we all experience is starting out listening and, before the communication has been fully conveyed, starting to think about what our response will be. Our brain has moved out of hearing–listening–understanding mode and into future-response mode.

In his aforementioned book, Dr. Stephen Covey writes, "Most people do not listen with the intent to understand; they listen with the intent to reply." Like passive or distracted listening, this also leads to the possibility that you will not truly get to real understanding.

A more negative version of this is when a leader experiences a feeling of defensiveness because they don't like what they are hearing, even before they have heard the speaker out completely. In this case, they might start to form arguments in their mind or discount what they are hearing before the speaker finishes their statement. This is a big problem. It not only leads to poor communication between the two but also to divisiveness between them as they move in to defend their position. You've probably experienced this: you might have been talking to someone when, in the middle of what you were saying, they crossed their arms or frowned. It changes the entire tone of the conversation.

3. BECOME CONSCIOUS OF BIASES

These examples of pitfalls may be in the category of biased listening. This is a big trap that is often subconscious and usually has negative outcomes. This can include any situation in which the listener applies his or her own views, biases, or assumptions while listening. That is why the third skill, understanding, is so vital. It is why, when you say, "As I understood you, you meant that . . ." and the speaker says you were wrong, you remain open and committed to understanding them and their full statements, rather than trying to convince them that you are right.

To Prevent Bias

I'm an example of someone who has experienced biases from others about their leadership ability. You already know that I have a hearing loss. I think there is an interpretation on the part of some that "Donato may not be hearing everything we say" or "Donato may not be as sharp as everybody else because of his handicap." This is how an assumption made based on one element about someone ("Donato has hearing loss") creates a bias ("Donato is not as smart as he thinks he is")! Such biases can be applied to a handicap of any kind ("This guy is probably not as competent as a whole-bodied person"). I feel like a bit of a different breed because I've had to live with those biases, but luckily, I'm more conscious now of my own biases toward others because of it.

Other examples of bias are age-focused. Some people are of the opinion that members of the elderly population are not able to work as hard as younger people. On the other hand, some people might believe that members of the younger generation don't have enough life experience to deal with complex issues. Certainly there are many biases when it comes to race, ethnicity, sexual orientation, and so on.

First of all, you have to become aware of the bias or biases you evoke in others. Then, you can better look outward and say to yourself, *I'd better be careful about bias with this person.* What I've learned is that a lot of people are not even aware of biases.

You have to have an organizational structure that has built teams that dare to speak up and challenge you on your misinterpretations of a situation, be it because of an implicit bias you haven't acknowledged or because you have not unfolded the hear–listen–understand strategy to its full extent.

I have disciplined myself to receive training to ensure that I'm not bringing my implicit biases to the table. I do think a focus on how to identify and back away from bias is vital in communications training. I've always said the reason we have workplace bullying is because we bring our respective biases to the workplace and do nothing but react to others based on them. Now, I may be wrong, but I don't think somebody wakes up and says, "Today's the day that I'm going to ruin the boss's (or whoever's) life by acting on my ingrained biases." I don't think that happens. I think that we are the carriers of our forebears' influence on us, and just like we inherit our parents' money when they die, we also inherit what we learned from them through observation starting from the time we were toddlers.

In other words, those biases are created in us from our earliest upbringing, and we have lived with them so long that we don't recognize them for what they are. Or, we form these biases based on certain life experiences. Formal training wakes up our awareness and starts the process of undoing the unwanted habits of bias; acting on the new awareness is next. It takes time and attention, but new habits can be formed.

We move back to empathy, as the more developed your empathy skills, the more you're going to hear, listen with a compassionate lens, and try to understand fully and correctly what a speaker is feeling and experiencing.

Be Careful of Solo Decision-Making

As a leader, I choose not to let decision-making fall into the realm of a single person. That can potentially create more opportunity for bias.

If you want to have a program that reaches those who are in the minority population, the decision-making should not be left to one person. That individual's bias may enter the equation, with him asking himself, *Why should that minority person be given preferential treatment? They should work just as hard as we do.* That's one person's bias. Instead, decision-making should belong to a diverse team of individuals, including some with a horse in the race and some with no direct interest in it. This helps ensure a better-rounded strategy (e.g., curriculum) for any program intended to reach the minority population.

Organizations have to model through example how decisions should not be governed by any person's or even any team's specific bias (including a bias that might be specific to the board of directors or C-suite), but should instead be founded on facts, wide-ranging perspectives, and the observations of many.

Bias comes in part from not being willing to hear others, to listen to them, and then to fully and accurately understand their conveyed meanings. Bias comes from a leader assuming that others don't have anything to add to a topic. Bias comes from a leader believing that there is no need to have a conversation or to seek out others' input because an issue seems clear. Seek the input, conversations, and commentary of a diverse range of people. You will very likely surprise yourself as you become aware of how your personal biases have colored your understanding of circumstances and led to deep *mis*understanding.

Leverage All Inputs

One of the compassionate leaders interviewed for this book is Kurt Small, senior vice president and CEO of the government business division at Anthem, Inc. One thing I have observed about Kurt is that he is a very skillful listener. This may stem in part from his overall inclusive and compassionate mindset, but his focus on listening and inviting multiple inputs is critical to true understanding, especially in a complex industry like health care.

Kurt practices this in any process. He described listening to his customers: "In my business, we have multiple customers. We have not only Medicare or Medicaid beneficiaries but also state customers or state partners, and we're working with the broader Medicare program. To make sure we are always in sync and in alignment with our customers, it really starts with listening and leveraging all of the inputs we have to understand our customer. That reaches all the way from customer service to research, and involves engaging with the customer, observing the customer and their buying patterns, and, if something doesn't go as expected and we receive a complaint, how we understand that. So it's a constant focus on trying to integrate as much information or data as we can to get a holistic view of the customer."

Kurt makes such a good point about making sure to get your understanding right for the sake of the customer, and making sure to update your understanding as their situations change. "The customer expects us to deliver on our commitment," he said. "But they want to make sure we're listening to them, because their needs change. When a customer is trying to understand how a claim was ultimately adjudicated or a benefit was paid on their behalf or to secure care during a very challenging time, both very important things, the customer can ask you to engage in different ways on that, and that's why I think the listening is really important."

Turn Listening into Action

It's essential to follow listening with an action. Sometimes that is quite naturally the next step. For instance, if an employee asks their manager a simple question, "Can you help me prioritize my work?" the manager is likely to respond, "Sure, come back in at 2:10 this afternoon, and we'll work on it together." If the question is, "When is this assignment due, boss?" providing that date and time is often the only action needed.

But what if an employee makes a recommendation, or shares an idea with you, or asks you a question you're not sure you know how to answer? Immediate action is not always what you can provide. You might tell your employee that you'll get back to him later. This is commonly where a disconnect occurs. Imagine an employee comes to you and suggests a new initiative that they believe has merit. They provided their rationale and some details. You might find it somewhat interesting, yet you don't think it's good enough or fits your criteria for success (notice the instant application of bias). You also don't want to hurt their feelings (notice the empathy reflex). So you say in a sort of negligent, passing manner, "Great idea, I'll get back to you on that." No specific day or time. No suggested process for moving through it with them. You have already moved on. You quickly forget it. You've dropped that ball. You never get a group together to brainstorm the pros and cons of the suggestion. You never go back to tell the person how you really feel about the suggestion and why. This is a sure path to disengagement. In fact, it is indicative of your own disengagement!

On one hand, this is about a failure to hear, listen, and understand. On the other hand, it is about a feedback failure. Most employees prefer negative feedback right away to no feedback at all. In an IBM survey,[4] eighty-three percent of employees said they were open to participating in employee listening programs, such as employee surveys. But only thirty-eight percent of baby boomers and twenty-two percent of millennials thought their bosses would ever actually act on their feedback. If you're not taking action on the feedback you get, you're not actually listening to your employees. In fact, you may not even be in hearing mode, let alone listening and understanding mode.

To turn hearing, listening, and understanding into action: make sure you respond with a due date (for yourself and/or the other person); mark the calendar for your own follow-up when that deadline has arrived; alternatively, finish the loop yourself by going to the person with a process, a decision, or preferably, more questions that put you squarely in understanding mode. Listen some more, understand accurately and deeply. Confirm that your understanding matches the employee's positions. Only when you take action—be it for or against the individual's issue—will your decision garner respect. The other person thinks, *Ah, okay, that's not the decision I would have preferred or expected, but he asked me a lot of questions and got a team together to discuss other points of view. Hats off. He respected my suggestion.* Trust in you is intact or even deepened.

Understanding Can Lead to Improvements and Innovation

Sometimes listening for more complete, deeper understanding, or listening with fresh ears and no assumptions or biases can lead to revolutionary thinking. Sometimes it leads to an aha moment or a breakthrough insight. This approach can drive customer satisfaction to new heights, propel greater numbers of new product innovations or improvements to those in existence, activate the team's process improvements, and much more.

One of the compassionate leaders we learned more about in our interviews really distinguishes herself by her ability to turn understanding into action. I've long admired the senior senator from Massachusetts, Elizabeth Warren. Senator Warren has great passion for what she believes in. She cares deeply about her staff and constituents. She's curious and thorough, and this leads her to roll up her sleeves to make sure she understands the people or situations she confronts. She was never satisfied with being a person who just wrote about problems; she always wanted to do something about them.

A great example is her work on bankruptcy, something that affects a lot of people's lives, and a topic she is an expert on. Before entering politics, Elizabeth Warren was an attorney, first practicing independently before teaching law and researching issues around bankruptcy and personal finance. When she started studying bankruptcy, the conventional wisdom (or bias) was that people going through bankruptcy were irresponsible, running up debt, gaming the system, or in financial trouble through some fault of their own. She discovered, though, that these reasons only explained a small percentage of bankruptcy cases and were, for the most part, biases on the part of attorneys and courts.

One of the things she did was go to the courthouses and observe where the decisions were being made. She thought about a time of financial distress in her childhood. When she was twelve years old, her father had a heart attack, and her mother had to get a minimum-wage job to make ends meet. She remembered thinking, *Well, my family got through this without going through bankruptcy proceedings, without having to resort to the courts to wipe away our debts. So you know, honestly, what's wrong with these people that they're not doing that?* She subscribed to the conventional bias that bankruptcy was due to the individual's own failings.

So, she went into that courtroom, observed those people, and saw that they really looked no different from her family members back in Oklahoma. And as she got deeper into her study, she realized that a lot of them were just people with medical emergencies that were no fault of their own. She explained the reality that she finally understood: "Medical problems, job losses, and family breakups had laid these families low. Most had hung on and tried to repay long past any reasonable chance of doing so. As I saw it, the families in bankruptcy were mostly good people caught in a bad situation."

As she dove deeper into a conventional bias to understand it, she saw it for what it really was. Senator Warren was ultimately successful by listening, developing compassion and empathy toward these folks, and understanding what they were going through, rather than making assumptions about who they were.

Later, she was asked to advise the Commissioner of the National Bankruptcy Review Commission, where she fought to oppose legislation meant to severely restrict consumers' right to file for bankruptcy. This led to her later coming up with the idea for, and serving on the congressional oversight panel overseeing, the Troubled Asset Relief Program (TARP), which had oversight for government bailout programs. And she stood up for the Consumer Financial Protection Bureau, which has protected millions of consumers from traps hidden in mortgages, credit cards, and other financial products.

Senator Warren demonstrates the idea of action as a result of hearing, listening, and understanding, as opposed to just hearing or just (biased) observing. Not content just to point out problems, she delved into understanding why they exist so that she could take appropriate remedial actions. The process has always been something that's motivated her. And she has been well-served by her own advice: "Don't be so focused in your plans that you are unwilling to consider the unexpected."

END-OF-CHAPTER EXERCISES

PRACTICE BETTER COMMUNICATION

Are you multitasking during a conversation? (This is even more prevalent in the Zoom era, when we can turn off our cameras!) Consciously put your phone down, shut the door, and listen.

Are you feeling checked out or disengaged? Lean forward and get curious. Come up with follow-up questions that allow you to have an even more interesting or engaging conversation.

Does it seem like others aren't satisfied with your comments at the end of a conversation? Make sure you understood the speaker, and confirm or validate their perspectives. Practice repeating back what you heard to make sure you understand.

Part III

Cultivating More Compassionate People

Chapter 10

Cultivating Compassion within Yourself

THE DALAI LAMA SAID, "If you want others to be happy, practice compassion. If *you* want to be happy, practice compassion." These words sum up this virtuous loop of compassion and provide a compelling reason to adopt this as a practice.

As much as compassion helps your organization, as I have already discussed at some length, *it helps you just as much or more!* Practicing self-compassion first makes the compassion you express to others more powerful and meaningful. Those are compelling reasons to take steps to become a more compassionate leader.

The Personal Rewards of Compassion

Practicing compassion has huge personal benefits for the leader who practices it. For me, there's nothing more meaningful than seeing someone else happy. When you value that happiness in others on your team, they feel appreciated. They feel respected. And you enjoy the happiness and satisfaction that you've brought to that person by helping them navigate through a challenge in their life or helping them grow as people. You also benefit from the richness of those connections that compassion creates.

One of the best parts of my year is when the Tramuto Foundation awards its annual scholarships to high school students. As part of our scholarship program, one of our board members is assigned to mentor each of these students as they go through college and beyond. We act as sounding boards, and we try to find ways to help bring out their greatest potential. There have now been more than 100 scholarship recipients through our program, and we keep in touch with all of them. Watching them grow and develop and hearing from them over the years is incredibly rewarding.

Just two days before writing this, I received a text message from Oliver Higgins, a 2017 Bangor High School scholarship recipient. When I presented the awards at the high school in 2017, Oliver was in the crowd with his parents, who walked up with him to accept the award. He was very shy. I saw a bit of myself in him. I said to the board, "I want to mentor him." Actually, Jeff and I mentored him together. Fast-forward four years. In 2020, I connected him to Tidesmart Global through their CEO Steve Woods and suggested that they hire Oliver as an intern over the summer. Steve's company has a division focused on logistics; Oliver is studying logistics, so it was a great fit. Afterward, Steve said he was the best intern that he's hired in twenty years. Oliver's part-time work turned into a full-time job.

The note I received from Oliver said, "I can't begin to thank you for your advice. It always helps me grow." Let me tell you, when I get these letters, it lights me up.

Compassion Is Good for You

Being more empathetic and outward-focused and taking more compassion-driven action leads to great rewards. In studies, practitioners of compassion widely report that they are happier and have better relationships. They even live longer! The rewards of practicing compassion are immeasurable.

Research by Ed Diener and Martin Seligman, leading experts and researchers in positive psychology, suggest that we can improve our mental and physical health by connecting with others in a meaningful way. Research by Stephanie Brown at Stony Brook University and Sara Konrath at the University of Michigan suggests that it might even lengthen our lives.[1]

Why do we feel happier and why are we healthier when we're compassionate? It appears that the act of giving is as pleasurable as the act of receiving, if not more so. A brain-imaging study at the National Institutes of Health showed that the pleasure centers in the brain (parts that activate when we experience pleasure from things like dessert, money, and sex) are just as active when we observe someone giving money to charity as when we receive money ourselves![2]

Another reason compassion may boost our well-being is that it can help broaden our perspective beyond ourselves. Studies show that depression and anxiety are linked to a state of self-focus. When you do something for others, on the other hand, that state of self-focus shifts to a state of other-focus.

Helping other people can make you feel energized and create a deeper connection with those you help. Compassion may boost your well-being by increasing your sense of connection to others. As I touched on earlier when describing the epidemic of loneliness, one telling study showed that lack of social connection is a greater detriment to health than obesity, smoking, and high blood pressure. On the flip side, strong social connection leads to increased longevity.[3] Social connection strengthens our immune systems, helps us recover from disease faster, and may even lengthen our lives.[4]

Awareness and Self-Awareness

I was thrilled to get the benefit of wisdom that Laurie Cameron shared for this book, especially as it relates to self-awareness, one of the dimensions of compassion that I feel most strongly about. She's a long-time management consultant turned founder of Purpose Blue, a business offering practical programs for companies to cultivate better performance, stronger teams, and greater well-being through mindfulness and compassion. She's also a mindfulness teacher, speaker, and author. Since she is someone who has taught more than 10,000 people how to be more compassionate, her thoughts on how awareness fits with cultivating compassion were of great interest to me.

"I teach awareness and self-awareness as the fundamental path to compassion because, once you start to see your own imperfections and your own patterns and your own hurt, that translates to how you're relating to other people," Laurie explained. "When people learn to look inside, they understand the fragility of the human experience, and the tenderness that we humans have gone through, this journey of pain and hurt and loss and joy and all of that. Until we really look at that in ourselves, it's easy to be impatient and judgmental with others. Once you start to bring that lens of awareness to yourself, then compassion just opens up. It starts on the inside."

First, Be Present Where You Are

Cultivating self-awareness makes us kinder to ourselves while being more compassionate leaders. There are many ways to develop self-awareness. Meditation is one; journaling and self-reflection are others.

Laurie starts with present-moment awareness through a process she calls a three-center check-in. She said: "The first step on the path is learning to be present. That's when your attention is in the same place as your body. Sounds simple, but it's actually hard. We always have something on our mind; we're either thinking about something in the past or something in the future. So being mindful and present and aware means that we're tuned in to our direct experience as it's happening in the here and now. If we can't do that, we can't be empathetic. If we can't be empathetic, we can't be compassionate."

The first step of the three-center check-in is to pause and ask yourself what's going on in your body. Observe any physical sensations.

Is there tightness in your chest? Is your heart beating fast? Then, you check in on your emotions. What emotion is that behind the tightness in your chest or the rapid heartbeat? Is it fear? Embarrassment? Then, only after the first two steps, we go to the third center, our thoughts. There you ask yourself, *What is the thought or the belief behind what I'm feeling?* Our brain is a meaning-making machine, so it's helpful to notice what beliefs might be creating your thoughts.

"Practicing this check-in," said Laurie, "actually retrains part of your brain called the insula that is associated with interception, the ability to notice your thoughts. This area of the brain is also associated with empathy, so as you practice this over time, your antenna gets finer and finer tuned, you get better at discerning your own emotions, then you get better at discerning the emotions of others. And now you're crossing the bridge to empathy, which leads to compassion."

Live an Examined Life

The way I practice self-awareness is by examining the highlights and the lowlights of my day. It's a daily task where I literally sit and look back through the calendar on my phone to reflect on all my meetings and conversations. When you do this kind of reflection, you have to be willing to be honest with yourself. Socrates said it well: "The unexamined life is not worth living." I think you have to stay aware of how your actions impact your own life and, importantly, others' lives. For example, you had a conversation with a colleague that didn't go as well as you would have liked. Maybe you used an impatient or harsh tone with them. Reflecting on this should include how it might have made them feel, not just how it made you look or feel.

When I was in a CEO role, I was on the phone once with an executive in my company, Kim, and the whole executive team. She got very aggressive with me on this call in front of everyone. I gave her enough chances to stop it. Then, I finally had to say, "Kim, it's obvious you have something to say and I have something to say. Who would like to go first?" My tone was definitely not the warmest. In fact, it had the effect of shutting her down completely. When I reflected on it later, the whole thing bothered me. On the one hand, I did nothing wrong, technically, because quite honestly, I was the CEO of the company, and where she was taking the conversation was, quite frankly, not appropriate. But then I thought about how she was feeling. You could tell she hung up very abruptly, clearly upset. So, I sent her a text late at night. I said, "I apologize for what I have done on my end." The next morning, we talked on the phone, and she started crying. I started crying. She said, "Just the fact that you were aware of my feelings . . ." She started apologizing, saying, "You know, I was wrong." Well, you know what, we were both apologizing for what we owned. We built our relationship stronger from there. Self-awareness gave me an opportunity to reclaim my leadership position and reset that conversation and our relationship.

People have lots of distractions and stress in their days, and that makes them less observant of others, which makes them less likely to tune in. Now, what I could have done in that conversation, because I had the power, was to just leave it at that or to further admonish her privately for what happened in the meeting. But self-awareness brings your compass back to where it needs to be, and it's an opportunity to reclaim what you lost. It's an opportunity to reframe a relationship that might have gone south. I think that's what compassion, what leadership, and what a growth mindset does: it lets you relinquish your power. And in many respects, by relinquishing it, you get twice the power back.

It's so important to me that people leave meetings or conversations with me feeling good. The late poet, memoirist, and civil rights activist Maya Angelou said, "I've learned that people will forget what you said, people will forget what you did, but people will never forget how you made them feel." In the case of my conversation with Kim, I heard from her boss the next day after she and I talked through our differences. She said, "I had a conversation with Kim, and she said you made her feel like a million dollars." In turn, that made me feel great.

Self-Compassion

One of the most important practices when developing compassion is also one that is often overlooked: cultivating compassion for yourself. This has a couple of dimensions in my mind. One dimension is about self-talk, or how you talk to yourself, making sure you are kind and forgiving to yourself as opposed to a negative critic who is always putting yourself down. The other dimension is the concept of putting yourself first in the sense of really committing to taking care of yourself. This includes structuring your life and priorities to optimize your health as well as to allow yourself joy and pleasure in your life.

Celeste Aliberti is an expert on self-compassion, a psychotherapist, and a trained clinical social worker who infuses her client interactions with a dimension of compassion and mindfulness. She explained self-compassion: "It's really about having a loving relationship with yourself. This means at every moment you're treating yourself with love and respect in the same way that you would treat someone else who you love."

How's Your Inner Dialogue?

Treating yourself in a loving way sounds simple enough, but it's not always easy. Even today I'll still catch myself saying unloving things to myself, but I quickly stop and change them to kinder sentiments.

Celeste Aliberti described very common situations in the workplace where we sabotage ourselves with negative self-talk: "Many people judge themselves, put themselves down, rather than being patient or forgiving," she said. "The key is to be mindful of this and to change the dialogue. When critical words enter your mind—things like, *I didn't do a very good job in that meeting* or *I'm terrible at this or that*—that's when it's time to bring in love. Let's face it, we all do it. We all have interjects of our parents, of our culture, that create this negative self-talk. When you feel this kind of dialogue starting, step back and think about talking to yourself with kindness and patience, as if you were talking to a much younger version of yourself or talking to a child. Then say more compassionate things to yourself, such as, *It's okay, you're doing your best and that's probably better than you're giving yourself credit for.*"

She went on to say: "It's not always easy to change this. It takes some time because it often becomes an embedded pattern. Positive self-talk is not something most of us are taught. We're taught at a young age—as kids—to be good little consumers, to always look outside ourselves for external or material sources of comfort or gratification. Our whole culture is programmed this way. We aren't taught to look inside ourselves for the answers, but that's where we'll find them."

One of the compassionate leaders I spoke with is Brad Fluegel, a former Walgreen's executive and now a health-care investor and advisor who articulated this well: "A lot of compassionate, successful people are harder on themselves than a lot of other people. It's something I've actually worked on a lot over the years. I think at this point in my life I show myself a lot more compassion than I did when I was thirty. And that's working really hard to not take on the echoes of what was put into my head when I was growing up. The self-talk that says that I'm never good enough. I think that generates the whole imposter syndrome that, probably, many of us have been through. I think now I'm much more compassionate to myself than I ever have been before in my life. A part of that is just being more accepting of yourself and knowing there are things that are good about you and things that are less good about you and forgiving yourself for some of them or trying to take steps to make those things better."

What is the outcome of changing our internal dialogue? For Brad, changing this dialogue allows him to work from a place of confidence. As Celeste said, "Self-compassion leads to empowerment, it leads to allowing your creativity to flourish. When you put yourself down, your creativity and confidence are smashed. When you develop a loving relationship with yourself, all aspects of yourself are empowered and uplifted! You are working for yourself, for your own growth and joy."

Give Yourself Permission

Getting self-talk to a forgiving and kind place will take you far, and it really does happen with practice. The other dimension of self-compassion that has actually been a little hard for me is making myself a priority. Even though I've worked extremely hard in my career, I still feel a little guilty about enjoying the fruits of my labor. Now that I've gotten the hang of it, though, I realize it's an expression of self-compassion and self-care.

Thasunda Duckett articulated this so well during our conversation. "Many times you're watering everyone else's flowers," she said, "and not realizing that you're thirsty for the same thing. So what I've learned is that I had to take a moment, give myself permission, and to realize that it wasn't selfish, it wasn't arrogant. It was allowing me to refuel so that I can make more impact, because when I am overtaxed, when I am pouring and pouring, I am not replenishing. Then, I cannot make the impact.

"So what I do now is a couple of things. I protect my soul and my spirit. I surround myself with people who mean me well. I make sure I'm kind to myself by taking time to smell the roses and being grateful for the work I have accomplished. Self-care is about knowing what brings you joy, and allowing yourself to do those things."

I think one of the kindest things Thasunda described doing for herself was giving herself permission to stop trying to balance her life and work. So many of us beat ourselves up for working too much if we aren't spending enough time with our loved ones, or conversely, we kick ourselves for taking time off with our loved ones when we should be working. It's a no-win situation that is brutal on you.

Thasunda's approach is incredibly kind and empowering. She explained: "I choose to live my life like a diversified portfolio. I don't believe in work-life balance anymore. I realized that when I was trying to balance my life I was failing at everything. I felt like I was failing at motherhood, I was not feeling great about work, I was feeling guilty that I don't do enough for my parents, I felt I was not connected to my friends as much as I would have liked. So, what I decided to do is to live my life like a diversified portfolio. I intentionally took the time to write down everything that matters to me—being a philanthropist, being a mother, being a daughter, being a friend, being an executive, etc. Then I allocated a percentage of time to each. I don't have 110 percent; I only have 100 percent. For everything that matters to me, I would allocate at least one percent.

"What it allowed me to do is to have permission to not live my life in judgment and failure," she continued. "When I'm working these long hours, I understand that it's earnings season, so I need to weight my allocation toward work. But it also gave me permission to recalibrate, just like you do with your money in the markets. When my dad was battling prostate cancer, I needed to reallocate more of my time and show up as a daughter to remind him of all the things he taught me, to play it back to him when he was at his weakest moment. I know that I may not be the best mom when I'm traveling. But over time, I'm a really good mom. I don't put 100 percent into my marriage and my children, maybe they're at thirty percent, but within that thirty percent I give 100 percent. I give it all that I have. And that allows me to show up with joy; it allows me to be intentional."

Make It a Daily Practice

I've mentioned that my practices of cultivating compassion include a few things: self-reflection, prayer, meditation, and mindfulness. These methods are used to cultivate more empathy and compassion through clearing your mind of racing thoughts in a way that allows you to connect with your own heart and soul. These practices open up our hearts and create more awareness of what people are going through around us.

These practices are some of the most widely used to develop a personal practice of cultivating compassion. There's a big bonus to these, too: They reduce stress, adding to the numerous benefits already mentioned. We all know stress is a literal killer and often operates on overdrive for leaders at any level. Meditation and mindfulness practice is one of the most powerful ways for an individual to stay grounded and stave off the effects of stress. This is also powerful in developing self-compassion, awareness, empathy, and compassion for others.

Meditation Is a Proven Performance Booster

Meditation is perhaps the most commonly recommended practice for developing compassion. This is why meditation enjoys a very long history. A great number of studies show its effectiveness in stress reduction, in calming the noise of the mind, and in calming the body and heart.

Meditation's benefits are scientifically measurable. Cognition, just one measure of your brain's effectiveness and presence, improves with meditation. A 2018 study by the University of California Davis Center for Mind and Brain found that meditation increases the ability to sustain mental attention, with the benefits lingering even after seven years. Improved cognition—thinking more clearly—supports critical thinking and the ability to think clearly during the management of crises and other typically high-stress times.[5]

Many of us know a bit about meditation or practice it already. There is no right or wrong way to start, and you can use fifteen to twenty minutes of quiet time or doing-nothing time as meditation, just as you can close your eyes and silently repeat a single word over and over in your head in rhythm with your breathing until you reach a quieter state. Look for some ways to start and block off time in midmorning and the early evening. Doing so will help you recenter, release stresses, and think more clearly.

Compassion Is a Two-Way Street

My conversation with the youngest leader interviewed for this book, Jordan Mittler, is a great example of the rewards of compassion. Jordan is a high school student with a passion for technology. He turned this passion into service when he launched the not-for-profit initiative Mittler Senior Technology, which teaches seniors how to use technology to stay connected to family, friends, and community.

He explained what prompted the idea: "It all started with my grandparents, who always needed help with simple things like sending a message or making a phone call with their smartphones. It was just amazing to me how something I've found so easy, they had so much trouble with. I knew that if my grandparents were having trouble, it's probably an issue in the lives of lots of seniors. I reached out to nursing homes, churches, and senior centers in my area, and I got a group of around twenty seniors signed up to take my first class with me. I taught them computer and smartphone basics. After the first class, I really enjoyed it, so I decided to do it again. And, it continued from there. When COVID-19 happened, I moved the class to Zoom. Now, I get seniors from around the country and the world.

"It's especially useful for seniors to use a program like FaceTime to see their grandchildren when they're isolated in their homes and can't see their family. When I show them something like that, their faces light up, and they think it's the most amazing thing ever. Even for something as simple as increasing text size, they fall back on the chairs. I've taught the same lessons ten or fifteen times already, and those reactions make everything that I'm doing so worth it. I know that my one hour spent teaching them is going to change the way they live their lives. That's why I do it."

Like Jordan discovered, compassion pays big dividends when it comes to well-being. It also makes things easier for you as a leader. People who are compassionate build more community and connection. Studies show that when you feel more connected to others, you have higher self-esteem, are more empathic to others, and are more trusting and cooperative.[6] And, as a consequence, others are more open to trusting and cooperating with you. Being compassionate helps you be more successful.

Don't Confuse Compassion with Sacrifice

One quick caution: A common mistake people make is thinking that compassion is just selflessly helping people, or worse, that compassion requires that you sacrifice your own well-being for the well-being of another. This is not so. That's simply called sacrifice, and when it comes to the day-to-day practice of leadership, I don't recommend it. It's not sustainable. It's a finite, one-way process and a slippery slope. Compassion is best practiced as a relationship, as an interaction—even as a transformation.

Homeless advocate Sister Mary Scullion of The Sisters of Mercy Catholic order, who I mentioned in a previous chapter, defined compassion in that way. She said simply, "Compassion is transformation." Then, she expanded on that: "When you talk about compassionate leadership, you're talking about leadership under which the community experiences transformation in a very human way. When you're touching another person's suffering in some way, you're different from that experience as well as, hopefully, the person themselves. It isn't about sacrificing yourself. It's okay to have personal growth and gain as part of your goal in being compassionate to others. Help given from one to another is simply transactional—a one-way distribution of services." If someone does this too often, it drains the giver and becomes a sacrifice. True compassion is relational—a two-way street, a relationship between the giver and the receiver by which both are transformed.

Worth More Than Money

My partner Jeff and I have an inn and a restaurant in the small coastal town of Ogunquit, Maine. We used to have two restaurants. Selling one of them brought us invaluable personal rewards, not necessarily financial.

Several years ago, we acquired the restaurant called Five-O (named after the street address) and quickly transformed it into a destination spot in this seashore community. We had an amazing team of hard-working, passionate employees. They took so much pride in their work and really were—and still are—the heart and soul of the business. Once the business matured and we decided to open another restaurant, Jeff and I had the idea to work out a structure that would allow the managers to buy the restaurant and benefit from the rewards of ownership. When we shared our intentions with the management team, we were met with some blank stares. This level of compassion is not a norm in the restaurant industry.

We didn't give it away. Instead, we created a situation that would allow the managers to do this largely on their own. First, we created a long-term incentive program that vested over a period of three years so that they could have a down payment. We then came up with a price and discounted fifteen percent from market value. We then financed the loan for a ten-year period with an interest rate that was fair and equitable, allowing them to also avoid any of the large bank fees business owners are strapped with. Today, they are full owners, and they and the restaurant are thriving.

If we had sold this on the open market, we probably could have made $200,000 more. But it was more valuable to us to see the satisfaction and pride of these three managers who have worked with us and enjoy the satisfaction of helping them get there. That $200,000 wouldn't have brought me as much satisfaction. During the first month of the pandemic, we reached out to the management team to offer our assistance in helping them navigate the new abnormal and, in showing compassion, we eliminated one month's rent and stopped their loan payment until they could get back on their feet. Today, they still operate a very thriving and successful business.

Eyes Open, Heart Full

A key component of this practice is cultivating an intentional outward awareness similar to mindfulness, though mindfulness is also about inner awareness. To me, practicing outer awareness can be described as getting out of your own head and maintaining an outward focus in the present moment. I think of this as a forward-leaning engagement with people and the world, a proactive noticing of what's happening for other people. It's being awake and engaged. It's a lens through which to look at the world.

I interviewed actor, producer, altruist, and compassionate leader Matt McCoy for this book, and he described this well. Matt is a talented actor who has enjoyed a successful career and a longevity that not every actor in Hollywood is fortunate enough to experience. After our in-depth discussion about compassion, I suspect his success stems at least in part from his amazing attitude and the compassionate way he lives his life every day.

When I asked Matt how he defines compassion, he said: "I think it's an awareness. It's being open to noticing that something is needed for someone else. It's being aware of people. You don't need to look far in this world to find someone who needs help. I think what comes back at you when you are open is tenfold. When I speak of compassion and the kindness that I try to carry with me through the day, it's in small ways. I'm much more about small things than I am about big things because few of us are in a position to do big things. So, I try to make my life about little things, and that's where compassion comes in for me."

For many, their faith inspires some of this awareness of others. "My faith is a big part of my life," Matt told me. "I was raised Catholic. Our parish here in Los Angeles, St. Paul the Apostle, is a big part of our life, and all of our kids went through Catholic school. My son still practices his faith with his wife, but my daughters do not, and that's okay. There's no better religion out there than 'do unto others' as far as I'm concerned."

He told me that it goes back to some of the philosophies of Albert Schweitzer. After studying and practicing theology for a time, Schweitzer began studying medicine in 1905, when he was thirty. He earned his medical degree in 1913 at the University of Strasbourg in the east of France. He'd already enjoyed a professional music career and, from his young manhood to his middle eighties, was internationally recognized as a concert organist. He wrote and published extensively, and he opened and funded a hospital in Gabon, a country on the west coast of Africa. He was awarded the Nobel Peace Prize of 1952. He was a compassionate leader and an influential thinker. His words still inspire: "Happiness is the only thing that multiplies when you share it." I really believe that to be true.

Matt clearly embraces that belief. He explained: "I have to tell you I wake up every day with my eyes open and my heart full. I just go out there, and I say a prayer every day: 'If somebody needs help, let them find me. And if I need help, let someone be there for me.' I don't think there's a better feeling in the world than the feeling of doing something for someone. If you want to get out of yourself, do something for someone—volunteer or teach—the feeling that comes from doing things like that fuels me. And it should fuel anyone. That's enough for me."

Start with Yourself

Compassion begins within each of us. Many would say that compassion is something we're born with, though some may have more of a predisposition toward it than others. As we live our lives, compassion may grow and deepen, or perhaps for many of us it might go a bit dormant as we face difficulties and become caught up in our busy lives. Wherever we are on our journey, there is always opportunity to cultivate deeper compassion and to embrace this as a practice at any point in our lives.

Developing and strengthening your own ability to feel, express, and convey compassion as a leader has so many benefits for your organization. We've addressed many of those benefits throughout these pages, and all of them will lead to more engaged employees, better performance, better outcomes, and stronger results.

END-OF-CHAPTER EXERCISES

START A DAILY PRACTICE

There are many ways to begin. If you aren't someone who meditates or reflects, start with one step that you add to your day that can act as a jumping-off point. Here are some simple ways to get started:

- Self-Reflection: Buy a journal or notebook, or use the notes feature on your phone. At the end of the day, sit down and reflect on your day, bringing awareness to how things went. Is there anything you would do differently in the future? Did you have any interactions that you wish had gone better? Bringing attention to this can improve relationships and how you deal with issues in the future. An important note on this: If you feel that something didn't go well, resist beating yourself up! Use self-compassion to forgive yourself, to realize we're all human.

- Meditation: This is often done early in the morning or at the end of the day. Find a quiet place—your bedroom, patio, a garden, anywhere you can sit with little distraction. Start with five minutes of meditating. There are many great sources from which to learn how. (You'll find many on my website www.donatotramuto.com/compassion.) Or, try one of the popular apps like Breethe, Calm, or Insight Timer. This makes it very easy to start.

- Journaling: Aside from general self-reflection, there are additional ways to focus on things that can help you be more mindful and compassionate. You can note something that you're grateful for. This is a science-backed way to increase well-being. Another is setting an intention at the beginning of the day. This is a way of being mindful and conscious at the start of the day, which often actually then impacts the kind of day you have. An example of an intention might be: "Today I have difficult conversations coming. I will approach those with compassion and calm."

Chapter 11

Can You Teach Others
to Be Compassionate?

I T'S NEVER TOO LATE TO LEARN to be more compassionate. It's never too late for a leader to cultivate the conditions under which others in their organization can learn to practice compassion, too.

When I think about teaching compassion as a leader, I think it happens on many levels, and it is about creating the type of culture that allows compassion to thrive, something expressed throughout this book and specifically in chapter six. But it has to start with the leaders themselves through their words and actions. It needs to be made a stated value and a priority. Then, compassion needs to be embedded into formal practices and processes to make sure it carries through the organization.

From the standpoint of the leader, just talking about it will not be effective if it isn't also acted on throughout each workday. In the workplace or in an organization, helping people learn and grow has to be integrated into day-to-day relationships, communications, processes, and operations. It needs to be applied in the situations and settings where it's seen and felt by others. I believe the most impactful way leaders can teach compassion is by modeling it themselves—in other words, leading by example. Ongoing implementation and reinforcement from leaders and managers throughout the organization is the key driver that allows this to take hold.

When leaders talk the talk *and* walk the walk, every day, it sets a visible example of compassion in practice.

For nearly four decades I have been challenged to define my leadership style, and too often I would default to the "leadership du jour" offered to us by the latest and greatest leadership guru. When I launched Physicians Interactive in 2008, it finally occurred to me that leadership by example was the leadership style that has defined—and continues to define—me.

Compassion Is Contagious. Pass It On!

Leading by example is not a choice a leader makes. Every action they take sets an example whether it's meant to or not. Your choice isn't whether to set an example, but rather what kind of example you want to set, and choosing to set that example intentionally. As a compassionate leader, whether you're a CEO, a supervisor, or a project leader, you have great influence on those who work for you, with you, and around you.

Outward compassion creates a chain reaction: It's been shown that employees of compassionate leaders are more likely to act in a helpful and friendly manner toward other employees, even when they have nothing to gain.

One study that looked at this scenario proved that when people are treated with kindness, they want to extend the kindness toward others, further proving that compassion creates a chain of more compassion.[1]

Another study showed that leading by example indeed positively increases reciprocity.[2] The more the leaders contribute, the more followers contribute. This is parallel with the statistic from a Gallup poll that showed that more engaged managers have more engaged employees.[3] A direct and powerful correlation.

Compassion is indeed contagious!

Since you're already influencing your teams and coworkers, make sure that your actions align with the values you express. I've seen so many leaders talk about company values and then act in opposition to those values. A workplace study found that only twenty-six percent of workers strongly agree "that managers embody the values they expect from their employees."[4] That's a very low percentage in my book. This type of disconnect leads to alienation and lack of trust, and it undermines the values the company is communicating. I think it's worse than not communicating any values at all.

Practice What You Preach

My good friend Phil Johnston has been an example of compassionate leadership throughout his career. His daily actions convey respect toward others and exemplify what it means to truly connect with people by understanding their pain. His leadership style is one of understanding, not just of the head but also the heart. Phil was a businessman, politician, and Regional Administrator of Health and Human Services for New England under President Clinton and previously Secretary of Health and Human Services in Massachusetts under Governor Michael Dukakis, who was a very compassionate leader as well.

I asked Phil how he built a strong team, and he told me, pretty bluntly, that first he had to get rid of all the bullies. Holding people to a high standard of respectful conduct, even if it means firing those who don't get on board, is a very meaningful way to express your commitment to these values. It's sometimes necessary to protect your culture and the employees who work for negative leaders. Preaching compassion while allowing people on your team to behave badly is setting a negative example. You are, in fact, contradicting yourself.

When I interviewed Phil for this book, he explained: "I've made it a point to hire people who are nice people, who are smart and talented. And then if I saw somebody who was misbehaving or mistreating people, if they didn't change quickly, they would be out the door. I had a big organization of 40,000 employees; I was in charge of seventeen state agencies. I think it's important to set a bar to establish a standard. That's what I did through my hiring and in the way I interacted with my employees. Everybody understood that both the governor and I would not tolerate disrespectful or bullying behavior. By the time I got through appointing people as commissioners and so on, I think we had a really good team. We had very decent people running those organizations."

He made it sound so easy, but I know it's very difficult for many managers to fire employees. Sometimes they have a decent relationship with an employee, but the employee doesn't treat coworkers well. In other cases, firing someone is just hard emotionally. You may feel sorry for the employee you let go or worry about their ability to feed their families. But it does not do them or anyone any favors to allow them to continue their bad behavior unchecked.

Phil agreed that firing people was not always easy. "I started out running the RFK Children's Action Corps (now called the RFK Community Alliance) when I was twenty-five-years old. I had a very hard time firing people then. There was a woman there who was a director in the organization, and she was an alcoholic, which I didn't realize. When she would drink, she would be unbelievably abusive to people. I was very shocked. She pushed me over the edge one day, and I fired her. It was such a clear-cut situation that led to immediate improvements for the team, and after that, I didn't have any problem firing people. I feel that if you're so bad that you're abusing people, I don't want you in my life or in my organization." This also goes back to how toughness fits with compassion, mentioned in chapter four.

Phil summed it up like this: "You have to practice what you preach. If you go out as Secretary of Health and Human Services and talk about being helpful to poor people, mentally ill people, and people in prison, you'd better be that way in your own life and with your own team. And you'd better be training your own staff and those who work out in the field the same way. I learned that from my mother, who was a devout Catholic and really practiced what she preached, even if it was difficult."

If you're telling your team that compassion is an organizational value, that you care about creating a safe and respectful workplace, it's important to show that you're going to walk that path yourself, even if it means doing the tough work of addressing the people who are toxic to your culture in order to protect and reinforce the values you're expecting from the rest of your team.

Make It Official

Establishing compassion and related values like respect and trust in your organization, and communicating those values to your leadership team and your organization, is a first step. Leading by example brings this idea to life, models the behavior, and reinforces the message. To make this more formal, this value needs to be incorporated into your processes.

There are many opportunities to incorporate compassion into your daily activities, and I'll give you a few of them. One place to incorporate this is into your communication strategy, whether it's executive communications or internal communications. A leader can reinforce this message and show people what it looks like in practice by publicly recognizing individuals who took compassionate action in their jobs. As discussed in chapter six, Zeel founder Samer Hamadeh gave a great example of this when he rewarded one of his employees who showed empathetic values with a thank-you and a $100 gift card.

Perhaps at company or department meetings you make a point to share a story of an employee who took an extra step that was compassionate. For example, you say, "I want to take a moment to thank Shannon for stepping up to do *X*." These stories can be conveyed through internal communications, employee newsletters, etc. In one-on-one communication, try to *catch* your employee doing something right. When an employee mentions something that they did or that someone did for them, celebrate that moment. When an employee has a success—maybe a big sale or their division exceeded their goals—point out not only the strong performance but also whether they did this by nurturing their teams, collaborating, or treating their employees or customers with compassion and kindness. Make a note to mention these examples in your next check-in meeting with that employee.

It's important to make these values part of the expectations you set for your employees in clearly stated goals. Explicitly communicate the expectation that employees proactively show compassion and respect to one another, that they think in terms of the well-being of teams and of the collective good, not just about their own needs or success.

To complete the loop, make cultural practices and priorities part of an employee's review discussions. Make part of their review about how they support their coworkers, how they support the culture, and, when possible, set team goals, not just individual goals. Then reward team success. This helps strengthen how teams work together, driving greater satisfaction among employees and greater performance.

The Network Effect

Kurt Small of Anthem, Inc., who I mentioned earlier, believes the power of example can multiply itself throughout an organization.

"I believe compassion can be taught," he said. "It can be taught in early years, and it can be taught later on in life. It happens through people's life experiences. Maybe they experience a sickness in the family and now understand what that's like for others or how it impacts the people around them. I believe experience is a powerful teacher. If you combine experience with spending time talking about compassion and reinforcing it, that's where I see life-changing events.

"I believe compassion is cultivated by intentionally carving out time in the busy world that we live in to talk about it. What leaders focus on has a significant impact on the organization. If you spend time doing that and emphasizing it in meetings or in conversations with your team, people understand the importance of it. And then, if you follow that up with reinforcements, both in how you interact with folks and how you rate and reward individuals, that reinforces the importance of it further. Then, people tend to devote more time to it, which gets better outcomes.

"If you reward individuals and reinforce the importance, you'll end up getting the networking effect from it. If you're communicating that with the leadership team and actually doing it yourself, leading by example and reinforcing that, then leaders on your team will start to do that. If leaders do that with their teams, their teams will do that with their teams, and then very quickly, you have the impacts in a broader organization."

An important thing to note here as you think about communicating values like compassion is that you may be working against some headwinds. For some, you're not just giving them a skill to add to their toolbox; you may be actually asking them to change. Keep in mind that the first reaction to needing to make a change is resistance to changing! Many people who don't currently think about or act on compassion have reasons for that. It's helpful for a leader to understand that and keep these factors in mind as they communicate with the individuals who work for them.

The Importance of Unlearning

Because of Jim Dlugos's experience as an educator and college president, I was interested in asking him whether he thought compassion could be taught. His answer was as much about unlearning as it was about learning. Learning is easy from a blank slate, but when previous learning interferes with new learning, getting the point across is challenging.

Jim told me: "I think people are born with a high tendency toward compassion, and then many of the things that we impose on young people over the years lead them astray. People ask the same question about creativity: Can you teach creativity? I think you have to unteach what people have learned first and get them back to where they began. I think a big part of teaching is articulating that there are reasons that are not the fault of anyone in particular. It's just simply the result of the system of education that has emerged over a very long period of time. Or, in the case of compassion, the result of living our lives. We have to sort of bring them back to where they began and connect with them again and then bring them forward from that place.

"So, I think compassion can be taught, and it can be taught at any level. It begins with talking about what compassion means or how someone understands it or finding examples of things to talk about that demonstrate it in the environment they're in now. In this process, you're actually listening to them. So, it's tapping into what was there at the beginning that they have somehow become less attached to over time. I do believe that a lot of what our society has done to folks over the years is to make them less in touch with their inner angels."

Fear Drives Compassion Underground

Jim also believes that the fierce competitive forces that we learn from a young age take away from our proclivity toward compassion for others. I mentioned Jim's views on this earlier, and he further explained: "What we need to unteach is this notion of competition where there are winners and losers. I think that's the thing that has to be sort of unlearned. There's competition of the sports kind, and there's also economic competition that becomes very clear very early to children. They know what they have and what they don't have, and they are bombarded every day all day long. By commercials on television, or on the Internet, which reinforce that consumer culture that we find ourselves in, or that we've chosen to live in. I think it's a big source of some of these challenges. I also think fear is a big driver. It drives compassion underground."

Fear is caused by all kinds of events and circumstances, real or not. In the workplace, it can be caused by a focus on winners and losers. By praising only a few people, we may inadvertently make our employees feel that their jobs are in jeopardy. If we work in a low-trust culture, fear can be pervasive. Jim went on to say, "Fear leads to closing in on oneself. If compassion is the art of being open to others, anything that causes me to close in, to have a higher level of anxiety, to have a higher level of fear, to have a higher level of potential sense of loss, is fear. I think all of those things need to be unpacked and unlearned to lay the groundwork for cultivating compassion."

Workplace Programs

Low-compassion, low-trust, hard-driving workplaces not only drive compassion underground, they also create stress and anxiety. It's pervasive; it is a financial drag on companies.

Workplace training programs of all types and subjects have long been known to pay off high dividends in employee engagement as well as higher top-line revenues and increased profits to the bottom line. When eradicating stress and anxiety and building compassion and trust is the goal, workplace programs again take the lead in providing effective outcomes.

As an example, Aetna saw that for every highly stressed employee, the company lost $2,000 in health-care costs, not to mention all the lost productivity.[5] The company explored ways to reduce stresses, for instance, through regular mindfulness practices, such as those touched on in the previous chapter. Aetna, in fact, did implement mindfulness programs. They resulted in health-care costs falling seven percent and a savings of approximately $6.3 million. Productivity gains were $3,000 per employee, an eleven-to-one return on investment.

I've been heartened to see more and more companies adopting programs that address well-being while also creating a more positive and compassionate culture. Some of the biggest and earliest companies to do this include Apple, Google, and Nike. Apple and Nike offer employee meditation rooms. I mentioned earlier the work Google has done, starting with Project Aristotle. This resulted in a well-known and highly regarded employee meditation and mindfulness program called Search Inside Yourself, created by Chade Meng-Tan. Meng-Tan later captured the program in a book of the same name. The course includes things like attention training and self-knowledge mastery. Instructors set up exercises that pair up employees to sit across from one another and recognize in one another their roles in life outside of work, their hopes and dreams and challenges. It's a practice in compassion that allows colleagues to see one another as human beings rather than cogs in a colorful corporate machine.[6]

Better Than Brain Surgery!

I touched on mindfulness and meditation in chapter ten, but I'd like to reiterate that such training programs in the business world are not by any definition marginal or zany or alternative, and they have not been for a long while now. Nothing is more mainstream in the business-training arena than mindfulness and meditation training, alongside places and times during a workday to escape into quietness and calm. Why is it mainstream? It's all about the money, from a purely business standpoint; people who are calm and clearheaded perform better for you. But from a compassionate leadership perspective, it is all about a tremendously enhanced quality of work life for your employees. People who are calm are happier, eventually healthier, and more focused and in the moment in their work.

In short, meditation enhances your quality of life and quality of performance on the job. Consistent meditation—that is, done at least once daily for a minimum of twenty minutes—pays big dividends in your calm, clarity, and composure. And those positive effects linger on well after your session has ended.

Your ability to learn, to think (even under great strain, as in during a crisis or while breaking all records to meet an "impossible" deadline), and to process all kinds of disparate information for decision-making—all that capability is enhanced by meditation. Your memory and mental focus improve, meaning your mind wanders less often during those many daily meetings your work involves.

Daily meditation also teaches the brain emotional self-regulation. In other words, you learn how to calm or otherwise self-govern or

self-control your anxieties, fears, and other negative unwanted feelings; your tendency for knee-jerk reactions gradually dissolve into a
more thoughtful thinking-before-action posture.

Consistent, regular meditation for one or two twenty-minute peri-
ods per day, accompanied by mindfulness throughout the day, have
been proven to preserve the brain's youthfulness, reduce depression,
reduce body pain, and reduce anxiety.

Formal studies from places like Harvard, UCLA, Johns Hopkins,
and Yale have demonstrated pretty amazing things[7]: one eight-week
meditation course yielded actual visible brain changes in the region
that governs learning and thinking,[8] another showed decreased
aging activity among meditators,[9] and yet another showed improved
memory and higher performance on tests after just several weeks
of meditation.[10]

Simple Steps Yield Big Dividends

Purpose Blue founder Laurie Cameron, mentioned in a previous chapter, helps companies institute mindfulness- and compassion-driven
processes that help create higher performing teams. Some of these
are quite simple yet very powerful. It definitely starts with the leader's
own actions, then those steps or processes are shared in one-on-one
interactions and within teams.

There are ways to implement small steps that are easy for a leader
and powerful for teams. Laurie gave a great example: "One simple
way is by doing check-ins at the beginning of team meetings that
connect team members at a deeper level. So many people are all
Zoomed out. We all have fifteen meetings before the end of the day.
People rush into the meeting. There's an agenda. Half the people are
multitasking, and seventy-five percent of them have their video off.
That's the way it is now. So, I teach how to create real connection in
a team, Zoom or not. One way is to really, truly check in with each
member at the start of a meeting. You take the ten minutes, which
makes some people go into a cardiac arrest thinking they're going

to waste ten minutes doing a check-in, but we know that there is an immediate payoff in engagement, productivity, and performance because you're engaging people as a whole human being and creating real connection. Especially now with so much remote work, we don't know what people are doing with the eight or ten hours for which they're getting paid each day. We want to engage them, not because we're trying to squeeze them for productivity, but because we care. There are many tools and ways to do this, like check-ins that get to the deeper level of how people are really doing, engaging them, and uniting your teams."

Mentoring Matters

As a compassionate leader, you are naturally attracted to helping people, and one way of doing that is through formal or informal mentoring. Mentoring is not telling someone what to do but guiding them through thinking about their own best strategies and approaches, their own best learning and becoming. Mentoring requires time and patience. It has to be a farmer's mentality. Take time, set the conditions, and build the environment—seasons, not seconds.

I've mentioned my foundation's work giving scholarships to college-bound students and the mentoring that's provided. When you look at that program, I believe the mentoring is the real value. It far exceeds the value of the dollars given. Mentoring is a valuable way to teach values like hard work, initiative, setting goals, or compassion. Whether it's mentoring kids or mentoring younger professionals, it's a powerful practice.

I've had the good fortune to get to know Jim Geraghty through my work with the RFK Community Alliance. Jim is a managing director for Morgan Stanley Private Wealth Management and the chairman of the board of the RFK Community Alliance, which I've spoken about previously. Jim is the embodiment of the value of mentoring, both in how mentoring changed his life and how he now impacts others by mentoring them.

Jim told me his story: "I grew up in public housing in a veterans' housing project. My father was a prison guard. He was sick a lot, in the hospital a lot. Most of the kids growing up there didn't have many opportunities. Some of them went to prison and not many went on to college. I was an exception. I went to an Ivy League college, Brown University, and have since enjoyed a successful career and many years of highly satisfying community involvement.

"What made the difference for me? Mentors, teachers, other parents, people who helped me and opened up opportunities for me at the right time. This is why I've devoted much of my life since then to mentoring others.

"I was able to come from where I grew up, do the things that I've done in my life, in part because I had teachers and mentors and other athletes and coaches who took an interest in helping me. Of course, much of my success was due to my own hard work as well, but mentors opened doors for me and shared wisdom that I didn't have. Even though we struggled at times, my parents made a positive impact on me, too. My father, who was a six-foot-three, redheaded Irish barroom-brawler type of guy, taught me respect. He always treated everyone with respect, even the prisoners. He told me, just because they're prisoners doesn't mean they should be treated with disrespect.

"I remember when I was around 11 years old. Hockey back then was a big deal because of Bobby Orr, and high school hockey programs were a big deal. I couldn't go to hockey camps because we couldn't afford to. So one day my mom got a call, out of the blue, from the hockey coach. We didn't know him. We had no connection. But he had heard of me and the situation that my family was in. He said to my mom, 'I would love for your son to come to the hockey camp.' My mom told him we couldn't afford it. And he said, 'I want Jim to be my guest.' I said yes, and the rest is history in a sense. I went on to play hockey, benefiting from the inspiration and confidence I got from coaches and other players. It ultimately led to my ability to go to college.

"I've done a lot of mentoring, one-on-one and through organizations. I worked with an organization called NFTE, the National

Foundation for Teaching Entrepreneurship. I was the chair of the New England board. We had a curriculum in public schools in the city of Boston. The students who participated came up with ideas for businesses. Then they would develop a business plan that we would bring to businesspeople to evaluate and give feedback. At the end of the year, there was a competition within the school, and then among the eight public schools in Boston.

"I volunteered mostly in a public high school in Charlestown. There were three young inner-city boys who, at the time, were fifteen. They were captains of the football team. I took an interest in them, I mentored them, and I introduced them to my friends in different networks. Oftentimes kids growing up in public housing do not have access to mentors who can help change the trajectory of their lives. Being someone who grew up in a similar situation, I have a firsthand experience for how important that is."

Jim told me about one of his favorite mentees. "Jason grew up in the Lennox housing project in Boston. I met Jason when he was fifteen and mentored him through high school and all through college. When he graduated, I helped to get him an interview for a job with Elizabeth Warren, which he got. I helped opened those doors for him, but he is a very, very talented, gifted young man, so it was up to him to walk through that door and shine. From there I encouraged him to apply to law school and he got into Northeastern law school, an amazing achievement that brought him so much pride. I will never forget when he called me the night of the new student cocktail reception, and he said, 'Jim, I'm on the top of a Northeastern building having a glass of wine, looking down at the Lennox housing project right now.' So close, yet he had come so far."

Jim's approach was not, "Hey, you need to do this, let me do this for you," but, "What do you want to achieve? Where do you want to go to college? What field do you dream of working in?" He'd facilitate that by helping those he mentored meet the right people and learn the right things.

The power of mentoring is invaluable. Many of the themes are the same for the workplace. Spend one-on-one time with key members of your team or with a mentee to offer an ongoing connection, or use it as an opportunity to convey values and lessons learned in the framework of trusted relationships.

END-OF-CHAPTER EXERCISES

TRY THIS WITH YOUR TEAM

There are mindfulness programs that can be incorporated into the workplace. On my website, www.donatotramuto.com/compassion, you will find online tools, companies, and programs that you can tap into.

There are also simple ways to begin to cultivate more compassion among your team members. Try the simple but powerful meeting technique of going around the table (or Zoom) and asking everyone how they're doing or what's happening in their lives. Spending a few minutes per week on this can produce big dividends.

Chapter 12

What Every Leader Needs to Know about the Future Workforce

L ET'S FACE IT, A LOT HAS CHANGED over the last couple of years. I understand that anyone of any generation in any era could say that, yes! But most agree that the change we are experiencing now is on an accelerated course. Much of what we knew about the workplace five or ten years ago has changed, in many cases, completely. Businesses who said in February 2020 that they were on a controlled path of change that they would need five years to achieve found that the pandemic accelerated that timeline to mere weeks!

Change calls for sharp awareness from leaders. Two major shifts stand out to me that are fundamentally changing what the workforce needs from its leaders.

The first is the generational shift in the workforce, from one that is baby boomer–centric to one that is predominantly made up of millennials and Gen Zers. The latter account for more than half of our workforce now and will make up more than two-thirds of it by 2030. With that shift, there is a need for leaders to become attuned to a whole new set of understandings, perceptions, and skills.

Technology is the second major driver. Technological change continues to accelerate. This change doesn't only require us to choose and implement technology or use technology to evolve or disrupt our businesses. More broadly, it's changing the nature of the skills we need in our workforce—and not necessarily in all the ways you might think. We don't just need more technically savvy workers, we need people with more finely tuned human skills, and we need leaders who understand how to bring these competencies out in proper proportions across their workforce.

The COVID-19 pandemic has certainly acted as an accelerant, moving many emerging trends along faster. What was once theoretical became reality fast. As a result, leaders have had to refocus on their people and their culture far more than most of them would have. Much of this focus also speaks to a company's readiness to withstand disruption. According to a recent O.C. Tanner workplace trends report, "Fifty-seven percent of companies anticipate major changes to their culture as a result of the pandemic. As companies emerge from the challenges of 2020, they have two choices: to enter 2021 bruised or poised to thrive. The determining factors will be their people and their workplace culture."[1]

It's because of these dramatic shifts that compassionate leadership is emerging as the core of modern leadership. The fundamentals of compassionate leadership align with what leaders need to successfully adapt to the trends that are shaping our future: developing and caring for your people, creating community, accepting and optimizing differences, celebrating authenticity, cultivating successful collaboration, and putting stakeholders over shareholders.

The Future Is Here

I remember years ago when executives would talk about the need to change strategies and competencies to adapt to the coming digital and technical revolution. It struck me then, and still does in some cases, that the future was already happening, even as executives referred to it as something to address later. I think we're in the same boat now as we talk about how future generations will change our workplaces and society. That future is happening now.

Demographics Are Destiny

A quick look at who leads our workforce compared to who makes up the workforce should be enough to get any leader's attention:

THE LEADERS

The average age of a CEO in the United States is fifty-nine. The majority of CEOs are white men. The average age for a C-suite member is fifty-six.[2] White men continue to be the dominant group leading listed corporations: They held ninety-six and four-tenths percent of the Fortune 500 CEO positions in 2000, and still held eighty-five and eight-tenths percent of CEO spots in 2020.[3]

THE WORKFORCE

Approximately fifty percent of the workforce is comprised of people in their forties and younger.[4] This number will be seventy-five percent by 2025. Only about half are white, compared to seventy-five percent of baby boomers who are Caucasian as of 2015.[5]

PUBLIC LIFE

It's not much different in politics. The average age of the 117th US Congress in 2021 is fifty-nine, compared to the median age in the US population of thirty-eight, according to the US Census Bureau. In Congress, seventy percent are men and twenty-eight percent are women. Seventy-two and a half percent are white, twelve percent are black, nine percent are Hispanic, four percent are Asian/Pacific Islander, one percent are Arab, and one percent are American Indian.[6]

Compare this to the US population, where sixty-two percent of people are white. And, looking ahead, Pew Research Center predicts that by 2065, our population will be less than half white, with twenty-four percent being Hispanic, fourteen percent being Asian/Pacific Islander, and thirteen percent being black.[7]

To state the obvious, the majority of our leaders in business and politics are older, white, and men, while those they lead are, on average, much younger and of a more diverse ethnicity and race. This creates a divide and sets us up for disconnects.

For businesses to be future-ready, or even just to be in sync with today's customers and stakeholders, leaders need to understand their workforce and their customers.

In many cases, leaders will also need to change their beliefs and jettison their biases about those who are different from themselves. As in any relationship, you can't ask other people to change to be more like you. You have to meet them where they are and create the best possible ways of working that accept and embrace the reality of your coworkers and employees.

While it's clear that many in leadership resist this change, which is already upon us, the best are already adapting to, and benefiting from, this shift.

Culture Clash

With leadership being homogenous and the workforce being much different in composition (to generalize), leaders will need to tune in to the potential disconnects and pitfalls they might confront in order to avoid them or successfully navigate them. Some examples are hiring biases, leadership style, and openness, or lack thereof, to a younger perspective.

LIKE HIRES LIKE

Leaders have a subconscious tendency to hire people like themselves. A Caucasian man CEO hires Caucasian men as managers and so on. This cannot reasonably continue.

Sixty-nine percent of younger generations who see their management teams as diverse—regarding gender, ethnicity and race, and educational and cultural backgrounds—believe their workplace is motivating or stimulating. In the opposite scenario, thirty-one percent of younger generations who see a lack of diversity among management find their workplaces less motivating.[8]

COMMAND AND CONTROL DOESN'T CUT IT ANYMORE

Leaders from the old command-and-control, top-down, "I'm-the-leader-so-I-have-all-the-answers" mentality have a very hard time with younger generations. You need to start interacting, calling on and acting from your workforce's suggestions and needs. Leaders need to move from a know-it-all mentality to a learn-it-all mentality, as Microsoft CEO Satya Nadella describes it.

The members of the rising workforce have confidence about their own ideas and opinions, want to voice them, and want and expect to contribute. Likewise, when younger generations are not taken seriously, are not allowed or encouraged to voice their opinions, or, worse, are met with disdain when sharing their opinions, they become disengaged and look for new jobs (leading to expensive and time-consuming employee turnover). Remember that people don't usually quit jobs, they quit managers.

GENERATIONAL BIASES

There are real differences in how baby boomers and rising generations have grown up, and therefore, in how they interact, live, and communicate. Let's take diversity as an example. Older generations grew up in a less diverse workplace, so if they suddenly find themselves in a very diverse workplace, it may make them feel defensive or set them up for biases. Younger workers are more comfortable with diversity; their generation is just more diverse. In fact, when I asked Austin, the teenage son of my writer and collaborator Tami Corwin, how he defined compassion, his answer was a wonderful reflection of his generation. While many of our leaders defined compassion (appropriately) as empathy combined with action, helping alleviate suffering, and helping others grow and better their lives, Austin added an important element. He defined it as noticing when someone needs help, and helping them, even if they're different from you. My generation has a lot to learn from those who are up and coming!

The bias that the older ones lead the younger ones is also false today, with younger managers leading sometimes much older team members. Older leaders will need to reexamine their old beliefs and misperceptions about generational, gender, or other types of diversity. Their past stereotypes will often show themselves now as negative and sabotage their best leadership efforts. If older leaders aren't careful, they may come across as out of touch.

Leadership needs to change because the workforce *has already changed* and is changing even faster as we move forward. The generational shift is impactful and unstoppable. It will eventually change everything as baby boomers retire and younger generations take their turn in more senior positions (many are already in them).

How do you approach this shift that has already occurred and help your organization benefit greatly from it? Through compassionate leadership, which offers leaders the skills that will make them more successful, such as embracing differences, listening without bias, expressing empathy, understanding and compassion, and committing to the development and well-being of your people.

Regardless of your age, you must embrace the needs of the rising workforce coming in behind you and position your business and teams to benefit from the skills and capabilities of that workforce. If you do not keep up and even blaze the trail for others, your business will soon lose its relevance. Whether baby boomers, millennials, Gen Xers, or Gen Zers, we all face the same nagging desire to belong, to be respected, to be embraced, and to feel part of something bigger.

The Digital Divide

A quick note on the discussion of generational differences as it concerns technology. Trying to describe these differences with general statements can lead to the implication that we should look at an entire generation as a homogenous group. That is not something I want to encourage. General statements cannot be applied to everyone, of course. There are those in older generations who are driving the changes we're all experiencing and are excited by them, and there are those in younger generations who have not adopted or embraced technology for a variety of reasons. Often, it's more about mindset than it is about age. That said, I think it's worth looking at differences between generations from as factual a standpoint as possible to encourage understanding.

A study by marketing firm Epsilon quantified how different generations reacted to emerging technology trends. There is quite a contrast between generations, and the difference grows with the span of years between them. In short, the younger the generation, the more fully and unquestioningly they embrace tech in all its forms and usages, from social media to virtual reality to AI. While Gen Z is all-in, millennials have a similar embrace of new technology, yet are not quite as all-encompassing.[9]

The younger workers are more focused on knowing where information is and how to find it and are often happy to be digital nomads, knowing that all they need is an internet connection to find the information they want. Older generations, referred to as "digital immigrants," are often seen as slower to embrace technology, as you might guess. Yet it is traditionally the older population who are in roles of leadership.

Crossing the Divide

Understanding such differences helps leaders optimally deploy their organization's human resources. A few examples:

Younger workers' expectation of having and using new tech on the job might be denied by older leaders who don't see the need, leading to frustration, disengagement, poor productivity, and employee turnover. Know this and adapt.

Older leaders' expectations that younger staff not only know where to find new knowledge but possess a library of understanding that enables them to fully use the new information might not be met, to the frustration of all. Understand the younger context and adapt.

Older generations may look at the younger generations as knowing more than they actually do. Younger people may have high digital confidence but a low digital competence: They have grown up using their smartphones and computers for schoolwork and for social connections, but that doesn't necessarily mean they have a truly broad-based, higher-level-tech skill set applicable to your workplace. Understand the holes in their tech skills and adapt.

When it comes to the differences in how generations embrace and view technology, principles, and practices, compassionate leadership can help cross the divide, bring teams together, and bring out the best in everyone.

1. **Listen.** I have discussed this vital, vital skill of listening to understand, listening with empathy and curiosity. Actively working to understand others brings awareness of biases that exist and may stand in the way of collaboration.

2. **Accept That You Don't Know What You Don't Know.** Two compassionate leadership traits—humility and self-awareness—will save you from the trap of assuming you know more than you do or assuming you have a real handle on something that you may not. Resist a know-it-all attitude.

3. **Resist Stereotypes.** Younger leaders must stop assuming that all older generations are slow, or not wired to understand new things, or that they cannot learn. Older leaders must resist the young-people-are-lazy stereotype. All leaders must resist false beliefs about other-race, other-gender, other-nationality, and other-age team members!

4. **Learn from Other Generations.** Learn also from other industries, other types of business models, and other countries' ways of doing things. Learn intergenerationally and globally.

5. **Embrace Change**. We're not all wired for change; it takes intention and practice. But change is coming whether you like it or not. Create more openness and opportunities through curiosity!

Future-Proof Your Workforce

We know that technology is changing our workplace, but we should not forget that without *people*, there is no workplace, no product, no service, no sale, no customer care.

The Future of Work report from McKinsey modeled skill shifts resulting from AI and automation that will take place through 2030. It found that the demand for technological skills will gather pace. But it found another shift that I don't think leaders are paying enough attention to yet: the "accelerating increase in the need for social and emotional skills, skills that machines are a long way from mastering." The report stated, "While some of these skills, such as empathy, are innate, others, such as advanced communication, can be honed and taught."[10]

Some organizations have been doing things backward banking on high-tech tools instead of people and their wide-ranging knowledge and approaches to fulfill the mission. We need to get better at our human skills, like compassion, creativity, and courage. Hard skills used to be everything, with soft skills taking second place, but now, your and your organization's soft skills are the future.

Fundamentals of compassionate leadership such as collaboration, trust, embracing diversity and differences, and open communication are essential for the team-oriented organizations of the future and as the foundation for all you do. Promoting compassion-driven characteristics like adaptability, agility, a growth mindset, re-skilling, empathy and compassion, continued learning and development, and openness will set great leaders apart in the future.

What Younger Generations Need from Leaders

When I wanted to get added insights from a compassionate leader who truly understands how to get the best from the younger generations, I turned to my friend Janine Francolini, founder of The Flawless Foundation, an amazing organization with a mission to normalize the conversation around mental health.

Like many of the compassionate leaders we interviewed for this book, Janine's life experiences led her to her life's mission and the founding of her foundation. "I had mental-health challenges as a young child that went untreated because of a lack of awareness, education, and treatment options," Janine explained. "These challenges escalated to a life-threatening point when I was a teenager. I finally received extensive treatment, which saved my life, but my story is all too common."

Perhaps in part because of the suffering she experienced as a child and adolescent, Janine was drawn to the education field, ultimately landing her dream job as an admissions director at a prestigious school in New York City, which included a coveted spot for her son. In her admissions role, she was interviewing 500 children and families a year for only ten spots. One day she had an epiphany that changed the course of her life.

"When I went to graduate school," she said, "my goals had been to teach and nurture children. Instead, my days were spent judging, testing, and eliminating. A light bulb went off for me. To everyone's surprise, I resigned from my position and relinquished my child's spot at the school. That's when the journey toward creating Flawless Foundation began. As I came to better understand the dire state of our education and mental health–care systems, I was called to action."

Janine launched her foundation at her kitchen table without much of a plan but with a great deal of passion and empathy for those she serves. Since then, the impact of the foundation has grown, as it has advocated for and partnered with others to promote mental-health awareness and treatment across the country.

I asked Janine to give me her perspective on what matters to the younger generations, and what they want from their leaders. "They care a lot about being satisfied in their work, making a difference," she said. "Work-life balance is important to them. In general, they won't stick it out in a job that they don't find fulfilling. They want to work with leaders who are authentic and inspiring. What has helped my organization is to let my team know in words and actions that I prioritize their well-being above all. It can seem counterintuitive, but giving them time and space to be at their best always works out in the long run."

Janine went on to address a misunderstood aspect of this generation. "There is a misperception that younger generations don't have a good work ethic," she said. "It takes some explicit training and communication, but once the skills are taught, they are extremely responsive. Instead of being frustrated, implementing systems and training goes a long way."

This leads back to one of the strongest features of compassionate leadership, connecting your people to your purpose, making sure your employees understand your mission and how each of their contributions connects to the broader goals. Younger generations need to be understood, not admonished or mocked. They need leadership that fits their needs rather than the leadership that current leaders think should work for them but doesn't.

Before you protest too much, this is not to say that if younger workers are not doing their jobs, they should be indulged. All employees should have and meet clear performance expectations. They should be given complete training and usable feedback, be recognized for their real accomplishments (not just that they showed up), and be held accountable if they don't deliver on their goals.

An Earlier Perspective

My collaborator on the original research highlighted throughout this book, Dr. Adam Leach, is also a high school counselor, teacher, coach, union president, and member of the Tramuto Foundation board. Adam has observed kids growing up and entering college and the workforce for decades. He provided valuable insight on forces that might shape young people today. Considering this can help bring older generations a better understanding of what drives (or does not drive) the youngest generations and how to get the best from them.

Adam explained: "Just like adults, younger generations represent all walks of life, so I hesitate to generalize, but I think it is appropriate to look at student leaders to offer relevant insight. Twenty-five years ago, the top ten percent in the class were driven to prove themselves. They were very individualistic and focused on their résumé. These are the current thirty-five- to forty-year-olds. Today it's different. There's less emphasis on title and prestige. I have more students who believe that a state university (at a lower cost) is as good as going to Yale. More kids are considering issues such as student debt, when in the past it was the brand name of the school that was the only factor. However, parent and societal attitudes haven't budged a bit. I still see overwhelming pressure on kids to get into a 'good' school.

"My observation," Adam continued, "is that parents our age (in their fifties, give or take) do things a lot differently than our parents did. When we were kids, the emphasis was on child-adult interaction, and when it came to peer-to-peer interaction we were on our own to figure it out. Today, we construct the peer interactions of our children (play dates, Little League practice) and we have missed good opportunities to mentor them with adult interaction. I think a lot of problem-solving skills and the development of emotional regulation came with a lack of micromanagement by parents. I don't think this is our fault. Grandparents move to Florida, two-parent working households, etc., have caused the paradigm shift.

"If I had to pick one big difference in teens today, it's that they are programmed to wait for instruction (again, recognizing that this is my bias). I can give one example. When I was a varsity soccer coach, I had an athlete who was late for practice. When I asked him why he was late, he said he couldn't get a ride. He only lives two miles from the field. The idea that a seventeen-year-old could walk two miles to practice was not even something that entered his mind. My biased reaction was 'Get off your a** and walk.' What I saw was a lazy yet perfectly fit and capable young man. Yes, he was someone who didn't think outside of what was familiar (or permitted). His mother always brings him to practice. In his mind he had to wait for her. Leaders have to look beyond their own bias (experience) and avoid thinking, *In my day, I would have left my mom a note and walked.* What I should have done was say to him, 'Help me understand this. Why didn't you just walk to practice; you only live a short distance away?' I could have said, 'Next time, walk,' and used it as a learning opportunity. I think compassionate leaders need to be teachers, coaches, and mentors, not just bosses and supervisors.

"Life has changed, and that is what I would say is relevant in compassionate leadership with regard to teens and young adults. Leaders need to know that younger generations had different childhood experiences than we did, and compassion is the effort to understand that difference.

"Young people still look up to their adults. Leaders need to understand their power and know that the younger people are watching their every move and will emulate them."

Don't Fear Flexibility

A few months before the pandemic, I read an article in the *New York Times* about how younger generations were going to "save us all from office life." Little did they know the coming pandemic would make this article even more prescient. The article featured a twenty-something-year-old who left her job as a project manager in the corporate office of a bank to join a branding and design firm. She didn't leave because she got a raise or a higher level of seniority. She left because the work–life balance was better for her.[11]

At her new company, everyone works from home on Tuesdays and Thursdays at whichever hours they choose. In contrast, at the bank, she said, people judged her for taking all her paid time off. At her new job, taking time off is encouraged. This flexibility is why she doesn't mind answering work emails while sitting by the fire on a camping trip. She said, "A client calls me at eight o'clock at night and I'm happy to talk to them, because that means the next day at ten a.m., I can take my dog to the vet. It enables me to make my career more seamless with my life. *It makes it feel more like people are human.*" Many of her friends have chosen their jobs for similar reasons, she said. "That's how millennials and Gen Zers are playing the game. It's not about jumping up titles, but moving into better work environments," she said. "They're like silent fighters, rewriting policy under the nose of the boomers."

Older generations were raised on the commute, long hours, hard work, sacrifice, striving to get to the top. Younger workers are pushing back. They expect flexible hours and flexibility to be in or out of the office when needed, they expect flextime, paid maternity and paternity leave, and paid vacation time.

A survey by PWC, an accounting and consulting firm, found that for millennials, work is a *thing*, not a place.[12] Millennials are largely unconvinced that what they would have to give up is worth such a sacrifice.

Staying Because of Belonging

Younger workers want to learn, grow, and be involved. They are known to be more than happy to leave a job if they don't like the culture, and it is culture that provides them with learning opportunities and a chance to make a contribution.

Trust your younger employees—and base that on first explaining the expectations you have of them and the fact that you have given them the tools and resources to meet expectations. The latter might be training courses or software tools. Build their trust in you—and base that on being a communicator who likes the face-to-face, listens to them, acts to provide what they say they need to do the job, and so on. Encourage all staff to speak up and participate with ideas, suggestions, process and procedural modifications, and so on. Listen and make them see, through your subsequent actions, that you trust them and believe in them as full-fledged participants in the business.

Younger generations want to belong, and that comes with wanting to have a voice that is heard. I recently had a young former employee named John call me because he was interviewing for a job. The hiring manager was older, in his sixties. John is bright, high performing, and not afraid to share his opinions and views. For some old-fashioned leaders, that leads to an uncomfortable feeling. I would say the majority of young people now are either direct and not afraid to speak up, or they are confident in their opinions, whether they speak up or not. John told me that when he spoke up respectfully but directly in his interview process, the traditional leader with whom he was interviewing defaulted to seeing him as being argumentative, not getting on board. The leader saw John's direct and confident communication as a red flag. I told John that the leader's reaction to him was a bigger red flag. He's not going to take the job.

For many decades, older leaders have led with a sense of authority due to hierarchy, where the lower in the hierarchy you were—and, what is more, the younger you were—the less you would be heard. No one would ever come to you for brainstorming, innovations, solutions, or resolutions. That has dramatically changed and is continuing to change—and this is for the best. If you are that hierarchy-entrenched leader, climb out of the foxhole and start chatting and listening to everyone up and down your organization.

Collaboration Is a Driver

If you don't meet workers where they are—in the younger set's case, in a sharing, collaborative, participative space—there's going to be a higher turnover in your company. Many millennials will not tolerate in their workplace what our parents tolerated. Our parents needed the paycheck. And at the end of the day, they don't become paychecks, they become "pain checks." One of my cousins is dealing with a pretty horrible boss who doesn't listen to anyone, just pressures his employees for more productivity. My cousin is staying because he's within a few years of retirement; he's trying to stick it out just for that reason. I don't think any millennial, though, would look at it the way my cousin is looking at it. They don't want to go to work for a "pain check." In fact, even a paycheck is less important than their quality of life, well-being, and sense of belonging, contributing, and feeling valued.

Janine Francolini summed it up this way: "They are creative and passionate, and they dream big. The examples of peers being successful from startups, social media influencers, and technology inspire them to think out of the box. They are open-minded and not as linear and narrow-minded. We get the best out of them by being in close relationship and expressing our care for them on all levels. Relationship is key. We must also be role models of our values. My team knows that their health and well-being always come first, and that foundation of care goes a long way in creating a healthy, vibrant team. We start our weekly staff meetings with each team member sharing what is really going on with them—including me. They are all connected and concerned about each other. I was so touched when I had to take a week off to take care of my ailing mother and the team of college interns sent me flowers and a beautiful note." That kind of leadership is a win–win.

Leaders: Be Open to Change

Leaders first and foremost have to be open to change, to fully embracing it, to implementing new strategies, and to trying new ways of leading. I mentioned having a growth mindset earlier. When it comes to these dizzying changes in the workplace, we all have to keep learning.

We have to address any obstacles in the way of change, including our own fear of it. Change was a feared theme in our compassionate leadership survey. The responses expressed the sentiment that current practices were generally acceptable, and change was not welcome or a priority.

When we asked survey respondents to rank the elements important to compassionate leadership, "change" was dead last for senior leaders, and that escalated with age. Seventy-eight and a half percent of senior managers aged forty-five to fifty-four ranked change as the least important element of compassion, while 100 percent of senior leaders sixty-four and over ranked this as least important.

This also demonstrates the potential for cognitive bias; fear of change can make it difficult for one to consider new ideas that would replace previously held thinking.

When it comes to fear in the workplace, much of our fear revolves around fear of losing a job or fear of failure. This is more pronounced for older leaders because they see the workplace as more competitive, whereas the younger generations would rather be collaborative than competitive.

The younger employees often think, "If I don't like my job, I can leave it for one that I might like better, where I feel I belong." Or they may consider taking a year off to travel.

I believe that those over fifty have a lot more fear. They have the fear that if they lose their job, they won't be rehired again. Or they fear losing their paycheck when they're closer to retirement, especially if they haven't saved enough for that. They're afraid of diversity because more and more companies and boards are looking for more gender, racial, cultural, and overall diversity. So, it makes perfect sense that white men who make up most of those jobs in the C-suite have something to fear.

Fear is a paralyzer. Fearful people can't seem to act in their own best interests; they see an enemy in every person around them. They put up a whole range of defense mechanisms—including skepticism and distrust of everyone—which might just be what sabotages them. The compassionate leader simply does not operate from fear of change, or fear of the future, or fear of failure. The compassionate leader operates from a certainty that change will occur on a daily basis and makes sure that his lines of communication to his team are wide open and working in all directions. When the leader has his team's back, the team steps up more courageously in the face of change.

Challenge Yourself

When I was a CEO, I advised my team of executives to create their own executive advisory boards. I told them they were the CEO of their teams. I suggested that they create a board from colleagues, people who reported to them, and even a board member. I told them this group should include young and old from as many diverse perspectives as were available, really. The purpose was to give that senior executive an opportunity to stay in touch with differing viewpoints up and down the hierarchy, to help them continually develop, to help them grow, and to give them a group from which to solicit feedback that might even challenge their own views.

If you're a leader, I recommend some version of this. You can do it officially or unofficially. It allows you to gather intelligence that will make you stronger, prepare yourself for change, and open your eyes to what's really going on. The best leaders challenge themselves to overcome their fears, to lean into areas that might make them uncomfortable. They stay open to learning from anyone, in or out of their organization.

Another strategy is sometimes called reverse mentoring, in which older leaders or employees specifically look for younger mentors to help them keep up with specific areas they are not as naturally adept at or just don't have the same experience in.

I've been fortunate because my foundation board members mentor kids as they head into college. We offer mentoring to each scholarship recipient, but for me, those relationships end up offering me the benefits of some reverse mentorship opportunities, too. I have disciplined myself to make sure that I have young people who can help the older board members understand the various trends and changes that are happening before us that sometimes we wouldn't necessarily see or understand as quickly. Once you have younger people on a board or in an advisory group, resist the temptation to shut the person down if he offers recommendations or opinions that do not seem appropriate or sophisticated. You have to listen, question, and learn. You have to help young people step up, give them their due credit for contributing and even just for the courage they've had to share their experiences.

Update Key Roles

Organizations have had similar roles, similar job descriptions and expectations, and similar structures for as long as I've been in the workforce. The C-suite is generally the same crew of leaders: CEO, COO, CFO, etc. There have been some welcome additions, like chief sustainability officer or chief diversity officer, though I'm not sure they have the same clout or credibility in the boardroom. It's time to stand back and rethink our senior roles and our governance. I have three recommendations, in particular: one for your human resources function, one for CEOs, and one for boards.

Elevate Human Resources

As we head into a future that focuses more on people, my first recommendation is that leaders need to rely much, much more on their human resources department to help them transform their way of thinking. Why? Because human resources is your people department! Human resources should not be looked at as a transactional cost center, but as a true profit center in charge of identifying, attracting (aka recruiting), understanding, developing, and appropriately deploying the organization's most valuable assets: its people.

When you listen to earnings calls, human resources is never invited. When I was CEO at a public company, I used to make sure that my head of human resources was present at all C-level and board-level meetings. Human resources touches every key aspect and every moving part of the organization. Thus, I think you need human resources to be part of everything at C-level, too, and just decide to make your human resources manager your CHRO, your chief human resources officer.

Human resources is no longer a transactional function alone. It's a transformational one. It's a problem-solving unit. It's at the helm of your leadership development pipeline. Human resources is a key driver of your organization's culture. And if your human resources team isn't there yet, they should transform as well.

Give CEOs Term Limits

My second recommendation is that CEOs should have term limits, like politicians. Leaders often come in, set an agenda for change or transformation, meet it, or not, in a three- to five-year period, and from there they sometimes stay around too long. I never stayed longer than a four- to five-year time period in the positions that I had. The reason I believe some senior leaders should be limited to a specific term is because bringing in new leadership ensures fresh thinking, evolution, and new relevance for the organization.

Of course, there are amazing leaders who continue to transform themselves and their companies, but many do not. My point is that getting used to changing and adapting as their way of life, so to speak, is the only way companies will grow and remain competitive.

Over the last couple of decades, CEO age has actually been trending up as people retire later, so the average CEO tenure is pretty long. There is, however, pressure from companies to add younger executives, to add younger directors to the board as the demands for digital insights, technology experience, and fresher thinking become more pressing.

If the CEOs are going to stay in the job, that is fine, as long as they and their boards make sure that leadership is adapting itself and the business to the changes in the marketplace and the world. It may mean bringing younger and/or more diverse people to the table, whose perspectives are represented along with your CEO. We're on a bit of a collision course right now, with a large number of young leaders (some in their thirties) coming up through the ranks, running into a large number of middle-aged leaders (some in their fifties and up to their seventies) staying in their jobs longer. I think it is going to take some time before this change takes place, but it needs to happen.

A Note to Boards

As my third recommendation, I believe the board of directors needs to be changed more often. If they are largely traditional or homogenous, then, unfortunately, you're not going to get the kind of dynamism you want and need. No doubt, a well-chosen board has immense experience represented among its ranks. But if you don't have the right kind of thinkers on the board, you will miss out. You won't get everything you need from them.

In my view, boards look for the most senior board members they can find, with the most impressive pedigrees, who are not necessarily known for moving into a generation of new thinking. Of course, it's critical to have plenty of governance experience in the group. But younger people—people with different experiences and backgrounds from the mainstream, entrepreneurs from other industries and business sizes, individuals practicing nontraditional careers—might add new dimensions and ask questions the traditional thinkers will not.

CEOs don't always want to challenge senior board members, and that can transform into an unhealthy environment as well as less than stellar outcomes. Compassionate leadership is about *impact*, and the question each board member needs to ask of themselves as they serve on the board is, "Have I made enough of an impact to ensure the level of trust that will drive value for all stakeholders?"

I recall one incident when I discussed with a member of the board an opportunity to sell the company, and he indicated that he did not want to forfeit his monthly retainer and liked the idea that his curriculum vitae revealed that he held a board seat on a public company. Imagine the kind of impact it had on me, and, more importantly, the residual impact it had on the employees, the investors, and others. Compassionate leadership will always put the greater cause ahead of any individual's self-interest.

END-OF-CHAPTER EXERCISES

SELF-REFLECTION: BE AWARE OF YOUR BIASES

Take some time to do some honest reflection about your own biases toward others you work with. But before doing that, acknowledge that it's normal to have these biases. We all have them, whether we're aware of them or not. But the more aware we are, the less they will affect our behavior negatively.

Now, think about your colleagues, employees, or bosses at work, especially those who are different from you. Do you hold beliefs about them that may be negative or may be arising from a generational bias? For example, "They are lazy and entitled," or "They are out of touch." If so, consider where that feeling is coming from. Do they trigger any of your own fears or feelings of discomfort? Also, consider a new approach to working with them. What do they bring to the table that is different from what you bring? How can you leverage that? How can you get to know them better? If you do, you will find that they likely have much to offer, but you may need a new way of working with them to optimize it.

Chapter 13

It's a Movement!
How You Can Join

I'VE ALWAYS HAD A PREDISPOSITION toward compassion. I've practiced this more intentionally at some points than I have at others, whether it was when challenges in my life overtook me, or when I was swept up in all-encompassing projects or roles. This changed when I lost my friends on 9/11. It stopped me in my tracks and caused me to search deeply within to make sense of such a horrible loss. I recognized that my impact on others was crucially limited and focused only on business. This resulted in a heightened awareness of life and my place in the world. Before that time, I had a lot of different areas of focus, I worked hard to be successful, and I did keep compassion and kindness in the mix of my daily life. But now, I measure my life solely by how much positive impact I have on others. I still work hard, I take time for myself, I have a lot of variety in my life, but I have one lens through which I see all of it—the lens of compassion.

The recent pandemic only underscored this clarity about what really matters. Since that inflection point on 9/11, I've devoted more and more of my time and focus to deepening my practice of compassion and helping to cultivate an environment of compassion in every organization or community I'm a part of. Compassion isn't the only thing I do, but it's part of everything I do. I don't always do it perfectly, but I always try to do it.

As I reflected on this, I remembered the story of Saint Thomas More, who served Henry VIII as Lord High Chancellor of England in the 1500s. Thomas More did not support King Henry's marriage to Anne Boleyn. King Henry was outraged. Rather than take his title away, King Henry stripped him of his power. That's when Sir Thomas More (later Saint Thomas More) said, "I feel like a mathematical point, I have a position but no power. No magnitude." I see this with CEOs and leaders now. Many have the title, but they're not using their position to create magnitudes of power. I'd much rather commit my life to contributions that have an outsized impact on others. I want my actions to have magnitude.

When you think about all the challenges that we're faced with now, perhaps even greater than the challenges that Thomas More was faced with—civil unrest, political division, loneliness, hunger, the changing workforce, what's happening to our planet—there are so many things that are coming at us. And, like it or not, these are all our problems. We are all so interdependent, we all need to care about the issues that affect us collectively. You as a leader can choose to have the position and use your power in an outsized way, or be powerless when it comes to impact, which would be equivalent to what Thomas More expressed. My hope is that you take this as an opportunity to really make a difference. You don't have to change the world yourself, but everything each of us does, big or small, moves us in the right direction. And, once enough of us do it, we create a tipping point into real change.

The Twenty-One Percent Rule

There is recent research that shows that if you engage three and a half percent of the population in nonviolent protests or campaigns, you will bring about societal change. A political scientist at Harvard,

Erica Chenoweth, looked at hundreds of campaigns over the last century and found that, in fact, every single time a movement or action engaged three and a half percent of the population affected, there was real change.[1] This includes the suffrage campaign led by Susan B. Anthony, the push for Indian independence led by Mahatma Gandhi, and Martin Luther King Jr.'s campaign for civil rights.

For me, though, I want to raise the ante on moving toward a more compassionate world, starting with businesses. I once worked with a great executive at United Healthcare, Jeanine Rivet, and she said that to make a cultural change in an organization, you need twenty percent of your workforce to get on board to make the transformation. Based on her observation, here is what I propose: Let's take that twenty percent and add another one point, making it a goal to get to twenty-one percent of corporate CEOs, executives, leaders of all kinds to commit to compassion to really push us up to and over that tipping point. If enough of us get on board with this movement, we will absolutely see change. I think twenty-one percent is a great goal.

In the number 21, the 2 represents the idea that it takes two or more to transform, and the 1 means it begins with one person: you.

Let's imagine what that could look like. Since there are about 3,300 CEOs on the NASDAQ, we need 693 of them to commit to this compassion movement. If there are, say, ten people in the average C-suite of those businesses, we need two to three of them from each company to join us. We do the same calculation for the number of employees we have and so on, to build twenty-one percent buy-in for our change.

I'm not being naive here, thinking we can get everyone to join or to commit formally to this. Some are not in the place to do it or don't have the resources or desire. But I do think there are enough of us ready to take the next step. I'm more confident than ever that we are experiencing a real change in our culture to one of more compassion. I'm energized and encouraged as I see others increasingly joining me in this commitment, in this daily practice to better themselves and the world, and, yes, to create stronger businesses and organizations in the process.

Together we have the opportunity, as Saint Thomas More stated, to move from individual mathematical points to a collective magnitude that can change the world one act at a time.

Companies Can Change the World
(and Many Already Are)

Larry Fink is the CEO of BlackRock, an American multinational investment management corporation based in New York City. Founded in 1988, BlackRock is today the world's largest asset manager, with $8.67 trillion in assets under management as of January 2021.

In 2019, Mr. Fink wrote a letter to CEOs. In it he told them, "The world needs your leadership." He expressed many of the sentiments that I have shared with you: that "profits and purpose are not inconsistent, but they are inextricably linked"; that attracting and retaining the best talent requires this focus on purpose, and that the only way to lead in these complex times is to embrace a long-term approach to business that allows proper stewardship of people and resources; that considers diversity, sustainability, and investment in human capital. He wrote, "As a CEO myself, I feel firsthand the pressures companies face in today's polarized environment and the challenges of navigating them. . . . As CEOs, we don't always get it right. And what is appropriate for one company may not be for another. One thing, however, is certain: The world needs your leadership. As divisions continue to deepen, companies must demonstrate their commitment to the countries, regions, and communities where they operate, particularly on issues central to the world's future prosperity. Companies cannot solve every issue of public importance, but there are many—from retirement to infrastructure to preparing workers for the jobs of the future—that cannot be solved without corporate leadership."

I literally cheered when I read this letter. And he's not the only influential leader expressing similar sentiments. Unilever CEO Paul Polmar recently tweeted about his belief in "business as a force for good. Purpose, passion, positive attitude." In my interview with Bruce Broussard, he said, "I believe that politics is not going to solve our problems. I think business leaders are needed to take responsibility, and I hear a number of my colleagues really taking this on."

Also, in 2019, the influential US CEO organization Business Roundtable redefined a corporation's very purpose as to promote an "economy that serves all Americans." Traditionally, an organization that works on ensuring a thriving economy, the Business Roundtable issued a purpose statement signed by 181 CEOs who committed to lead their companies to benefit all stakeholders—customers, employees, suppliers, communities, and shareholders. In the statement, Jamie Dimon, chairman and CEO of JPMorgan Chase and then chairman of the Business Roundtable, said, "Major employers are investing in their workers and communities because they know it is the only way to be successful over the long term."[2] My friend Alex Gorsky, chairman and CEO of Johnson & Johnson, said of the statement, "This new statement better reflects the way corporations can and should operate today. It affirms the essential role corporations play in improving our society when CEOs are truly committed to meeting the needs of all stakeholders."

It makes perfect sense that these companies would want to help all shareholders. Strong economies are made up of strong communities, strong companies, strong families, and strong and healthy individuals. After all, as John F. Kennedy often said, "A rising tide lifts all boats."

The Collective Power of Businesses

I do believe there are more and more enlightened and empowered leaders, men and women leaders alike, from established household-name businesses and brand-new startup businesses and everything in between, who are fully embracing their power and influence to make change. I've seen many examples in recent years of groups of companies coming together to address a societal issue or a crisis. Take Project Gigaton, launched by Walmart in 2017.[3] This is an initiative that was created to avoid one billion metric tons of CO_2 emissions from the global value chain by 2030. Walmart's suppliers are inspired to reduce upstream and downstream greenhouse-gas emissions from this chain. There are 3,171 suppliers who have signed on.

Among the many initiatives I could name are the following examples through which you can inspire yourself and your employees:

Keep Americans Connected was launched by AT&T, Charter, CenturyLink, Comcast, Cox, Sonic, Sprint, T-Mobile, and Verizon, among others, when the coronavirus pandemic began. This pledge prevented "any potential abuses from US Internet service providers during the ongoing novel coronavirus pandemic." For sixty days after the pledge was taken, the companies were asked to keep services for residential and small-business customers open, waive late fees that occurred due to the economic aftermath of the virus, and open public Wi-Fi hotspots to any individual who needed them. Many industries made similar moves to protect workers and business owners when they could not work or operate their businesses in a lockdown.[4]

Another initiative came after the murder of George Floyd, when fashion designer Aurora James created the *15 Percent Pledge*.[5] This pledge had major retailers commit fifteen percent of their shelf space to black-owned brands. James was frustrated over the low representation of black-owned businesses in major retailers, despite black people making up fifteen percent of the US population. Sephora was the first company to take the pledge, followed by Macy's, Vogue, Athleta, Banana Republic, Gap, Old Navy, Yelp, and others.

The World Business Council for Sustainable Development (WBCSD) is a CEO-led organization with more than 200 leading businesses, including Accenture, Apple, Bloomberg, Deloitte, Google, Philips, and Verizon. They work together to create a sustainable world by making sustainable business more successful. The companies represent a combined revenue of more than $8.5 trillion and 19 million employees. The goal of the council is to "create a world where more than 9 billion people are all living well and within the boundaries of our planet, by 2050."[6] Members co-create solutions and learn from one another to create the best tools and expertise to create a positive impact on societies, shareholders, and the environment.

Use your sphere of influence and your networks to build your own meaningful initiative. Pick up the phone. Corner people at conferences, trade shows, meetings, and events! It takes only one—you—to start the momentum.

The Double Bottom Line

All of the sentiments of these enlightened, conscious company leaders speak to what I've long called "the double bottom line"—the idea that a company can measure its success by producing 1) strong financial results and 2) a positive impact on the people and the community at the same time. This impact can touch employees, partners, suppliers, and the community where companies do business, and be a part of the greater good in the world. Companies can serve their people, their customers, and the communities in which they operate using the same set of compassionate leadership skills.

The idea of doing good for the greater society at large doesn't always mean writing checks—far from it! I've given many examples showing that how a company or organization carries out its day-to-day business makes an impact in and of itself. Choosing compassion can happen on the most micro level: how you interact with one person in one interaction at a time. Or, when you make a decision or a policy that sets higher standards within your company or with your suppliers or partners. It can mean standing up or speaking up for issues that will promote the health or welfare of your employees or customers, even when that's difficult. No doubt, there is difficult terrain to navigate when trying to address societal issues that have the potential to be polarizing or cause negative reactions from some groups, but if a leader sticks to their values and considers the welfare of their stakeholders, I believe these very focused values will guide them to make decisions that are best for them, the business, and the community.

It Takes a Village

Working toward a double bottom line is perhaps first expressed in how your own business, or your part of a business, can better impact your customers. It is also expressed in how you forge partnerships (with other for-profit businesses, nonprofits, nongovernmental organizations, government) to collectively solve problems.

I spoke with Tom Riley, president and CEO of Seniorlink Inc., a leader who believes that being part of solutions for his constituents "takes a village," and that it requires many different approaches. His constituents are seniors. For example, he has served on the Governor's Council to Address Aging in Massachusetts. The council is a multidisciplinary group focusing on making their state the most age-friendly in the country. "It's not just about the government stepping in," Tom said. "It's about partnership with industry. It's about creating standards for industry to become certified as age friendly. It's about providing resources to folks, the lower socioeconomic range. . . . It's about how to solve some of the loneliness problems. I'm also on the board of a company called Angels Innovation, a spinoff from Hasbro. You've probably seen these animatronic cats and dogs for kids. There have been studies done with AARP, with Brown University, and with United Healthcare around the impact of using these sorts of tools to help people, especially individuals who have Alzheimer's and dementia, overcome their loneliness. So, I guess what I'm saying is, get active. There's no single answer to these problems."

Tom doesn't see any other way to live life and do business. It's no longer a question of whether or not to lead this way. There isn't a choice to make between success and compassion; it's all integrated. Tom observed how this affects him as a leader and as a person. "I think it's pretty clear," he said. "Compassionate leadership results in strong relationships. Stronger relationships result in lower turnover and higher performing teams. Higher performing teams find a way to validate themselves in the work they do and the mission they adhere to. I get so much out of my compassionate interactions with those around me that I don't see it as a one-way street. I get so much in return from those interactions that it feeds me."

The Infinite Power of One

It was an honor to meet Dr. Zane Gates while working on this compassion project. His life story is a testament to the power of how one human can impact another, and how this can go forward and make an impact on others far and wide. He believes that compassion is expressed by how you act and how you live; words are only "icing on the cake."

Dr. Gates is an internal/family medicine physician with a general practice in Pennsylvania, and he is also the cofounder of Empower360/Spark360, a health-care company that helps companies incorporate workforce health and well-being into their work culture. Like many leaders interviewed for this book, his life informs his work and vice versa, and his early experiences continue to fuel him. Two major things influenced the course of his life: where he was raised, and the woman who raised him. And, an important mentor whom he met along the way cemented that course.

He explained: "I was unfortunate yet greatly fortunate to have grown up in a housing project. I've never seen my father. My mother had only an eighth-grade education. People called our neighborhood The Zoo. When you live in a place like that, everywhere you go, you're looked down upon. But, having had that experience gives me the ability to see other people's struggles and empathize with them. This generates compassion."

Zane's mother's actions gave him so many early examples of compassion. "My mother had this friend," he told me. "She completely loved this lady. But if you looked at this lady, she didn't smell so good. She didn't have any teeth. Her clothes were dirty. At first glance, you thought she was a mess. But what you didn't know was that she had a very abusive husband who used to beat her and take the money that she needed to do the wash. She didn't have transportation to go see a dentist, and though she cleaned her children's clothes, she wouldn't clean her own. Everybody looked down at her, but this lady was a beautiful woman with a beautiful heart. My mom showed me that she should be treated just like anybody else.

"Being compassionate is understanding that everybody you meet is special first and flawed second," Zane continued. "That guy who is the CEO of an organization may have had a lot of accomplishments, but he's flawed. And that person who lives in the project, who is just as flawed, is also just as worthy of respect. My mom, who was making $3,000 a year fighting to stay off of welfare would give her last dollar so she could help someone get something to eat. To me, when you see somebody who has nothing but does something, it fuels you to want to make a difference.

"My mom had me when she was forty-six with a man who supposedly couldn't have kids. She had a heart attack when she was seventy. I was only twenty-three, in my first year of medical school. She had something called the green medical card that didn't cover much of the costs of her medical care. I remember watching her pull change out to try to get her high blood pressure medicine. When she had the heart attack, she didn't get a stent or a CT scan. She couldn't go to Pittsburgh and get the new angioplasty that existed. She just had a heart attack. They gave her heparin, and she died.

"A few years earlier, I had told her that I felt that I'm supposed to do something big that's going to help millions of people someday. And she looked at me, and she said, 'I know that's why you were born. I know that I was not supposed to have a kid at this age. You were born for a reason.' Knowing that this beautiful woman who was doing everything she could to do right had to go through what she did, I never wanted anybody to ever go through that again. So, that's one of the events that really fueled me to try to make a difference in the world."

Pay It Forward

"The other event that really influenced my life," Zane told me, "was when I was doing homeless work with a guy named Dr. Jim Withers

(J. W.), one of my greatest mentors who does homeless health care. I was kind of lost as a medical resident. I was ready to quit. Then, Dr. J. W. and I started going out and seeing the homeless on the streets and on the banks of the Allegheny River. I really started to see these folks that everyone looks down on and see the problem. They are profoundly mentally ill with no support. I learned that yes, they need the same care as the CEO does.

"That led me to really understand what it means and what an honor it is to be a physician. And that all this beautiful science and care should be for everyone. No one should ever have to make the decision whether to take their insulin or feed their children. That's when I made the decision to deliver care to the poor and homeless. I opened up a free clinic for people who didn't have coverage. I got a van, I got drug samples, and I took medical care to the people. I wanted to give back to my community because my community had been good to me.

"We've helped a lot of people . . . and they often pay it forward . . . There was this drug addict who was in and out of shelters. No one cared about him. The Salvation Army finally got him into treatment. We worked hard together to get him through this. Now he owns one of the most successful drug rehabs in our area. He is outstanding. He's fought every addiction, gambling, heroin, and he's fine. He's helped thousands of people.

"I have a son, Shawn, who I adopted after working with him for years when he was in a foster children's program. His mom was in and out of jail. When Shawn was maybe one and a half years old, his dad died of a heroin overdose. The police found him dead, holding Shawn in his arms. I remember when I was young, I would look at all of these kids doing cool stuff with their dads and I would say to myself, *I wish someone would come in and rescue me* and *be my dad*. I got to do that for Shawn.

"I think back to when my mom once said to me, 'The world's been around for twelve billion years, and your life is a very short blip in it. So, you want to make your blip one of the brightest.' Doing for others. To me, that's how you do it."

Leaving a Value Legacy

We all have the power to impact others, as Zane Gate's mom did for him, and as he did for his son Shawn and so many others. I recently met and interviewed an amazing young man, Matt Dexter, whose story illustrates this "chain of compassion" beautifully. When I met Matt, I learned that he had been in the audience when I gave the commencement speech at Lasell University in 2018. In my speech, I talked about the difficulties I faced in my life, including the loss of so many loved ones, what I've called *bulldozer moments*, and how to rise up from those moments stronger and find your way by giving back. What I didn't know at the time was that my message resonated with Matt because he had suffered the enormous loss of his mother to stomach cancer when he was just thirteen years old.

He told me that my words helped inspire him to find a way to help others in the cancer community as part of his path forward. A few years prior, he had started the Christine B. Foundation to support those affected by cancer in Eastern Maine, an organization and mission he is devoted to fully. We all lose loved ones, but we don't all devote our lives to helping others who were affected by the same illness. I asked Matt where he learned compassion. Not surprisingly, his mother was a big influence in his life. "My mother was fearless, dedicated, and loving. Her own mom died when she was thirteen, which taught her to live her life to the fullest." He continued, "When we buried my mother, we chose a quote to represent her life from Mother Teresa that simply said, 'No large things, only small things with great love.' That really struck me at the time, and looking back now, that message compounded."

Matt's mom left a beautiful legacy of compassion carried forward by Matt. I read an article in a local Maine magazine, *Down East*, about Matt's work with the cancer community. He had just run 100 miles (in one day!) to bring awareness to the unfortunate fact that some patients have to travel up to 100 miles each way to get cancer treatments. He was quoted saying, "I learned early that life is short, and I've committed mine to this. I want to leave a value legacy. And there's no better time to start." Matt learned early that life isn't measured by how much we have in our bank account, but by our ability to have an impact, and he does this every day as he creates his own legacy of compassion that was inspired by his mom.

The More You Give, the More You Get

I was deeply touched when I heard the story of Karen Nascembeni, manager of the North Shore Theatre in Beverly, Massachusetts, and a very compassionate and involved member of her family and her community. Karen, a lifelong practitioner of doing for others, realized the benefit of that when she needed it the most. She is another moving example of someone who lives a life of impact.

Karen and her husband, Steven Richard, came down with COVID-19 together in March of 2020, before many people were even worried about the disease. After initially being diagnosed with sinus infections, they both quickly became very ill. They entered the hospital together on March 17, St. Patrick's Day. When Karen said goodbye to her husband as he exited her car in the emergency room ambulance bay, it was the last time she would see him. She was in a coma for thirty-one days, on a ventilator, and had at least two near-death experiences during that time. What she didn't know was that during the time she was in a coma, her husband died, as did her father-in-law and a friend. What she also didn't know was that there was a worldwide, round-the-clock outpouring of love and support for her that had been taking place in those thirty-one long days.

She explained: "I did not know that my sister, Sandra McArthur, was having to make life-or-death medical decisions on my and my husband's behalf. I did not know that my friends and family were hanging onto my sister's every word in her nightly eloquently written Facebook post updates. I did not know that people were praying for me around the world, that the North Shore Music Theatre costume department was sewing masks, or that T-shirts, wine glasses, and coffee mugs were being designed by my friend, Nate Bertone, with my portrait on them and two of my favorite sayings, 'Hello, Darling' and 'Come On Party People,' and that these were being sold to raise money for the Steven T. Richard Memorial Photography Scholarship Fund, which Nate also created, along with a Postcards for Karen campaign. I did not know that homes and businesses were placing candles in their windows in honor of Steven's passing and in the hope that I would survive this dreadful virus."

What Karen described was the paradox of the more you give to others, the more you get back in return. She also saw that this ordeal that she endured resulted in her own community stepping up. She said, "It was like, through their compassion and love for me, they all became leaders. There has been this ripple effect throughout the people in my life. They're all doing for others." Amazingly, Karen, too, continues to help others affected by COVID-19. "If I know people with COVID, as soon as I hear, I go and I leave food on their porch, because people were so good to me that I just want to pay it forward every chance I get." Karen's story is one of strength and courage and commitment to creating these positive ripples throughout her own community and certainly beyond.

See Something, Do Something

I recently listened to a talk by a Buddhist monk that resonated with me. He explained very simply that the only purpose in life, the only thing that will ever make you happy, is to think about others first.

This practice takes many forms. It can be a series of small acts that accumulate over time, as in the example I mentioned earlier of actor Matt McCoy. Or it can become your entire life's work, as in the case of Dr. Zane Gates. We don't all have immediate clarity about what it is that we're meant to be doing. But if you live with outward awareness, get outside yourself, and focus on others, there are opportunities almost every day to check in on someone, to see if they need anything. Or, quietly notice someone's pain and take the step to see if you can do something to help. As Matt McCoy told me, he goes through life with his eyes open and heart full, in case he sees someone who needs his help.

I have lived by the words of the late congressman and civil rights activist John Lewis: "If you see something that is not right, not fair, not just, you have to speak up. You have to do something." Similarly, if you see someone who is in need and you are a witness to it, ask yourself what you can do to help. Small acts are important. You will never really know if that one small act, seemingly easy and insignificant at the time, is what gets a bigger ball rolling toward bigger positive outcomes somewhere down the line. Small daily acts are very much a part of the practice of compassion.

One of the great inspirations in my life is my brother, Michael Tramuta. He started out as a teacher and a coach in the small town where I was born, Dunkirk, New York. Along the way, he noticed kids who needed help, who no one else was helping, so he did. He started by coaching kids at neighborhood playgrounds, collecting coats for the kids who didn't have them. Later, he noticed rising chemical dependency among young kids. He explained: "At that time, in the eighties and nineties, it was an epidemic. Kids were using alcohol, marijuana, then so much cocaine. Kids were getting into trouble in school, getting into trouble at home, being kicked off the team, and nobody was doing anything to help adolescents. I tried to go to the superintendent of schools, to the athletic director and show them what I wanted to do with the kids. I'd say, 'Let's try to help. These are kids, and they're sick.' And that would be nixed, because they didn't want to take a chance on it. So finally, I just did it on my own. I started a program on Thursday nights to help kids with addiction. Anywhere from seventy-five to 100 kids would join in that group, kids who wanted to get better.

"I remember we had 110 kids who were at the bottom of the barrel," Michael continued. "They were in sixth, seventh, and eighth grade, and they were six grade levels below in their reading proficiency. They were failing everything in school. We went to the teachers and wanted to take their books and do their work in our class. We hit a brick wall. The teachers said, 'We don't want other people doing my stuff.' Well, the kids kept failing! So we started to do programs that would help them. We didn't look at them as kids that were six grade levels behind. No. We looked at them as children who needed help, and we helped them with a reading lab we had. We had phonics. We had everything that they might need to give them an honest shot."

My brother Michael was in a position to understand these kids more than some might, because many years ago he was addicted to alcohol. He also worked hard to overcome it.

He tells the story of one night when hitting a very rock-bottom place, when his wife told him she would not bail him out again. He prayed and asked God to help him. Michael believes that He did, because that night my brother made the decision to get sober. He told me that God gave him compassion, and he knew that he would now have the ability to give compassion to others. His challenges and his foundation of learning to work hard and treat others well gave him the will and the skill to step up for these kids, a job that wasn't always easy.

He told me: "You have to be tough but have compassion to work with some of these kids. Some are hard-core drug addicts. I work with guys from Washington who are making $150,000 a week on the streets. I would tell them, 'If you go down this road, I can tell you what's gonna happen.' They'd say to me, 'You're a chump, you do this job for $10 an hour. I make $500 in two minutes carrying a package across Sycamore Street.' And I'd say, 'Yeah, but you're going to jail. I'm not.'

"We used to ask kids, 'What would you want to put on your tombstone?' One kid sticks out in my mind; he was eighteen years old. And he looked at me. I'll never forget it. He said, 'Nothing. I don't want anything on my tombstone. I don't want anybody to know that I was ever here.' And I looked at him, I said, 'Why, Jimmy?' He said, 'Would you if your mother tried to cook you in the oven at 350 degrees when you were four years old?' He was a child out of wedlock. His mother didn't want him. So the compassion was not just feeling sorry for him, but understanding what that kid must have been through. When people become drug addicts and alcoholics, the pain is so enormous that it has to be something you pick up on as a teacher or a coach or counselor. In other words, their pain is so big, you just can't not see it and feel it. Basically, that was my compassion to see that and to say, 'You know what, I'm going to do something. I'm not going to quit.'"

Compassion Begets Compassion

Michael gave to others his entire life. In fact, he is eighty years old as I write this and he is still working with kids to help them get over drug and alcohol dependency. What he gives, he gets back in spades, and it keeps him going. He talked about how those he took care of took care of him at his most painful moment. "My first wife died in childbirth. At the time, I was the head basketball coach at school, in 1972–73. We had a great team. They were the greatest kids. It was almost like they would do everything I asked them to do. Without them? I'm not sure I would have made it through that year. They were tremendous to me. Amazingly, that year, we had the best team in the history of the school. We were number one in New York State. They were a joy to work with. And, we got five kids into college on scholarships.

"To this day, I still hear from people who I helped years ago. There is a guy who has been sober now for twenty-seven years. He has called me every year since the day he became sober. That was 1995 on July 4. He was part of the guys from New York City; his father had breakfast with John Gotti every morning. He calls me every year and thanks me. And I say, 'No, don't thank me. You did this.'

"I'd be walking in a Walmart, and I'd see one of the kids I helped, grown up now with their kids, and they'd come over and they'd say to their family, 'I want you to meet my teacher. He taught me how to read. If he hadn't, I would never be able to be here.' You know, when somebody tells you something like that, it's amazing, because you really never know. You're out there doing the best you can and you don't get much feedback at times. But we felt we had done a good job. The compassion was to help them self-actualize. And many of them did great. And when they went further than just this city—they have, some of them, become judges and lawyers, doctors, counselors, too—they learned you have to be willing to take a risk or go the extra mile to help others. I used to make my guys go to the food kitchens and distribute food to the poor. I say to everyone, just do it, just do little things, little acts of kindness, you know, and don't expect anything back. Sometimes it's about one person having an idea and not giving up on it."

The good you do is cumulative. It is like a little snowball that rolls and rolls, getting bigger and bigger. Or like a ripple in a pond, spreading out and touching far-off banks that aren't even visible.

Ripples of Hope

I've mentioned that one of my personal heroes was Robert F. Kennedy. In June of 1966, he visited South Africa during a period of great unrest over their system of apartheid. He was invited by an anti-apartheid student organization to speak at the University of Cape Town. The speech he gave, referred to as the "Ripples of Hope" speech, still reverberates far and wide today. This was no doubt one of the most powerful speeches given during my lifetime, and the core message still moves me.

A portion of this speech speaks to our own individual power to make change: "Few will have the greatness to bend history itself, but each of us can work to change a small portion of events, and in the total of all those acts will be written the history of this generation. Thousands of Peace Corps volunteers are making a difference in isolated villages and city slums in dozens of countries. Thousands of unknown men and women in Europe resisted the occupation of the Nazis, and many died, but all added to the ultimate strength and freedom of their countries. It is from numberless diverse acts of courage and belief that human history is shaped. Each time a man stands up for an ideal, or acts to improve the lot of others, or strikes out against injustice, he sends forth a tiny ripple of hope, and crossing each other from a million different centers of energy and daring, those ripples build a current which can sweep down the mightiest walls of oppression and resistance."

Having grown up with such reverence for Bobby Kennedy made the night I received the RFK Ripple of Hope Award a true high point in my life. When I accepted the award, I said, "I accept this award, not for what has been achieved but rather for what still needs to be accomplished." My sentiment was that this award was not necessarily honoring my achievements; it was honoring my humanity. What is great about compassionate leadership is its recognition of our humanity, its recognition of our frailties.

The last line of my speech quoted Horace Mann. He was the great educator who said, "Be ashamed to die until you have won some victory for humanity." To me, that's what compassionate leadership is about. Be ashamed to be a leader until you've won a victory for each one of your employees.

We're all looking for the Abraham Lincoln, Robert Kennedy, Martin Luther King Jr., or John Kennedy to lead us. Be that person yourself. Do small things, small, compassionate actions every day.

I don't think it's going to be one person anymore who leads the charge. I think it's going to be all of us, working as one unit toward a common desire for change, toward an agreed better outcome. I think we have to do this together, and it's why this book is so important. If you're waiting for a Dr. King or a John Lewis or some other hero to step up and change things for us, you're going to wait a long time. I think what we need right now is us, doing this together, creating ripples of hope that become ripples of change.

Start today. Create some ripples that will eventually make an impact on far-off shores.

END-OF-CHAPTER EXERCISES

TAKE THE NEXT STEP

One of the messages I most want to convey in this book is that we all have the power to be a positive impact on others and the world. The best way to start is by taking small actions that accumulate to create bigger collective changes and a more compassionate world. I have always maintained that it makes no difference how much you give, what makes the difference is that you gave. It makes no difference how much you do; what makes the difference is that you did something. Start today and look for an opportunity to help someone, even if it's just listening a little more intently when someone shares something with you or perhaps taking a moment to follow up with someone in your life who has had recent struggles to see if they need anything. At work or in your organization, consider implementing any of the ideas from this book; just pick one that resonates with you and try it. Any step you take will help strengthen your "compassion muscles," and you'll reap the benefits of a more satisfying life. For more ideas about how to get involved and join our movement toward a more compassionate world, please explore the resources offered on my website at www.donatotramuto.com/compassion. I look forward to connecting with you!

TRIBUTE PAGES

THE PROCEEDS FROM THIS BOOK will be shared among the following organizations in tribute to the work they are doing to make our world a more compassionate place.

Robert F. Kennedy Human Rights
Workplace Dignity Program

Robert F. Kennedy Human Rights' newest program, Workplace Dignity, was created to provide leaders with actionable, practical tools that foster a new understanding of the workplace where the dignity—the inherent value and worth—of employees is centered, creating a workplace culture in which all can thrive. The Tramuto Foundation provided a three-year grant to launch the program, recognizing that advancing the dignity of all workers, whatever the work they do and wherever they do it, is not only the right and humane thing to do, but also deepens engagement, enhances productivity, and promotes retention.

The program recognizes that human rights don't end at the workplace door.[1] Workers are entitled, in the words of the UN

Declaration of Human Rights, to a workplace that is "just and favorable." But all too often there is a gap[2] between what employees report they are experiencing and what employers think their workplace and its culture are delivering. Organizations can close that gap by refining the day-to-day actions and behaviors of their leaders, and more structurally, through organization-wide processes and policies (impacting recruiting, on-boarding, communication, benefits, and more). The program provides tools for change in each of these areas. It also celebrates dignity champions and practices in a range of workplaces, strategically supports dignity-advancing legislation, and incorporates workplace dignity as a content anchor in other RFKHR programs.

To learn more, visit: http://rfkhumanrights.org/our-programs/workplace-dignity.

Robert F. Kennedy Community Alliance

For more than fifty years, the RFK Community Alliance (formerly RFK Children's Action Corps) has served as a beacon of hope for at-risk youth and families in Massachusetts. With a focus on child welfare and juvenile justice, the RFK Community Alliance has created community-based initiatives and residential treatment and juvenile justice programs.[3] The organization works with national organizations and state agencies to ensure that proven and developed methods are used to help at-risk children. With tools that help them heal and grow, families can overcome the most difficult of challenges.

In collaboration with the Doctor Franklin Perkins School, the Community Alliance serves approximately 2,000 children, youths, and adults annually who are faced with emotional, psychological, health, environmental, and social issues. With the use of community-based services, educational services, foster care and adoption, and residential treatment, a brighter future for all children is possible. To learn more, visit www.rfkcommunity.org.

St. Joseph's College Institute for Integrative Aging

The Saint Joseph's College Institute for Integrative Aging was created after the Maine college adopted a plan to think about the future in an entrepreneurial manner. The plan included a commitment to using the institution's assets to help promise its financial stability and to serve its students, community, and region. The Institute for Integrative Aging provides a creative, age-friendly learning environment for older rural adults. These adults work alongside younger students, who are becoming well-equipped to support a rapidly growing aging population through the development of new courses and certificate programs.[4]

Social isolation and loneliness are pressing issues in older rural adults. However, the Institute for Integrative Aging combats those issues with programs structured around intergenerational connectivity, health and wellness activities, education, and support in nourishing their emotional, intellectual, creative, physical, and spiritual selves. The college is changing the culture of education through these programs and creating a new generation of integrative aging professionals who exhibit respect and compassion. Through the Institute for Integrative Aging, the community at Saint Joseph's College will have a better understanding of the aging process and what is necessary to live the healthiest life possible. To learn more, visit www.sjcme.edu/centers/institute-for-integrative-aging.

Scholarship Funds in Memory of Maeve and Gideon McKean

After the loss of Maeve McKean and her son Gideon in 2020, several fellowships were created in their name to honor their leadership and compassion.

McKean was the executive director of the Georgetown Global Health Initiative, where she promoted the intersection of health, data, law, policy, and diplomacy[5] to create breakthroughs in global health issues. Her passion for social justice was seen by the Global Health Fellows she mentored and her students at Georgetown Law and School of Foreign Service. To sustain McKean's legacy in the promotion of global health, Georgetown University and the McKean family created the Maeve McKean Excellence in Global Health Award. Students who aim to improve health outcomes for vulnerable and marginalized communities, both within the United States and internationally, are supported through this award. Awarded annually, the fellowship includes providing a student or group with resources to travel to the World Health Assembly or other experiential learning activities that fit their curriculum.

McKean served as the first-ever senior advisor for human rights in the State Department's Global AIDS Program, having been appointed to the post during the Obama Administration.[6] Inspired by her devotion to improving the health rights of people around the world, the University of Maryland, Baltimore's School of Medicine, and the Institute of Human Virology created the Maeve Kennedy McKean Global Public Health Fellowship. Students awarded with this fellowship will work with the university's Center for International Health, Education, and Biosecurity team to help mitigate and end the HIV epidemic in Africa.

Other awards and philanthropic programs honoring Maeve McKean include a fellowship by the Women's Law and Public Policy Fellowship Program and the O'Neill Institute for National and Global Health Law, which supports a student to work in Washington, DC, each year on public health issues; the Maeve McKean Cluster Cares Fund, which helps families in the Cluster community of DC receive support to pay bills, buy groceries, and take care of daily tasks during the COVID-19 pandemic; and the 2020 Distinguished Partners for Women Peace and Security Award, which provides awards and financial support for seven organizations in conflict-affected countries.[7] To learn more, please

visitwww.maeveandgideon.org,https://maeveandgideon.org/donate/
oneill-institute-fellow/,orhttps://maeveandgideon.org/donate/maeve-
mckean-cluster-cares-fund/.

Boston University School of
Public Health (BUSPH)

As a top-ranked graduate school, Boston University School of
Public Health offers access to innovative research, scholarship, and
public health practice. BUSPH offers a top-tier education with an
on-the-ground mission to improve the health and well-being of
populations worldwide, particularly the underserved. BUSPH is
committed to igniting and sustaining positive change that leads to
health and well-being around the world. Proceeds to BUSPH from
the royalties of this book will create a Compassionate Leadership
Student Scholarship in promotion of social justice, human rights,
and equity across local and global communities. To learn more, visit
https://www.bu.edu/sph/.

Tramuto Foundation

Donato Tramuto was scheduled to board United Flight 175 from
Boston to Los Angeles on September 11, 2001, with his good friends,
Ron Gamboa and Dan Brandhorst, and their three-year-old son,
David, who had been visiting with Donato and his partner, Jeff,
in Ogunquit. When Tramuto experienced a sudden toothache on
September 10, he decided to visit his dentist near the Boston Logan
Airport and changed his flight back to Los Angeles to one departing

later that evening, a routine flight that he made almost every Tuesday. Ron Gamboa, Dan Brandhorst, and David, however, boarded United Flight 175, as scheduled. Theirs was the plane that hit the second World Trade Center Tower in New York City.

When learning the news of his friends' tragic passing, Tramuto was in anguish, describing the experience as the worst "bulldozer moment" he has had in his lifetime. Several weeks after the event, Tramuto decided that he needed to make a living tribute in honor of his friends. A few months later, the Tramuto Foundation was born. With the help of his good friend, Dr. Mary Jane England, then president of Regis College in Newton, Massachusetts, the foundation began focusing its efforts on awarding annual college scholarships to graduating seniors who have successfully overcome a difficult situation in their life,[9] with the goal of helping these scholars turn adversity into success.

For the past twenty years, two students each year from Bangor, Ogunquit, and Wells, Maine, and other areas across the world who show their potential in overcoming adversity are chosen for the Tramuto Foundation Scholarship. In 2006, the foundation advanced its mission to award multiple grants annually to organizations whose mission it is to make the world a better place. Every five years, the foundation holds a gala to celebrate the achievements of grant scholars. At the time of this writing, the Twentieth Anniversary Gala is being organized for September 11, 2021. All scholarship laureates will be recognized, and eight organizations across the globe will be honored at the event. To learn more, please visit http://tramuto foundation.com.

NOTES

INTRODUCTION

1. "The US Workforce Is Becoming More Diverse." (2005, November). The National Center for Public Policy and Higher Education. http://www.highereducation.org/reports/pa_decline/decline-f1.shtml.

2. "Millennial Generation is Bigger, More Diverse Than Boomers." (n.d.). CNNMoney. https://money.cnn.com/interactive/economy/diversity-millennials-boomers/.

3. Hougaard, R., Carter, J., and Beck, J. (2018, May 15). "Assessment: Are You a Compassionate Leader?" *Harvard Business Review*. https://hbr.org/2018/05/assessment-are-you-a-compassionate-leader.

CHAPTER I

1. Workspan Daily. (2020, January 22). "Average Age for C-Suite Member Is 56." World at Work: Total Rewards Association. https://www.worldatwork.org/workspan/articles/average-age-for-c-suite-member-is-56.

2. Crain Communications, Inc. (2018, June 16). "50 Most Influential Physician Executives – 2018." *Modern Healthcare*. https://www. modernhealthcare.com/awards/50-most-influential-physician -executives-2018.

3. Lwala Community Alliance. (2020). "Lwala 2020 Annual Report." https://lwala.org/wp-content/uploads/2021/02/2020-Lwala-annual -report_compressed.pdf.

CHAPTER 2

1. Gallup. (2020). "State of the American Workplace 2020." https:// www.gallup.com/workplace/238085/state-american-workplace-report -2017.aspx.

2. Businessolver. (2020). "2020 State of Workplace Empathy." https:// www.businessolver.com/resources/state-of-workplace-empathy.

3. Parthasarathy, H. (2005). "Expressing the Big Picture." *PLoS Biology* 3(3), e105. https://doi.org/10.1371/journal.pbio.0030105.

4. Feloni, R., and Mullineaux, M. (2020, July 29). "Humana's CEO Said the Coronavirus Crisis Has Confirmed the Value of a Stakeholder -Driven Strategy." JUST Capital. https://justcapital.com/news/humanas -ceo-explained-how-the-coronavirus-crisis-has-confirmed -the-value-of-a-long-term-stakeholder-driven-strategy/.

CHAPTER 3

1. Korn Ferry. (2019, November 4). "Purpose Pays." https://www.kornferry. com/about-us/press/purposepays?utm_source=instagram&utm_ medium=social&utm_term=&utm_content=article&utm_ campaign=organic.

2. Glassdoor. (2019). Mission & Culture Survey 2019. https://www. glassdoor.com/about-us/app/uploads/sites/2/2019/07/Mission-Culture -Survey-Supplement.pdf.

CHAPTER 4

1. Zenger, J., and Folkman, J. (2017, September 20). "Why Do So Many Managers Avoid Giving Praise?" *Harvard Business Review*. https://hbr.org/2017/05/why-do-so-many-managers-avoid-giving-praise.

2. Gyatso, Tenzin, the Fourteenth Dalai Lama. "Compassion and the Individual." https://www.dalailama.com/messages/compassion-and-human-values/compassion.

CHAPTER 5

1. PWC. (2016, January). "Redefining Business Success in a Changing World: CEO Survey." https://www.pwc.com/gx/en/ceo-survey/2016/landing-page/pwc-19th-annual-global-ceo-survey.pdf.

2. Zak, P. (2019, November 27). "The Neuroscience of Trust." *Harvard Business Review*. https://hbr.org/2017/01/the-neuroscience-of-trust#:%7E:text=Leaders%20understand%20the%20stakes%E2%80%94 at,threat%20to%20their%20organization%27s%20growth.

CHAPTER 6

1. Jobvite. (2018). "2018 Job Seeker Nation Study." https://www.jobvite.com/wp-content/uploads/2018/04/2018_Job_Seeker_Nation_Study.pdf.

2. TINYpulse. (2018). "Employee Retention Report." https://www.tinypulse.com/hubfs/2018%20Employee%20Retention%20Report.pdf.

3. Shpak, S. (2018, May 21). "How Communication Affects Productivity Statistics." AZ Central. https://yourbusiness.azcentral.com/communication-affects-productivity-statistics-27004.html.

4. Buhler, Patricia M., and Worden, Joel D. (2020, July 30). "The Cost of Poor Communications." SHRM. Excerpted from Up, Down, and Sideways: High-Impact Verbal Communication for HR Professionals (SHRM, 2013). https://www.shrm.org/resourcesandtools/hr-topics/behavioral-competencies/communication/pages/the-cost-of-poor-communications.aspx.

5. Salesforce Canada. (2014, August 20). "How Soft Skills Are Crucial to Your Business." *Salesforce Canada Blog*. https://www.salesforce.com/ca/blog/2014/08/how-soft-skills-are-crucial-to-your-business-.html.

6. Solomon, L. (2017, October 25). "Two-Thirds of Managers Are Uncomfortable Communicating with Employees." *Harvard Business Review*. https://hbr.org/2016/03/two-thirds-of-managers-are-uncomfortable-communicating-with-employees#:%7E:text=A%20new%20Interact%20survey%20conducted,often%20uncomfortable%20communicating%20with%20employees.

7. Lipman, V. (2016, August 9). "65% Of Employees Want More Feedback (So Why Don't They Get It?)." *Forbes*. https://www.forbes.com/sites/victorlipman/2016/08/08/65-of-employees-want-more-feedback-so-why-dont-they-get-it/?sh=338892e914ad.

8. Murray, B. and Fortinberry, A. (2013). "The new capitalism: The greater the compassion, the greater the profit." *Effective Executive* 16(2): 43–50.

CHAPTER 7

1. McQueen, N. (2018, June 26). "Workplace Culture Trends: The Key to Hiring (and Keeping) Top Talent in 2018." LinkedIn. https://blog.linkedin.com/2018/june/26/workplace-culture-trends-the-key-to-hiring-and-keeping-top-talent.

2. "Nearly Half of Office Workers Value Community in the Workplace." (2018, June 28). *PR Newswire*. https://www.prnewswire.com/news-releases/nearly-half-of-office-workers-value-community-in-the-workplace-682214991.html.

3. Achor, S. (2011, August 23). "5 Ways to Turn Happiness Into An Advantage." *Psychology Today*. https://www.psychologytoday.com/us/blog/the-happiness-advantage/201108/5-ways-turn-happiness-advantage.

4. Mintzberg, H. (2009, August 1). "Rebuilding Companies as Communities." *Harvard Business Review*. https://hbr.org/2009/07/rebuilding-companies-as-communities.

5. Samdahl, E. (2017, June 22). "Top Employers are 5.5x More Likely to Reward Collaboration." Institute for Corporate Productivity (i4cp). https://www.i4cp.com/productivity-blog/top-employers-are-5-5x-more -likely-to-reward-collaboration.

6. Duhigg, C. (2016, February 25). "What Google Learned From Its Quest to Build the Perfect Team." *New York Times*. https://www.nytimes. com/2016/02/28/magazine/what-google-learned-from-its-quest-to -build-the-perfect-team.html.

7. Woolley, A. W., Chabris, C. F., Pentland, A., Hashmi, N., and Malone, T. W. (2010). "Evidence for a Collective Intelligence Factor in the Performance of Human Groups." *Science* 330(6004): 686–688. https:// doi.org/10.1126/science.1193147v.

8. Carmeli, A., Brueller, D., and Dutton, J. E. (2009). "Learning Behaviours in the Workplace: The Role of High-Quality Interpersonal Relationships and Psychological Safety." *Systems Research and Behavioral Science* 26(1): 81–98. https://doi.org/10.1002/sres.93.

9. Robison, B. B. W. A. J. (2021, March 23). "Fostering Creativity at Work: Do Your Managers Push or Crush Innovation?" Gallup. https://www. gallup.com/workplace/245498/fostering-creativity-work-managers -push-crush-innovation.aspx.

10. Catmull, E. (2008, September). "How Pixar Fosters Collective Creativity." *Harvard Business Review*. https://hbr.org/2008/09/how -pixar-fosters-collective-creativity.

11. Thompson, L. (2013, March 13). "Collaborate Better." Kellogg Insight. https://insight.kellogg.northwestern.edu/article/collaborate_better.

CHAPTER 8

1. Hewlett, S., Marshall, M., and Sherbin, L. (2014, August 1). "How Diversity Can Drive Innovation." *Harvard Business Review*. https://hbr. org/2013/12/how-diversity-can-drive-innovation.

2. Hunt, V., Layton, D., and Prince, S. (2021, March 12). "Why Diversity Matters." McKinsey & Company. https://www.mckinsey.com/business -functions/organization/our-insights/why-diversity-matters.

3. Castrillon, C. (2019, March 26). "Why Women-Led Companies Are Better For Employees." *Forbes*. https://www.forbes.com/sites/carolinecastrillon/2019/03/24/why-women-led-companies-are-better-for-employees/?sh=27db16c03264.

4. Dishman, L. (2015, July 9). "The Business Case for Women in the C-Suite." *Fast Company*. https://www.fastcompany.com/3048342/the-business-case-for-women-in-the-c-suite.

5. Glassdoor Team. (2014, November 17). "What Job Seekers Really Think about Your Diversity and Inclusion Stats." Glassdoor for Employers. https://www.glassdoor.com/employers/blog/diversity/.

6. Hunt, V., Layton, D., and Prince, S. (2021, March 12). "Why Diversity Matters." McKinsey & Company. https://www.mckinsey.com/business-functions/organization/our-insights/why-diversity-matters.

7. Lorenzo, R., and Reeves, M. (2018, January 30). "How and Where Diversity Drives Financial Performance." *Harvard Business Review*. https://hbr.org/2018/01/how-and-where-diversity-drives-financial-performance.

8. Hewlett, S., Marshall, M., and Sherbin, L. (2014, August 1). "How Diversity Can Drive Innovation." *Harvard Business Review*. https://hbr.org/2013/12/how-diversity-can-drive-innovation.

9. Dobbin, F., and Kalev, A. (2016). "Why Diversity Programs Fail." *Harvard Business Review*. https://hbr.org/2016/07/why-diversity-programs-fail.

10. Dobbin, F., and Kalev, A. (2016). "Why Diversity Programs Fail." *Harvard Business Review*. https://hbr.org/2016/07/why-diversity-programs-fail.

CHAPTER 9

1. Jose, R. (2015, December 7). "5 Reasons Why You Should Listen to Your Employees." *SHRM Blog*. https://blog.shrm.org/blog/5-reasons-why-you-should-listen-to-your-employees.

2. Curtin, M. (2020, February 6). "Employees Who Feel Heard Are 4.6x More Likely to Feel Empowered to Do Their Best Work." *Inc.* https:// www.inc.com/melanie-curtin/employees-who-feel-heard-are-46x-more -likely-to-feel-empowered-to-do-their-best-work.html.

3. ServiceNow. (2019, June). "The Employee Experience Imperative Report." https://www.servicenow.com/lpwhp/employee-experience -imperative.html?cid=pr:employee_experience_research.

4. IBM Institute for Business Value and IBM Smarter Workforce Institute. (2015). "Amplifying Employee Voice." IBM. https://www.ibm.com/ downloads/cas/08NLPNQA.

CHAPTER 10

1. Seppala, E. (2013, July 24). "Compassionate Mind, Healthy Body." *Greater Good.* https://greatergood.berkeley.edu/article/item/ compassionate_mind_healthy_body#:%7E:text=A%20study%20led%20 by%20Sheethal,well%2Dbeing%20and%20social%20connection.

2. National Institutes of Health. (2015, July 6). "Brain Imaging Reveals Joys of Giving." National Institutes of Health (NIH). https://www.nih. gov/news-events/nih-research-matters/brain-imaging-reveals-joys -giving#:%7E:text=A%20new%20study%20found%20that,even%20 at%20a%20personal%20cost.

3. Harmon, K., and Harmon, K. (2010, July 28). "Social Ties Boost Survival by 50 Percent." *Scientific American.* https://www.scientificamerican. com/article/relationships-boost-survival/#:%7E:text=Overall%2C%20 social%20support%20increases%20survival,%2Da%2Dday%20 smoking%20habit.

4. Cole, S. W. (2013). "Social Regulation of Human Gene Expression: Mechanisms and Implications for Public Health." *American Journal of Public Health* 103(S1): S84–S92. https://doi.org/10.2105/ ajph.2012.301183.

5. University of California—Davis. (2018, April 5). "Seven-Year Follow-up Shows Lasting Cognitive Gains from Meditation." *ScienceDaily.* https:// www.sciencedaily.com/releases/2018/04/180405093257.htm.

6. Lee, R. M., and Robbins, S. B. (1998). "The Relationship between Social Connectedness and Anxiety, Self-Esteem, and Social Identity." *Journal of Counseling Psychology* 45(3): 338–345. https://doi.org/10.1037/0022 -0167.45.3.338.

CHAPTER 11

1. University of California – San Diego. (2010, March 10). "Acts of Kindness Spread Surprisingly Easily: Just a Few People Can Make a Difference." *ScienceDaily.* https://www.sciencedaily.com/ releases/2010/03/100308151049.htm.

2. Qiu, H., Zhang, Y., Hou, G., and Wang, Z. (2018). "The Integrative Effects of Leading by Example and Follower Traits in Public Goods Game: A Multilevel Study." *Frontiers in Psychology* 9(1). https://doi. org/10.3389/fpsyg.2018.01687.

3. Gallup. (2020). *State of the American Workplace 2020.* https://www.gallup. com/workplace/238085/state-american-workplace-report-2017.aspx.

4. Qiu, H., Zhang, Y., Hou, G., and Wang, Z. (2018). "The Integrative Effects of Leading by Example and Follower Traits in Public Goods Game: A Multilevel Study." *Frontiers in Psychology* 9(1). https://doi. org/10.3389/fpsyg.2018.01687.

5. Change, T. B. (2018, November 21). "Does It Pay Off? The True R.O.I. of Mindfulness in Business." *Medium.* https://bthechange.com/does-it -pay-off-the-true-r-o-i-of-mindfulness-in-business-3c9185dd8d11.

6. Baer, D. (2014, August 5). "Here's What Google Teaches Employees In Its 'Search Inside Yourself' Course." *Business Insider.* https://www. businessinsider.com/search-inside-yourself-googles-life-changing -mindfulness-course-2014-8.

7. Davis, D. M., and Hayes, J. A. (2011). "What are the benefits of mindfulness? A practice review of psychotherapy-related research." *Psychotherapy* 48(2): 198–208. https://doi.org/10.1037/a0022062.

8. Luders, E., Cherbuin, N., and Kurth, F. (2015). "Forever Young(er): Potential Age-Defying Effects of Long-Term Meditation on Gray Matter Atrophy." *Frontiers in Psychology* 5(1). https://doi.org/10.3389/ fpsyg.2014.01551.

9. Hölzel, B. K., Carmody, J., Vangel, M., Congleton, C., Yerramsetti, S. M., Gard, T., and Lazar, S. W. (2011). "Mindfulness Practice Leads to Increases in Regional Brain Gray Matter Density." *Psychiatry Research: Neuroimaging* 191(1): 36–43. https://doi.org/10.1016/j.pscychresns.2010.08.006.

10. Fell, A. (2016, January 24). "Mindfulness from Meditation Associated with Lower Stress Hormone." UC Davis. https://www.ucdavis.edu/news/mindfulness-meditation-associated-lower-stress-hormone.

CHAPTER 12

1. Oakes, K. (2020, June 4). "Positive Product of the Pandemic: Culture." HRExecutive. https://hrexecutive.com/positive-product-of-the-pandemic-culture/#:%7E:text=When%20we%20asked%20those%20same,%2C%2057%25%20said%20they%20did.&text=In%20our%20wildly%20popular%20study,culture%20succeeded%20in%20doing%20so.

2. "Average Age for C-Suite Member Is 56." (2020, January 22). World at Work: Total Rewards Association. https://www.worldatwork.org/workspan/articles/average-age-for-c-suite-member-is-56.

3. Zweigenhaft, R. (2020, October 28). "Fortune 500 CEOs, 2000–2020: Still Male, Still White." *The Society Pages*. https://thesocietypages.org/specials/the-highest-paid-ceos-still-white-still-male/.

4. Deloitte. (2014, January). Deloitte Millennial Survey. https://www2.deloitte.com/content/dam/Deloitte/global/Documents/About-Deloitte/gx-dttl-2014-millennial-survey-report.pdf.

5. Frey, W. H. (2017, August 15). "Diversity defines the millennial generation." Brookings. https://www.brookings.edu/blog/the-avenue/2016/06/28/diversity-defines-the-millennial-generation/.

6. Congressional Research Service. (2021, March). "Membership of the 117th Congress: A Profile." US Census Bureau. https://crsreports.congress.gov/product/pdf/R/R46705.

7. Cohn, D. (2015, October 5). "Future Immigration Will Change the Face of America by 2065." Pew Research Center. https://www.pewresearch.org/fact-tank/2015/10/05/future-immigration-will-change-the-face-of-america-by-2065/.

8. Deloitte. (2018). 2018 Deloitte Millennial Survey. https://www2. deloitte.com/content/dam/Deloitte/at/Documents/human-capital/at -deloitte-millennial-survey-2018.pdf.

9. Taylor, J. (2018, March 16). "From Boomers to Gen Z: How Different Generations Adapt and React to New Trends and Technologies." Epsilon. https://www.epsilon.com/emea/insights/blog/from-boomers -to-gen-z.

10. Bughin, J., Hazan, E., Lund, S., Dahlström, P., Wiesinger, A., and Subra-maniam, A. (2021, January 23). "Skill Shift: Automation and the Future of the Workforce." McKinsey & Company. https://www.mckinsey.com/ featured-insights/future-of-work/skill-shift-automation-and-the-future -of-the-workforce?utm_content=107864459&utm_medium=social &utm_source=facebook&hss_channel=fbp-286401775642469&f bclid=IwAR2j_lMkf0MjmFIQFwspv2gLz8FKG6maq0j4jz4XqVg d1CNSgK6LuHN2WkI.

11. Miller, C. C., and Yar, S. (2019, September 21). "Young People Are Going to Save Us All from Office Life." *New York Times*. https://www. nytimes.com/2019/09/17/style/generation-z-millennials-work-life -balance.html.

12. PWC, USC University of Southern California, and London Business School. (2013). PwC's NextGen: A global generational study. PWC. https://www.pwc.com/gx/en/hr-management-services/publications/ assets/pwc-nextgen.pdf.

CHAPTER 13

1. Robson, D. (2019, May 13). "The '3.5% rule': How a Small Minority Can Change the World." BBC Future. https://www.bbc.com/future/ article/20190513-it-only-takes-35-of-people-to-change-the-world.

2. Business Roundtable. (2019, August 19). "Business Roundtable Redefines the Purpose of a Corporation to Promote 'An Economy That Serves All Americans.'" https://www.businessroundtable.org/business -roundtable-redefines-the-purpose-of-a-corporation-to-promote-an -economy-that-serves-all-americans.

3. Fund, E. D. (2019, November 8). "The Businesses That Are—And Are Not—Leading on Climate Change." *Forbes*. https://www.forbes.com/sites/edfenergyexchange/2019/11/08/the-businesses-that-are--and-are-not--leading-on-climate-change/?sh=2109437f7aa1.

4. Statt, N. (2020, March 13). "AT&T, Comcast, Verizon and Others Agree Not to Overcharge Customers during Coronavirus." *The Verge*. https://www.theverge.com/2020/3/13/21178451/fcc-coronavirus-keep-americans-connected-pledge-att-comcast-charter-att.

5. CBS News. (2021, March 8). "Meet the Woman on a Mission to Have Retailers Commit 15% of Their Shelf Space to Black-owned Brands." https://www.cbsnews.com/news/15-percent-pledge-aurora-james/.

6. WBCSD. (n.d.). "About us." World Business Council for Sustainable Development (WBCSD). https://www.wbcsd.org/Overview/About-us.

TRIBUTE PAGES

1. *Introducing Workplace Dignity.* (2021, April 30). [Video]. YouTube. https://www.youtube.com/watch?v=a9lDZ-D6Wds.

2. *Workplace Dignity Survey.* (2020, February 5). Willis Towers Watson. https://www.willistowerswatson.com/en-US/Insights/2020/01/2019-workplace-dignity-survey.

3. "Who We Are." Robert F. Kennedy Children's Action Corps. https://www.rfkchildren.org/about-us/who-we-are/.

4. "About the Institute for Integrative Aging." Saint Joseph's College of Maine. https://www.sjcme.edu/centers/institute-for-integrative-aging/about/.

5. "Georgetown University Maeve McKean Excellence in Global Health Award." Maeve and Gideon. https://maeveandgideon.org/donate/georgetown/.

6. "Maeve Kennedy McKean Global Public Health Fellowship." Maeve and Gideon. https://maeveandgideon.org/donate/ihv/.

7. "Fellowships and Funds." Maeve and Gideon. https://maeveandgideon.org/donate/msm/.

8. "Our Story." Health eVillages. https://www.healthevillages.org/our-story/.

9. "About the Foundation." Tramuto Foundation. http://tramutofoundation.com/about/.

ADDITIONAL RESOURCES

Visit www.donatotramuto.com/compassion to find:

- Recommended Reading

- Compassion-Related Websites

- Summary of Our Compassionate Workplace Survey

- Corporate Programs for Building Compassionate Culture

- Tools for Human Resources

- Organizations That Support Compassionate Causes

- How to Get Involved

- Bonus Book Content Including Video Interview Outtakes

Index

About the Authors

Donato J. Tramuto is widely recognized for his commitment to social change and transformational leadership in health-care innovation that led the *New York Times* to deem him "a global health activist." He has been a champion for compassionate culture throughout his career that has spanned numerous corporate, entrepreneurial, and philanthropic endeavors.

He is the former CEO of Tivity Health®, Inc., (NASDAQ: TVTY), where he served as a board member, chairman of the board, and later, CEO, championing a turnaround that moved the company toward profitability. Tramuto is an entrepreneur, innovator, and passionate champion of cutting-edge approaches to health-care access, drug safety, and addressing the social determinants of health (SDOH), defined by the World Health Organization as the conditions in which people are born, grow, live, work, and age. Under his tenure as CEO of Tivity Health and following his execution of a successful turnaround, he transformed the business model to center around partnering progressively, profitably, and collaboratively with consumers, payers, health-care practitioners, and employers in cutting-edge approaches to SDOH conditions, including nutrition, fitness, and social connection that improve health outcomes and reduce medical costs.

Before joining Tivity Health, Tramuto's record of bringing together social commitment with health-care innovation included his founding of Physicians Interactive Holdings (Aptus Health sold to WebMD in 2019), a global provider of insight-driven digital engagement solutions for health-care professionals and consumers. Reflecting a conviction that universal health care is a basic human right for all people, he launched Health eVillages in 2011, a nonprofit organization providing state-of-the-art mobile health technology in the most challenging clinical environments and working to broaden health-care access.

Tramuto is also the founder and chair of the Tramuto Foundation, which advances people's rights to education and health-care access, combats human right violations, and supports projects that foster a more compassionate world. He launched the foundation in memory his two friends and their three-year-old son who lost their lives on 9/11 when United Flight 175 crashed into the South Tower. Tramuto was scheduled to be on that flight, however, due to a toothache, he never boarded the plane. Since the launch of the foundation, over 100 young adults have received a Tramuto Foundation Scholarship to pursue their dream of a college education, and many organizations have received financial and partnership support, helping them deliver on their promise to make the world a more equitable place.

His three-decade-long commitment to compassionate leadership, social change, and innovation has earned numerous awards, including the prestigious Robert F. Kennedy Ripple of Hope and the RFK Embracing His Legacy awards, and induction into the PharmaVoice Hall of Fame for his leadership in the health-care industry.

Tramuto currently serves as a member of the Robert F. Kennedy Human Rights board and is chairman of its Leadership Council, where, in 2018, his foundation committed to funding a three-year, $1 million grant to address workplace bullying, leading a national initiative to address workplace dignity and inclusion in the United States and Europe. Tramuto is a member of the Brown University Healthcare Leadership Board, board member for Element3 Health, and chairman of the board for Cherish Health, as well as an advisory board member at the Boston University School of Public Health, Gryphon Investment, BioIq, Zeel Health, and Gento Health. He also serves as an executive in residence at Tidesmart Health, Sharecare, and Concierge Health, and as Honorary Scholar in Residence at St. Jospeh's College in Maine. He is the creator of a groundbreaking 360-degree public service campaign and annual summit addressing challenges unique to older adults, including the too-often overlooked issues of isolation and loneliness.

A proponent of lifelong learning, Tramuto holds honorary doctorates from the University of Massachusetts at Lowell, Thomas Jefferson University, Lasell University, and Saint Joseph's College, and is also the author of *Life's Bulldozer Moments: How Adversity Leads to Success in Life and Business*, now available in the United States and Italy.

Tramuto is a regular speaker on topics of workplace dignity, social justice, health-care access, and value-based leadership. He has frequently appeared in the *New York Times*, the *Boston Globe*, and the *Wall Street Journal*, and on CNBC, Fox News with Neil Cavuto, and Bloomberg News.

Tami Booth Corwin is an independent consultant, advisor, strategist, publishing and media executive, and creator/writer who helps companies, brands, organizations, and thought leaders communicate important messages to wider audiences and increase their impact through innovative deals and initiatives.

As a corporate executive, she has a strong track record of launching, growing, and transforming businesses and brands and driving significant audience and revenue growth. She's held several C-level leadership roles including president and editor-in-chief at publisher Rodale, and president at emerging internet/tech company SparkPeople. At Rodale, she grew the book division from $10M in revenue to over $50M by creating and implementing a new multi-platform, multi-channel content and revenue model, while also negotiating and launching game-changing deals and launching new brands such as *The South Beach Diet*, which grew into a half billion-dollar brand, and the book companion to the documentary film

An Inconvenient Truth by Vice President Al Gore, which helped to change the national conversation around climate change.

In 2005, she was named to the *Wall Street Journal's* 50 Women to Watch list for "leading a striking turnaround at Rodale's book division." That same year, she was recognized by the *WSJ* as one of 21 women "In Line to Lead," the youngest to be featured.

Driven by a passion for ideas and innovation, fresh thinking, a strong propensity for problem solving, and an ability to get things done, she has negotiated deals and led the development of hundreds of best-selling books, digital content, licensed products, strategic partnerships, and initiatives. She has consulted and led projects with diverse clients and project partners such as NBC Universal, Lifetime, Tivity Health, Christie's Auction House, Time Inc., Truth Bar, Nutrisystem, The South Beach Diet, CP Baker Private Equity, Yahoo!, SparkPeople, Vyv Tech, The Tramuto Foundation, and numerous authors, publishers, and thought leaders.

As an independent creator and marketer, she has written articles, blogs, and opinion pieces for clients, overseen photo shoots, shot photography for book and social, developed marketing and social campaigns for brands, produced videos and digital content, written television treatments, created websites, produced events, and developed book concepts.

As a board member at nonprofit Boston Cares, she worked to connect compassionate organizations with people in need by co-founding their Corporate Volunteer Program, underwritten by Fidelity Investments and launched with General Colin Powell. As a board member at the Charter Arts Foundation, she worked to support education and opportunity for students at one of the top arts high schools in the US. She is a longtime supporter and volunteer at Last Chance Ranch where she works with rescued horses.

She has appeared or been featured in media outlets such as the *New York Times*, the *Wall Street Journal*, CBC, *Ad Age*, *Publisher's Weekly*, *Boston Business Journal* and CNBC. This book, *The Double Bottom Line*, is the first book she has written.